Z SPECIAL UNIT

OSPREY
PUBLISHING

This is the happy Warrior; this is he

That every man in arms

should wish to be.

William Wordsworth

Z SPECIAL UNIT

THE ELITE ALLIED WORLD WAR II GUERRILLA FORCE

GAVIN MORTIMER

OSPREY PUBLISHING
Bloomsbury Publishing Plc
Kemp House, Chawley Park, Cumnor Hill, Oxford
OX2 9PH, UK
29 Earlsfort Terrace, Dublin 2, Ireland
1385 Broadway, 5th Floor, New York,
NY 10018, USA
E-mail: info@ospreypublishing.com
www.ospreypublishing.com

OSPREY is a trademark of Osprey Publishing Ltd
First published in Great Britain in 2022
© Gavin Mortimer, 2022
Gavin Mortimer has asserted his right under the
Copyright, Designs and Patents Act, 1988, to be
identified as Author of this work.

For legal purposes the Acknowledgements on p. 6
constitute an extension of this copyright page.

A catalogue record for this book is available from the
British Library.

ISBN: HB 9781472847096;
eBook 9781472847102;
ePDF 9781472847072;
XML 9781472847089

22 23 24 25 26   10 9 8 7 6 5 4 3 2 1

Maps by www.bounford.com
Index by Zoe Ross
Cover, page design and layout by Stewart Larking
Printed and bound in India by
Replika Press Private Ltd.

Editor's note
Imperial units of measurement are used in this book.
For ease of comparison please refer to the following
conversion table:

1 knot = 1.85km/h
1 mile = 1.60km
1yd = 0.9m
1ft = 0.30m
1 inch = 2.54cm
1lb (pound) = 0.45kg
1 stone = 6.35kg
1 ton = 1,016kg
1HP = 0.74kW

Osprey Publishing supports the Woodland Trust, the
UK's leading woodland conservation charity.

To find out more about our authors and books visit
www.ospreypublishing.com. Here you will find
extracts, author interviews, details of forthcoming
events and the option to sign up for our newsletter.

CONTENTS

ACKNOWLEDGEMENTS

First, I would like to thank my editor at Osprey, Kate Moore, for commissioning a history of Z Special Unit, one of the more obscure special forces outfits of the Second World War – at least in the United Kingdom, where their exploits have never received the recognition they deserve, unlike in Australia. Kate recognised that Z Special's was an important story that needed to be told. Her subsequent sensitive and supportive editing was of great assistance in producing the finished narrative. Also at Osprey, Cleo Favaretto is a diligent and decisive desk editor who made life easier in adding the finishing touches to the book.

Thanks also to my agent, Matthew Hamilton, for his support and sagacity.

I am grateful to the staff of the National Archives, the Imperial War Museum and the Liddell Hart archives at King's College, all of whom made the research easier with their efficiency. Similarly, I was helped by the archivists at Harrow School, Wellington College and Rendcomb College in unearthing information about the formative years of Ivan Lyon, Bobby Ross and Reginald Ingleton.

Although the lockdown prevented my visiting Australia to further my research, I was fortunate in being able to access the excellent Australian War Memorial. Their digitalised archive is a boon to historians and it furnished me with much significant information.

Still in Australia I would like to thank Peter Dunn, host of the website www.ozatwar.com, and Terry Gallaway, for granting me permission to use a couple of photos of Refuge Bay, and I received similar generosity from Harley Carey, the son of Sam Carey (and nephew of Walter), who sent me a wealth of information on his gallant family members.

In Singapore, I was fortunate to locate Jerome Lin, who allowed me to reproduce three photographs pertaining to Operation *Rimau* from his blog, 'The Long and Winding Road'.

I was delighted to make contact with Jeremy Chapman, the son of Walter Chapman, and he sent me several remarkable photographs, taken by his father during Operation *Rimau*. He also patiently and candidly answered my questions about Walter.

Finally, I would like to salute Michael Tibbs, the sole survivor of Operation *Rimau*, who, at the grand old age of 99, astonished me with his clarity and energy. He sent me a copy of his absorbing war memoir, *Hello Lad, Come to Join the Navy?*, an eloquent reminder of the courage and fortitude of all submariners. I dedicate this book to him, and all the men of *Rimau*, particularly those who lost their lives on the operation and who have no known grave.

AUTHOR'S NOTE

Z Special Unit was a section of Special Operations Australia (SOA) during the Second World War, which itself was an offshoot of Britain's Special Operations Executive (SOE). It was raised in April 1942, and soon Z Special Unit was born, a holding unit for Australian soldiers who joined SOA from the Australian Imperial Force. In time another holding unit was formed, M Special Unit.

Many of the men who served in this unit were unaware (for security reasons) that they were serving officially with Special Operations Australia, and there was further confusion in April 1943 when the Services Reconnaissance Department was established, its personnel recruited from the ranks of the SOA.

After the war, veterans' groups adopted Z Special Unit as the name of their associations, and several designed emblems. They were as confused as readers are likely to be by the subterfuge employed by SOA! For the sake of clarity, therefore, I categorize these operations as Z Special Unit missions.

Strictly speaking, Operation *Jaywick*, the first of Ivan Lyon's forays to Singapore, was an SOE mission and not connected with SOA, as it was financed from London. However, that could be considered splitting historical hairs, as it was planned and prepared in Australia, and for that reason it is designated a Z Special Unit operation.

INTRODUCTION: STIRLING EFFORT

On the evening of 24 April 1940, the Royal Navy submarine, Truant, slipped from its base at Rosyth into the Firth of Forth. Its destination was Norway, its cargo six British soldiers, all heavily armed and steely-eyed. 'At Rosyth these brave soldiers came on board,' recalled the Truant's commander, Christopher Hutchinson. 'I say brave because they probably never volunteered to dive in a submarine to start with. Secondly, not perhaps in war, and thirdly, having got them to their landing place I was to forsake them, and leave them with such weapons as they had: plastic explosive, cheesewire for silencing sentries, ghastly-looking knives. I'd never seen such a bunch of cut-throats, but I must say, I did admire them.'[1]

The soldiers were members of Military Intelligence (Research), MI (R), what would shortly be re-designated the Special Operations Executive (SOE), Britain's elite practitioners of clandestine warfare. They were led by Major Bryan Mayfield, a former regular officer in the Scots Guards, and under him were captains Bill Stirling, Peter Kemp, Ralph Farrant, David Stacey and Jim Gavin.

They had disparate talents and experience, but none was as distinguished as the 28-year-old Gavin. A noted scholar and athlete, Gavin had grown up in Chile and went from Cambridge University – where he read Mechanical Sciences – to the Royal Engineers. In 1936 he was selected to join the British expedition to Mount Everest led by Hugh Ruttledge. Described by one newspaper as the 'baby of the party' but with 'a tough physique', Gavin proved his worth on the unsuccessful but gallant attempt to scale the peak. On returning to Aldershot, Gavin and his squadron commander constructed a 35-foot yacht that won the Army sailing championships.

The purpose of Operation *Knife*, as the men's mission was codenamed, was to land in Sogne Fjord, north of Bergen, where a party of the Norwegian resistance would greet them. In partnership, using the explosives they had brought from Britain, the guerrillas would then launch a series of sabotage attacks on the Bergen to Oslo railway, now controlled by the Nazis following their invasion at the start of the month.

Eight hours into the voyage, the Truant hit a mine as it sailed on the surface of the North Sea. No one was killed in the violent explosion that rocked the submarine, but such was the damage that Hutchinson was obliged to return to Rosyth for repairs. The six soldiers retired to Bill Stirling's* country estate at Keir just outside Dunblane to wait while a replacement submarine was found. 'Exhilarated by the recollection of our recent escape and stimulated by the hope of another, more successful venture, we were yet able to relax enough to enjoy the superb hospitality which the Stirlings, undismayed by the imminent conversion of Keir into a hospital, lavished upon us,' recalled Peter Kemp.[2]

But there was no second attempt. The Allies admitted defeat in their campaign to wrest Norway back from the Germans and Operation *Knife* was cancelled. Kemp said the news was a 'severe blow' to their morale, except to Bill Stirling, who saw it as an opportunity. 'It was thanks to Stirling's imagination and initiative that our partnership was not, in fact, immediately dissolved,' said Kemp. 'It was Stirling's idea that the six of us, reinforced by a few selected officers and NCOs, should form the nucleus of a new training school. We should begin with cadre courses for junior officers from different units of the army. Mayfield was to be commandant, Stirling chief instructor.'[3]

Stirling, whose family had deep connections within government and the Royal Family (his mother was a friend of Queen Mary, George VI's mother), went to London with Mayfield and swiftly won over the War Office for their irregular warfare training centre. At that point in the war Britain was searching desperately for any means to hit back at the Nazis.

ABOVE A renowned mountaineer, Jim Gavin took easily to guerrilla warfare and in 1941 established the special training school in Singapore. (Author's Collection)

ABOVE LEFT Bill Stirling, the elder brother of David, founder of the SAS, can be considered as the father of British special forces in WWII. (Author's Collection)

---

* Together with his younger brother, David, Bill would found the Special Air Service in North Africa in the summer of 1941.

The site chosen was at Lochailort in the north-west of Scotland, an area that was as rugged as it was picturesque. Stirling knew it from his summer holidays when, in the company of his cousin, Simon Fraser, the Lord Lovat, he had hiked, climbed, swum, stalked and shot. The land was owned by Lord Lovat but he willingly leased it out in return for a place on the training staff as an instructor in fieldcraft. On 30 May it was designated the Commando STC (Special Training Centre) Lochailort, and the following week the first recruits arrived. With the enthusiastic backing of the new Prime Minister, Winston Churchill, they were there to learn the art of guerrilla warfare, what one of their instructors, Mike Calvert, famously summarized as 'the tactics of the materially-weak against the materially strong'.[4]

Calvert was a Sapper★ and had been recruited to Lochailort by Gavin, the chief demolitions instructor. Another instructor Gavin knew personally was Freddie Spencer Chapman, a gifted Arctic explorer and born survivalist, who assessed Lochailort as 'a training centre for smash-and-grab raids on targets in enemy-occupied territory, a sideline which, after Dunkirk, seemed the only possible form of offensive warfare'.[5]

For the rest of 1940 a steady stream of officers and NCOs from the newly formed 'Commandos' passed through the Lochailort course, their bodies and their minds challenged during four demanding weeks. 'It was a rather good course and again extremely hard physically,' recalled one Commando officer, George Jellicoe. 'It was practical training, some of it was deer stalking and poaching, and hunting deer ... we had a rather long taxing two or three days in the hills.'[6]

As well as mastering explosives, students learned other technical skills such as unarmed combat, close-quarter shooting and map reading.

To his annoyance, Mike Calvert was transferred after only six weeks as an instructor, joining the Military Intelligence Directorate in London, where with Peter Fleming (brother of Ian, creator of the James Bond novels), he began planning a guerrilla campaign in southern England in the event of a Nazi invasion. Once that threat had receded Calvert was off again, this time to Australia, where his task was to establish a training school along the lines of Lochailort. He sailed in October 1940 in the company of Spencer Chapman, a man who, in Calvert's estimation, 'talked like a liberal and acted like an anarchist'.[7]

★ Sappers is the nickname of members of the Royal Engineers, derived from 1856 when the Corps of Royal Sappers and Miners merged with the officer corps of the Royal Engineers to form the Corps of Royal Engineers.

Bill Stirling left Lochailort in January 1941, travelling to the Middle East with Peter Fleming, for what would prove a fruitless mission to recruit anti-fascist Italian prisoners into a guerrilla unit willing to operate in their homeland.

In March it was Jim Gavin's turn to depart Lochailort.★ On reporting to London, Gavin was promoted to major and informed that he was to establish a special training school in Singapore, codenamed 'Scapula', the purpose of which was 'to train all types of personnel – military and civilian, European and native – in irregular warfare'.

Gavin was introduced to his superior, Valentine St John Killery, a former executive with ICI and now the head of the Orient Mission, the SOE codename for their activities in the Far East. 'The immediate necessity for the new unit was a comprehensive War Establishment, without which we should have no official standing,' wrote Gavin. 'On the 4 April an establishment of 10 officers and approximately 50 other ranks was approved by the War Office. Meanwhile the stores had been ordered, and many interviews held with a view to selecting suitable officers and NCO instructors. Eventually it was decided to take out 7 officers and approximately 20 other ranks from the UK, and recruit the rest locally.'[8]

Gavin left England by air the following month and arrived in Singapore on 28 May. The Malaya Command had selected a site for the training school, but its surrounding countryside made it wholly unsuitable. Gavin therefore chose an alternative, at Tanjong Bali, 20 miles from Singapore, which boasted a large house 'with extensive grounds on an island joined to the mainland by two causeways . . . in a very secluded part of Singapore Island.'

Gavin and his HQ staff moved into Tanjong Bali on 14 July, and he christened their new home No. 101 Special Training School. Two days later the main party arrived from England, and the remainder checked in on 5 August.

Gavin had his school. All he now required was to recruit a handful of officers and men who knew the area and could bring this knowledge to their training.

Inverailort House, south of Lochailort, was the HQ of the Special Training School established by Bill Stirling in May 1940. (Author's Collection)

★ By now it had been decided to establish a large training centre for the commandos, and in March 1942 Achnacarry, 30 miles east, received its first intake.

CHAPTER 1
LYON HEARTED

It was only natural that Jim Gavin and Ivan Lyon should hit it off. The pair had much in common: tough, sinewy, resourceful and a streak of individuality that in Lyon's case was literally emblazoned across his skin. He called the tiger's head tattooed prominently across his chest, 'Rimau', the Malay word for the beast, and its scarlet eyes and gold and black stripes caused a sensation in the officers' mess of the Gordon Highlanders.

Conduct unbecoming of a British officer? Lyon cared not a jot. There was within a streak of iconoclasm despite a background that suggested he should be a rigid military type. He came from a long line of warriors, stretching back to an ancestor, David, who had been slain fighting the English at the Battle of Flodden in 1513. His grandfather had served in the Horse Artillery, while his father had reached the rank of brigadier-general in the Royal Field Artillery.

Ivan himself was born in Sevenoaks on 17 August 1915, and spent some of his early childhood in Brussels, where his father was British military attaché. Aged 12, Lyon was enrolled at Harrow School, where he made a name for himself as a sportsman if not as a scholar. He played in the back row for his house, West Acre, in the inter-house rugby competition, and later for the 2nd XV, and was an outstanding member of the cross-country team. He won the inter-house competition in 1933, recorded the Harrow School magazine, stating: 'The going was heavy over the 5½ miles course, which I. Lyon had mapped out with the help of one of the masters . . . the course consisted of two different circuits of about equal length.'

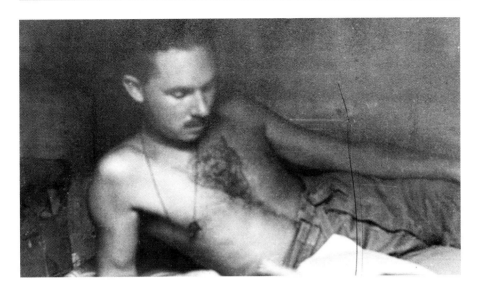

Ivan Lyon's distinctive tiger tattoo, the result of a night's drinking in Singapore, was the inspiration for 'Rimau', the Malayan word for 'Tiger'. (AWM 045422)

It was sailing, however, that most stimulated Lyon, encouraged by one of the Harrow masters, a Mr Gannon. On 10 April 1933 Lyon embarked on the school's 'Spring Cruise', a two-week voyage along the south coast of Cornwall. The yacht was the *Amy*, an 18-ton ex-Bristol Channel pilot cutter, and the crew consisted of Lyon and six of his peers, as well as a Captain Inskip, a retired master mariner who had served 29 years in sail. 'It has been said that this cruise, in comparison to the others undertaken by the Club, was a "pleasure cruise", but the initiated as well as the uninitiated learnt a great deal about matters that one does not come in touch with in the ordinary course of events,' noted the school magazine, a reference to the 'very fierce squall' encountered off the Lizard, the most south-westerly point of the British mainland.

It was a cruise that instilled in Lyon a love of the sea, a passion that remained with him for the rest of his life. He applied for a commission in the Royal Navy upon leaving Harrow in the summer of 1934, but was deemed unsuitable material for a naval officer; so Lyon followed family tradition and went to the Royal Military College, Sandhurst, and from there to the Gordon Highlanders as a second lieutenant.

In late 1936 Lyon was shipped out to Singapore with the 2nd Battalion aboard the troopship *Dorchester* and so began a fascination with the region that would, in time, be of inestimable value to the British military.

From the start Lyon eschewed the cosy and clannish expatriate community in Singapore. He preferred the authentic East to the artificiality of the Tanglin Club and Raffles Hotel, where officers, planters, businessmen and bankers frolicked in opulent indolence, to the exclusion of the indigenous population.

Unorthodox, audacious and innovative, Ivan Lyon proved himself a brilliant guerrilla leader. (Author's Collection)

Lyon's tattoo was the consequence of too many Tiger beers in one of the Singapore dive bars, where he preferred to do his drinking.

The British commander in Malaya in 1937 was Major-General William Dobbie, pious and austere, the polar opposite in character to the maverick Lyon. But Dobbie – a veteran of the South African War and the Great War – was also an astute military strategist, one of the few senior British officers who viewed with grave alarm Japanese ambitions in the Far East. He was also unsettled by the preponderance of Japanese spies in Singapore, quietly gathering intelligence that was sent back to Tokyo.

Dobbie lobbied London to establish a counter-intelligence department, and the fruition was the appointment of Lieutenant-Colonel Francis Hayley Bell as Defence Security Officer. Described by his daughter, Mary, as 'a strange, complex man, spiritually proud, with the heart of a lion; sometimes too strong',[9] Hayley Bell recruited Lyon part-time to his department, recognizing a kindred spirit, as well as a soldier bored with garrison life.

Hayley Bell soon infiltrated the Japanese espionage network, discovering plenty of intelligence that indicated they intended to attack Singapore, not from the sea, but from the north, coming through the jungle of Malaya. Dobbie believed him, but Whitehall didn't.

Lyon, meanwhile, was combining business with pleasure, sailing a 3-ton yacht, *Vinette*, among the islands of the Riau Archipelago, south of Singapore. As well as searching for evidence of Japanese espionage, he learned about the tides and currents, and the customs and attitudes of the islanders.

In late 1937 Lyon was invited to join the crew of the 12-ton Australian yacht, *Kewarra,* which sailed from Singapore through the Dutch East Indies to Darwin. The yacht's owner, J.A. Gagan, was a brilliant navigator and he helped Lyon hone his skill in the art of using a chart, sextant and tide tables.

By early 1938 Lyon was fed up with garrison soldiering; it challenged him neither physically nor mentally, and he was increasingly a peripheral figure in the officers' mess. He saved up his weekend leaves in order to embark on longer voyages, sailing up the eastern coast of Malaya in the *Vinette*. Then in the summer of 1938 he set out for Saigon, a voyage that would change the course of his life.

His navigation was not yet perfect and, according to the *Edinburgh Evening News*, 'running a little off his course, he arrived at the convict island (of Pulau Condore, now called Con Son Island) on which it is usually forbidden to land'. The island, 100 miles south of the mainland, was known as Vietnam's (then Indo-China) 'Devil's Island', where the French imprisoned locals and subjected them to brutal forced labour. The director of the penal colony was Claude Bouvier, then in his second term in charge of the settlement. Delighted at the appearance of his uninvited guest – particularly as Lyon was fluent in French – Bouvier insisted the Scot stay for dinner and the night.

If Lyon had any initial reluctance to interrupting his voyage, it vanished the moment he saw the director's daughter. Gabrielle was 24. She was beautiful, vivacious and elegant, and although divorced with a young daughter, Lyon didn't care. He was smitten, and one night extended to seven as he fell in love with Gabrielle. Though she detested Lyon's tattoo, she, too was enamoured, and a few months later accepted his proposal of marriage. They wed in July 1939, and their happy day made the papers in Britain: 'YACHT CRUISE ROMANCE SCOT MEETS BRIDE ON PENAL SETTLEMENT' ran the headline in the *Edinburgh Evening News* on 9 August 1939, continuing:

A young officer of the Gordon Highlanders who found a bride on a French penal settlement island off the coast of Indo-China, has just been married in Saigon, say reports reaching Singapore. He is

Lieutenant Ivan Lyon, of the Second Battalion Gordon Highlanders, who are stationed in Singapore. A keen yachtsman, Lieut. Lyon was cruising in the China Sea in his two-ton [sic] yacht, when he ran a little off his course and came to Pulau Condore, the French convict settlement island about 100 miles from the Indo-China coast . . . Lieutenant and Mrs Lyon are soon returning to Singapore.

There had been a significant change in Singapore when the Lyons took up residence in a military bungalow in Orchard Road. William Dobbie had been replaced as commanding officer of Malaya by Lionel Bond, and he took a dim view of Francis Hayley Bell's counter-espionage methods, which included the summary execution of captured Japanese agents. Hayley Bell had been dismissed in May 1939 and his Defence Security Office disbanded.

The outbreak of war in Europe had little immediate effect on the Lyons, but when France capitulated to the Nazis in June 1940, both Ivan and Gabrielle began working for the Free French. Ivan was appointed the liaison officer to General Georges Catroux, the former Governor General of French Indo-China, now the Commander-in-Chief, China, with the Free French movement, and Gabrielle was employed as a secretary in the Free French office in Singapore.

In 1941 Catroux was transferred to the Middle East, and in July that year Lyon first came to the attention of SOE. On the 15th of that month he was interviewed by Lieutenant-Colonel Alan Warren, a Royal Marine, who acted as a liaison between GHQ and the Orient Mission in Singapore. Instructed to complete a form, Lyon gave details of his background, education and qualifications. He could speak French and Malay, rated his physical fitness as 'A' and listed his dimensions as 5 feet 10, 145 pounds, brown hair, green eyes and a fresh complexion. Alongside 'distinguishing marks', he wrote: 'Tiger tattooed on chest'. He could ride, sail, drive, box, swim, ski and cycle, but could not sketch or read or transmit morse. Under 'special knowledge' he wrote 'D.R. [Dead Reckoning] navigation' and gave Australia, Malaya and the South China Sea as the regions he knew well.

SOE's assessment was that Lyon 'is under consideration for employment; he may be definitely engaged later when he will be advised accordingly'.

By early September 1941 Lyon had been despatched to 101 Special Training School (STS), where he was introduced to Jim Gavin and his second-in-command, Freddie Spencer Chapman. 'Training began one week after forming, and continued at full capacity until just before the fall of Singapore,' wrote Gavin subsequently. 'Instruction was given in demolitions and sabotage, use of weapons, unarmed combat, seamanship and communications; and over 10% of the time was spent in night-work.'[10]

The instruction appealed to Lyon's maverick nature; guerrilla fighting was his sort of soldiering, not the conventional life of an infantry officer. That war was coming with Japan was evident, but throughout the autumn of 1941 the 101 STS was training under a misapprehension. 'By the 8 December, plans were well under way for directing irregular warfare in China,' wrote Gavin. 'For providing a fifth column organisation in South Thailand; for equipping a strong "Stay Behind" party in the new territories, Hong Kong and for fostering sabotage in Indo-China . . . war came, however, too soon for any of these plans to yield good results.'[11]

Ivan Lyon was transferred from 101 STS to SOE (Orient Mission) on 14 February 1942. The next day the British surrendered Singapore to the Japanese, who renamed it Shonan (Sunny South) and wound the clocks forward an hour and a half to correspond to the time in Tokyo.

Lyon had seen his wife and baby onto a boat bound for Australia the previous month, and most of the staff of 101 STS had been evacuated by steamer from Singapore to Rangoon.

In the two months since the surprise attack on the US naval base in Pearl Harbor, Hawaii, Japan had proceeded to inflict one crushing defeat after another on the British, humiliating them in Hong Kong and Malaya, sinking their newest battleship, the *Prince of Wales,* as well as the battle cruiser HMS *Repulse*, and finally the fall of Singapore, described by Winston Churchill as 'the worst disaster and largest capitulation in British history'. The loss of Singapore hurt the most because it had been a symbol of British prestige in the region. Its loss, and the surrender of 125,000 Allied soldiers appalled Churchill, who bitterly reflected that the young soldier of this war wasn't a patch on that of the Great War. 'In 1915 our men fought on even when they had only one shell left and were under fierce barrage,' he wrote. 'Now they cannot even resist dive bombers. We had so many men in Singapore, so many men – they should have done better.'[12]

That they didn't was more to do with weak and incompetent leadership than lack of courage and fortitude. Freddie Spencer Chapman had been urging GHQ to despatch small guerrilla parties from 101 STS into Malaya ever since the Japanese had invaded on 7 December. 'Malaya would never have fallen had I been

LEFT Ron Morris, a coal miner before the war, joined the Royal Army Medical Corps and was identified by Lyon as an exceptional soldier. (AWM 045417)

BELOW Padang, on the western coast of Sumatra, was where Ivan Lyon sailed to Ceylon at the wheel of the *Sederhana Djohanes*. (Author's Collection) allowed to go ahead with my scheme when I first put it forward,' he subsequently claimed, rather brashly. 'My guerrillas, if their numbers had been strong enough, could so have completely disorganised the Jap attack that time would have been gained to allow our reinforcements to arrive from Australia.'[13]

Instead, he and the rest of the Training School were ordered to keep their 'noses out of things that could be handled perfectly by highly trained officers whose profession it was to learn the art of war'.

On 31 January Lyon was summoned to the office of Lieutenant-Colonel Alan Warren in the Cathay Building. Also present was Major Herbert 'Jock' Campbell, 37, once of the King's Own Scottish Borderers, but more recently a director in the rubber and palm oil business. Fluent in French and Malay, Campbell had been instructed by Warren to establish a supply route to Sumatra, but that was before the lightning advance of the Japanese through Malaya. It was increasingly likely that the supply route would now be an escape route. Warren asked Lyon to draw on his knowledge of the islands between Singapore and Sumatra to establish a staging post where evacuees could receive food and medical assistance.

Lyon was granted permission to enlist the help of one of the STS staff, a 22-year-old corporal in the Royal Army Medical Corps called Ron Morris, a coal miner before the war. Inevitably nicknamed 'Taffy' on account of his having been born in the Rhondda Valley, Morris 'had the Welsh means of expressing all his feelings in song [and] his clear tenor rang through all his waking hours'. Morris had an irreverent humour that appealed to Lyon; he was also stoic and efficient, traits that would be important for the task ahead.

On 6 February the staff of 101 STS were evacuated from Singapore on the steamship *Krait*. Lyon and Morris went as far as Pulau Durian, an uninhabited island at the northern end of the Durian Strait (about 35 miles south of Singapore), which had been selected by Lyon as their staging post. The *Krait* then picked up Jim Gavin from Java before proceeding to Rangoon.

For the next three weeks Lyon and Morris comforted and sustained hundreds of civilians and military personnel who washed up on their island having fled Singapore in any seaworthy vessel. Once they were ready for the next stage of their escape, the evacuees were re-directed to Prigi Radja (60 miles south), where Campbell had established a base.

By the end of February there were no longer any stragglers arriving at Pulau Durian, so Lyon and Morris set sail in a small boat, navigating their way up the Indragiri River to Rengat. There they met an Australian called Bill Reynolds, another of the unconventional characters that often come to the fore in a time of military crisis. The 49-year-old, a naval veteran of the Great War, had worked in the Malayan mining industry in the 1930s, where he spent his free time hunting tigers and also, it was rumoured, spying for MI6.

Reynolds was now in the same line of work as Lyon, collecting stragglers from Singapore, and in total he had rescued more than 1,000 people. He was about to embark on an intelligence-gathering operation but, before he set off, he arranged for a car to drive Morris and Lyon to Padang on the western coast of Sumatra. They arrived on 2 March, and made their way to the Oranje Hotel, where Lieutenant-Colonel Warren was trying to bring some semblance of order to the chaotic scenes at the port as 2,000 frightened soldiers and civilians clamoured to board the remaining vessels before the Japanese arrived. He had also to contend with the Dutch authorities, who officially ran the town, and who on 7 March – with the Japanese only 50 miles away – decided to prevent any further evacuation by the British in the hope of currying favour with the new dominant force in the region. One of the last vessels to leave contained several SOE personnel, mostly other ranks, among whom was Taffy Morris.

Warren, however, had been told of one vessel moored 7 miles up the coast, the *Sederhana Djohanes* (Simple Jack), a 65-foot Malay prahu. He had bought it with the last of the funds from the GHQ account, and the intention was to sail it 1,500 miles across the Indian Ocean to Ceylon. The dilemma that Warren faced was in deciding who merited a place on the small vessel. 'This boat was capable of taking twenty people on board and therefore [Warren] would, when the time came, choose such British officers as were in the port and choose from among them the ones he considered would be best for the war effort in the future,'[14] said Richard Broome, a member of SOE, who had worked under Warren in Singapore.

The selection had been discreet; panic was rife in Padang and Warren feared if word got out that there was a boat about to depart there would be pandemonium. He had decided to remain, believing it his duty as a senior officer to continue to command the demoralized men. Among those chosen by Warren were Ivan Lyon, Jock Campbell, Richard Broome and John Davis, a former policeman in Malaya who had been recruited by SOE. 'I was sent to stay on board and Davis was left on shore to make the final arrangements to get these officers off,' said Broome. 'When the Japanese had already invaded Sumatra and things looked pretty desperate, Davis appeared with these picked officers . . . and he brought with him a written order from Warren to me to take charge of this prahu to Ceylon.'[15]

For such a formidable undertaking, the *Sederhana Djohanes* was alarmingly under-equipped. With one short mast and one long, the vessel had been built to trade the length of the Sumatran coast, not cross the Indian Ocean. Described as 'broad in the beam and bucket-shaped amidships with an 18-inch freeboard',[16] *Sederhana Djohanes* had a mainsail, mizzen, staysail and jib, but the sails were so thin, recalled one of the passengers, it was possible 'to see the stars through them'. The navigational aids were similarly sparse: one chart of Sumatra's west coast, a sextant but no chronometer. They would have to use a wristwatch. As for traversing the Indian Ocean, all they had was a small wind map ripped from a pocket dictionary.

The men – 18 in total – assembled on the *Sederhana Djohanes* in the early hours of 8 March, whereupon Broome briefed them about the scale of their challenge. They had a limited quantity of food, only basic medical equipment, a couple of Lewis machine guns and 140 gallons of water stored in large drums, earthenware jugs and fuel tins. 'We never knew how long this trip was going to take us so we had to reckon for forty odd days and had to ration our water accordingly,' recalled Broome. 'We had one pint per day per head in this ration, which was to cover any kind of cooking you could do and all necessities.'[17]

Broome asked who had sailing experience; not the messing-about-on-a-river type but proper seafaring knowledge. There were a couple of Royal Navy officers among the party, but the two who stood out were Lyon – described by Broome as 'a very good lone yachtsman . . . a very good asset to our company' – and a merchant seaman called Garth Gorham, a skilled navigator.

The wind was kind to them on the first day at sea, 9 March, enabling them to cover nearly 40 miles. Spirits were high, buoyed by the adrenaline of embarking on such a bold venture. The *Sederhana Djohanes* also gave cause for optimism. 'The boat itself was extraordinarily good, awfully well constructed,' said Broome. 'Made of teak and she was ballasted with pebbles, it consisted of one huge hole covered with a penthouse roof, a poop astern and a small fo'c'sle which would each hold about four or five chaps but there always had to be people down below.'[18]

Among those on board the *Sederhana Djohanes* was an artillery major called Geoffrey Rowley-Conwy (later the Lord Longford), who had escaped from Singapore in a junk. He found Lyon a 'reassuring figure' at the helm; utterly focused on the task in hand, he bantered little with his companions, instead puffing on his pipe while 'staring beyond the line of the horizon into the closed country of his own thoughts'.[19] The pair made occasional small talk and Lyon described some of his past sailing experience: the cruise along the Cornish coast while a schoolboy at Harrow, a voyage from Munich to Dubrovnik in a sailing canoe, the trip from Singapore to Australia and the time he landed himself a wife en route to Saigon.

The tranquillity of the first day soon vanished as the weather turned, and the boom broke in the teeth of a fierce storm. Then one of the sails ripped. These were setbacks that could be rectified. More threatening were the coral reefs they had to negotiate on the west coast of Sumatra, an obstacle that Lyon skilfully circumvented. What they feared above all else, however, was not a natural foe. 'While we were in aircraft range of Sumatra we had Japanese reconnaissance aircraft over every day,' said Broome. He had organized a drill for such an event, which was for all the Europeans to go below decks while the two Malays (John Davis's police colleague and Broome's batman) would remain on deck in the hope the enemy pilot would mistake them for fishermen. 'All went well until one day this machine came over, swooped down and started firing, about three bursts,' said Broome. 'By the grace of god no one was hit. One or two bullets came through the deck but were stopped by the pebble ballast.'

Once they were well away from Sumatra the weather was capricious. A sudden storm might descend, followed by days of hot windless tedium. There was no space for the men to escape from their companions if they wanted some solitude. Hunger and thirst further chafed nerves. 'Our morale was usually pretty high except when we had contrary winds,' said Broome.

By early April they had covered over half the distance, but their doctor, Major Davies of the RAMC, was concerned at the state of some of the men. 'Sepsis is the main cause of my worries,' he wrote in his diary. 'The lesions are either fulminating ulcers resulting from trauma or a generalised eruption of vesicles and pustules usually in the axillae, belt areas, groin and buttocks.'[20]

The *Sederhana Djohanes* was similarly run down, the copper that lined the outside of the hull peeling away, making the vessel ever more vulnerable. Then on 12 April Gorham spotted what at first glance appeared to be a cloud on the horizon. He looked harder. It wasn't a cloud; it was land. To be precise, it was the 7,300-foot Adam's Peak on Ceylon.

The men's jubilation was short-lived. 'The great problem arose of what to do,' said Broome. 'We had no charts of the Ceylon coast and none of us knew the first thing about what the east coast of Ceylon was like. Those of us who had some experience of yachting or sailing knew we had to be jolly careful because if we carried on sailing straight for Ceylon we might strike a rock and the whole enterprise would be wasted.'[21]

Lyon and Gorham advised Broome that the prudent course was to sail round the south coast of Ceylon to a port called Hambantota. Broome agreed, but the decision not to take the shortest route to land 'rather upset the morale ...there was considerable dissent at this decision'. The men's mood deteriorated further when dawn broke on 13 April; land had disappeared because a rising south-westerly wind was pushing them back out into the Indian Ocean.

Lyon fought manfully against the wind for the next 36 hours, coaxing the *Sederhana Djohanes* back towards Ceylon, close enough for them to see the distant palm trees – and the size of the sheer cliffs against which the surf smashed. Morale plummeted, but soon soared when a vessel was spotted. The men – except Lyon – were so shattered that they no longer cared if it was friend or foe. But their luck was in. From the bridge of the cargo ship, the *Anglo-Canadian*, its skipper, David Williams, observed the curious craft heading in his direction. 'We made every kind of signal we could but they were suspicious,' said Broome. 'But eventually they came close and knew we were all right.'

The whole ship's company cheered the 18 men on board as they climbed unaided up a 30-foot rope ladder. The last to leave the *Sederhana Djohanes* was the man responsible more than any other for bringing them safely through their ordeal. Ivan Lyon had piloted the creaking craft 1,500 miles in 36 days and 13 hours in an outstanding feat of seamanship.

CHAPTER 2

OPERATION JAYWICK

The rescued men of the *Sederhana Djohanes* recovered their strength in the luxurious splendour of the Taj Mahal Hotel in Bombay. It was a brief interlude of indolence. They soon embarked on new adventures and only Lyon and Campbell were left in India. Neither was in particularly high spirits despite their magnificent accomplishment in crossing the Indian Ocean. It had been their own 'Dunkirk', a testament to their pluck and initiative, but that could not conceal the humiliating retreat from the enemy. Lyon had seethed with resentment from the moment he had left Singapore, but his imagination had been fired by his anger and a plan was now taking shape in his head. He shared it with Campbell in Bombay and then, as if destiny was validating his idea, whom should he encounter in Bombay but Bill Reynolds, the irascible Australian he had last seen at Rengat on the Indragiri River at the end of February?

Reynolds had some tale to tell. On leaving Rengat he had sailed his 70-foot Japanese coaster called *Kofuku Maru* up the Sumatra coast, through the Malacca Straits and across the Indian Ocean. The diesel engine had coughed and spluttered like an old man with asthma, but somehow Reynolds and his skeleton Chinese crew had nursed her to India.

Over a beer Lyon outlined his plan to Reynolds: he would lead a small team of guerrillas in canoes into Singapore Harbour, where they would sink Japanese shipping with magnetic limpet mines. What he needed from Reynolds was his boat, and his navigational excellence, to take them to the cluster of small islands off the east coast of Sumatra, from where they would paddle to their objective.

Reynolds approved of the plan. Like Lyon, he was also smarting from the bitter taste of defeat and the thought of punching back at the Japanese was one that appealed.

Now came the bigger challenge: convincing the powers-that-be. The first step Lyon took was to approach the Indian Mission,★ established by SOE in New Delhi and run by a former businessman called Colin Mackenzie.

Initially he was greeted with a mixture of scornful indifference, but then Lyon met Bernard Fergusson, a pre-war acquaintance and also a sailing enthusiast. Fergusson had arrived in Delhi in April to take up an appointment on General Archibald Wavell's Joint Planning Staff. The Commander-in-Chief, India, had an unenviable task: that of trying to restore morale after the debacle in the Far East, while also producing ways of striking at the Japanese. 'Many people in those days came into our office with plans for reconquest,' recalled Fergusson. 'Some of their ideas were useful: these were carefully noted, and filed away for future references. Some were fantastic and foolish: these we made a pretence of noting, and bowed their originators out of the room as quickly as in all civility we could.'[22]

The plan proposed by Lyon wasn't for reconquest, but it was audacious and, if successful, one that would embarrass and anger the Japanese, while demonstrating to the world that the Allies had the means – and the pluck – to attack them even hundreds of miles behind their lines.

Fergusson passed it to Wavell, who must have had a sense of déjà vu as he studied Lyon's submission. Almost two years earlier, in June 1940, when Wavell had been the commander-in-chief in the Middle East, he had received an idea for a long-range reconnaissance force to operate deep inside Italian-held Libya. It was the brainchild of Ralph Bagnold, who, during the 1920s while an Army officer stationed in Cairo, had explored large tracts of the North African desert in Model T Ford automobiles. Bagnold had stressed that as well as gathering intelligence on the enemy's strength and positions, there would also be the opportunity for some 'piracy on the high desert'. Now here was a man proposing to draw on his pre-war exploration of the South China Sea and the islands therein to create a force of similar boldness. Bagnold's idea had grown into the

★ This Mission subsequently became known as Force 136.

Long Range Desert Group, the unrivalled masters of guerrilla warfare in North Africa, and Wavell saw immediately the potential in Lyon's proposal.

So, too, did admirals Sir Geoffrey Layton, Commander-in-Chief, Ceylon, and Geoffrey Arbuthnot, Commander-in-Chief, East Indies. There was one issue that required consultation: where the mission should start. Wavell would have liked Lyon to base himself in India, no doubt because if successful some of the glory would reflect on himself. On 12 June, Wavell's staff cabled the War Office in London to inform them: '0.302 [Lyon's codenumber] has worked scheme for raiding Japanese Occupied Harbours particularly Singapore. This scheme has received approval of commander in chief India and commander in chief East Indies. Scheme involved using Reynolds's Japanese diesel engined fishing vessel ... expedition will start from Cookstown Queensland.'

Among other points made in the cable was the proposed starting date of the operation – February 1943 – and a promise that Lyon's draft plan would be sent by air shortly. This plan was summarized and despatched on 20 June and contained much interesting information:

> The C-in-C discussed at some length with 0.302 [Lyon] the relative merits of basing the project on India or Australia, and while at first somewhat doubtful or reluctant, he eventually decided that 0.302 was right in his preference for Australia.
> Captain Reynolds is a middle-aged Australian. He was at Zeebrugge [sic] and Ostend in 1918 with the Dover Patrol. His ship is exactly what 0.302 requires, and he proposes to charter it at the price of £100 per month.
> The suggestion to obtain volunteers from New Zealand was an after-thought on 0.302's part. It was agreed with the C-in-C that he would in the first instance attempt to obtain suitable Australian volunteers, as going down to New Zealand would add considerably to the time which would be occupied in travelling.*

As for the personnel so far recruited: Lyon was the leader, Jock Campbell the administrator, Reynolds the skipper, and Ron Morris, 'lately a private soldier in the RAMC now transferred to the IACC [Indian Army Corps of Clerks].' The rest would be recruited in Australia.

---

* Ironically, when Ralph Bagnold raised the LRDG in 1940, his first inclination was to recruit Australians, but their high command refused, so he selected New Zealanders, who proved eminently suited to the role.

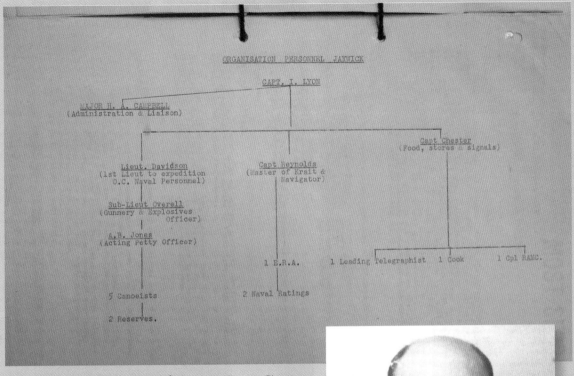

ORGANISATION PERSONNEL JAYWICK

CAPT. I. LYON

MAJOR H. A. CAMPBELL
(Administration & Liaison)

Capt Chester
(Food, stores & signals)

Lieut. Davidson
(1st Lieut to expedition
O.C. Naval Personnel)

Capt Reynolds
(Master of Krait &
Navigator)

Sub-Lieut Overell
(Gunnery & Explosives
Officer)

A.B. Jones
(Acting Petty Officer)

1 E.R.A.   1 Leading Telegraphist   1 Cook   1 Cpl RAMC.

5 Canoeists

2 Naval Ratings

2 Reserves.

ABOVE The command structure of Operation *Jaywick*, the name of which was inspired by a bad egg on a previous Lyon voyage! (Author's Collection)

RIGHT Francis Chester oversaw logistics for *Jaywick* and later operated in Borneo with Z Special Unit. (Author's Collection)

LEFT General Sir Thomas Blamey, Commander-in-Chief, Australian Land Forces, threw his support behind SOE Australia in 1942. (NAA 33035073)

Finally, the memo revealed the operation's codename, *Jaywick*, although it did not elaborate on its origins. It was not named in honour of the small Essex coastal town built in the 1930s for Londoners to enjoy the sea air, but rather it was a nod to a well-known air freshener, Jay Wick, that had been a topic of conversation on a pre-war cruise to Thailand. In a rough sea, a basket of eggs had smashed on Lyon's yacht, *Vinette*, their yolks seeping into the bilge to create a smell that wrinkled one's nose. If only we had some Jay Wick to purge our yacht of the evil stench, Lyon remarked to his companion. It was Lyon's ambition to purge Singapore of the evil stench of the Japanese occupier.

While Ivan Lyon had been making good his escape from Sumatra in March 1942, two British SOE majors, Grey Egerton Mott and Ambrose Trappes Lomax, had landed in Fremantle, Western Australia, from Java independently of each other. They received instruction from London to establish an SOE outpost in Victoria Barracks in Melbourne, and they had soon made the acquaintance of Commander Rupert Long, the Director of Naval Intelligence (DNI). Long was an advocate of special operations and with his support and encouragement, Mott – the senior of the two British officers – was introduced to General Sir Thomas Blamey, Commander-in-Chief, Australian Land Forces. He also expressed his enthusiasm for an Australian SOE, although he warned Mott that ultimate control would reside with General Douglas MacArthur, Supreme Commander of US Forces in the Far East. He had recently set up an HQ in Australia after being run out of the Philippines by the Japanese, and many of his staff were contemptuous of the British, re-dubbing their South-East Asia Command (SEAC) 'Save England's Asiatic Colonies'.

Nonetheless, MacArthur authorized the establishment of Special Operations Australia (SOA) on 17 April and he expressed no objection to Blamey retaining 'immediate control' over the organization or to Mott being its director.

Under the cover name Inter-Allied Services Department (ISD), Mott sourced a more spacious HQ in Melbourne using some of the funds provided by SOE in London (Mott estimated that SOA would require funding of £100,000 per year). The funds were channelled to Mott through a secret bank account at a Sydney branch of the Bank of New South Wales.

The HQ was called 'Airlie', a stylish house in the exclusive neighbourhood of South Yarra. Mott also took possession of a Guerrilla Warfare School at Wilsons

Australia's Prime Minister John Curtin (right) and General Douglas MacArthur, Supreme Commander of US Forces in the Far East. (NAA 11198588)

Promontory, some 130 miles south of Melbourne, a site originally selected by Mike Calvert and Freddie Spencer Chapman as their Special Training School. 'It was miles from anywhere and an ideal spot for commando training because it gave us a wide choice of different types of country within a reasonable area,' reflected Calvert. 'Mountains, plains, forests, sand dunes and sea.'[23]

Throughout these weeks ISD was shaped by external and internal forces. Though there were a few civilians and airmen in ISD, most of its personnel were Australian soldiers and in order to distinguish them as such Blamey categorized these soldiers administratively as Z Special Unit.

On 6 July, however, the Americans formed a new body, the Allied Intelligence Bureau (AIB), bringing under one roof all the irregular units in the Far East. No secret was made of the reason: to prevent the British and Dutch from operating independently of MacArthur. Mott was crestfallen. The creation of the AIB stripped him of his independence, intellectually and particularly financially, and the Englishman now had to deal with layers of antagonistic American bureaucracy.

Ivan Lyon arrived in Melbourne on the same day as MacArthur replaced the ISD with the AIB, with a letter of introduction from General Wavell. A week earlier Lyon had landed in Fremantle, whereupon he made his way to a hotel in Perth. He asked to see the register. Flicking back a few pages he came to the start of May 1942 and the entry 'Gabrielle A.G.M. Lyon and baby'. An Australian newspaper later explained the significance of that entry:

> At the hotel they vividly remember the tall, strikingly handsome Frenchwoman and the baby she tended with such loving care. They

sensed the anguish under which she laboured although she rarely betrayed it. Not a day passed without her inquiry for the cable that was so long in coming. One day it did arrive, and overjoyed she read its formal message. 'Safe and well. – I'. For months she had had no trace of her husband, but now it seemed he had slipped the enemy's clutches and got to India. She decided to go to him immediately in spite of persuasions of friends who told her the sea crossing was dangerous and that it would be better if she remained . . . not many weeks after Mrs. Lyon booked out, a military officer, the typical Englishman, booked in. It was her husband. 'Yes, they were my wife and child,' he told the booking clerk. 'Their ship has disappeared. I don't know what's happened to them'. And he added, 'Yes, war's pretty grim'.[24]

Gabrielle Lyon and her eight-month-old baby, Clive, had left Fremantle on 5 May bound for Bombay on the *Nankin*, a ship carrying both cargo and 162 civilian passengers, including Greeks, Africans, British and Arabs. Five days out, the *Nankin* was intercepted by a German vessel, and the crew and passengers were transported to Yokohama, arriving in the Japanese city on 23 June. For nearly three weeks the Japanese and Germans argued as to who was responsible for the prisoners: eventually, on 10 July, the Japanese marched the passengers off the ship and into captivity in Fukushima. One of the prisoners, Cecil Saunders, recalled: 'During the early part of our internment, the general treatment of the women by the Japanese authorities was really bad – in many ways worse than that of the men. One woman was knocked down on to the floor, kicked severely about the head, and might easily have been killed had the guard not been dragged off her by the interpreter.'[25]

The Japanese degraded the women in other ways: 'One woman, who gave birth to a child a few weeks after our arrival in Fukushima, asked for cow's milk for the child, as her own milk was no longer available,' said Saunders. 'She was made to go down to the office, bare and squeeze her breasts in front of the guards in order to show that she no longer had any milk to feed the infant.'

Lyon knew nothing of the fate of the *Nankin*, only that the vessel had vanished at sea, perhaps captured or perhaps torpedoed.★ When he arrived in Melbourne, therefore, Lyon was more determined than ever to have his revenge on the enemy, but first there were obstacles to surmount. In a memo written a

★ It wasn't until the spring of 1943 that Lyon learned his wife and son were alive and in captivity in Japan.

ABOVE Refuge Bay, to the north of Sydney, was chosen by Ivan Lyon as Camp X and here his men trained for *Jaywick*. (Author's Collection - Courtesy of Terry Gallaway)

LEFT Donald Davidson didn't look like a special forces soldier but beneath the bookish exterior was a brave and charismatic adventurer. (Author's Collection)

year later, Mott recounted how Lyon 'came to Australia to try and put the Project on its feet . . . after a number of abortive interviews at GHQ and elsewhere Lyon eventually, through the agency of the Governor-General [Alexander Hore-Ruthven, 1st Earl of Gowrie], was introduced to Admiral Sir Guy Royle and he, mainly through DNI [Commander Rupert Long], fathered the Project to the extent of providing Naval personnel, camp site, supplies and all the necessary organisation for their early training.' The money came from London, in total around £11,000 despatched by SOE in instalments.

Mott was intrigued by Lyon, whom he described thus: 'Though shy and peculiar on first acquaintance, [he] does seem to know his job, to know exactly what he means to do, and to have a real gift for leading his men.'

Jock Campbell and Ron 'Taffy' Morris arrived in Melbourne on 2 August, but Bill Reynolds was having more difficulty in making the passage in the *Krait*. Twice he set out from India only for the boat's engine to pack up on each occasion, forcing him eventually to transport the vessel on a cargo ship.

Lyon's most pressing task was to appoint a second-in-command, a man on whom he could rely, who was in prime condition physically and mentally, someone who was disciplined with a dash of unorthodoxy, an adaptable mind not a rigid one. It was while dining at the home of the Victorian governor, Sir Winston Duggan, that Lyon fell into conversation with the governor's equerry, Captain H. A. R. Tilney, erstwhile of the 14/20th Hussars, who suggested his brother-in-law might fit the bill.

Born in 1908 in Northampton, one of six children of a vicar, Lieutenant Donald Davidson had been educated privately at Cheltenham College. Tall, lean, balding and monocled, Davidson looked at first glance more a civil servant than a special forces soldier. But beneath the bookish exterior was the soul of an adventurer, a man who, like Lyon, had left England at a young age to escape the stultifying mores of the upper-middle class. On leaving school in 1926, Davidson sailed to Australia and worked on the sheep and cattle stations of Western Queensland. After a couple of years he was on the move again, travelling to Thailand, where he worked in the timber industry in the country's teak forests. The jungle became his home for six years, an environment which challenged, fascinated and excited him. In the late 1930s Davidson's timber company transferred him to Burma and once more he was able to explore one of nature's more inhospitable regions. By the end of the decade Davidson had been recruited by British intelligence and in his spare time he canoed Burma's rivers, gathering what information he thought might be relevant in the event of war with Japan.

When war broke out Davidson enlisted in the Royal Naval Reserve. He was now married, to Nancy, who shared his love of South-East Asia and in 1939 had written a book about the edible fruit, durian, which was published by Oxford University Press. Nancy gave birth to a daughter, Caroline, in the same Singapore hospital – and in the same month – as Gabrielle Lyon. The Davidsons had made the acquaintance of the Lyons in Singapore, albeit briefly, and while the men got on, Nancy's relationship with Lyon was cool.

Fiercely protective of her husband, she may have regarded Lyon as the first man she had met who was Davidson's equal – possibly his superior – physically and intellectually. 'Lithe and wiry, not very robust,' she wrote of him. 'Full of nervous energy, and with the habit of unbroken thought; he had no scruples in attaining his end; he strode over any obstacle of red tape or personality to advance his scheme.'[26]

When Lyon approached Davidson he was seconded to the Royal Australian Navy, but he was released and attached to the *Jaywick* operation as OC Naval Personnel. Also recruited by Lyon was Sub-Lieutenant Bertram Overell, a 22-year-old Australian, appointed gunnery and explosives officer, and Captain Francis Chester, in charge of food, stores and signals.

Chester was another Englishman who had defied his upbringing to live a life of intrepid originality. Born in Johannesburg in 1899 to British parents, he was educated at King's School, Canterbury, and from there he went straight to the Royal Military College, Sandhurst, and thence to the Western Front with the King Edward's Horse cavalry regiment. On demobilization, Chester had gone to North Borneo, where he spent the next 20 years as a rubber planter, becoming fluent in Malay and Dusun. When the Japanese invaded North Borneo in December 1941, Chester had fled, enlisting in the King's African

Rifles and serving in the Abyssinian Campaign. He was in India in the spring of 1942, working for SOE, who described him as a 'very courageous and determined leader. His organising ability is well above average and in all his work he has shown himself to be extremely capable and efficient.'

Chester – nicknamed 'Gort' on account of his physical resemblance to Viscount Gort, the British Field Marshal – had impressed Lyon when they met in India, and he was summoned to Australia in September 1942.

The first non-commissioned officer recruited by Lyon (other than Taffy Morris) was 20-year-old Acting Petty Officer Arthur 'Arty' Jones, from Guildford, Western Australia. His upbringing couldn't have been more different from the British officers; one of six children, he had left school at 14 to work as a grocer's assistant. Called up in January 1941, he had joined the Navy and spent 18 unsatisfying months waiting for some excitement. Described by Davidson as a 'typical sailor, smart and trim, beer-loving and bawdy, full of fun and rough pranks', Jones was on a gunnery course at Flinders Navy Base (HMAS *Cerberus*), south of Melbourne, when 'two funny-looking people came around . . . looking for volunteers for a different type of work which they said was very adventurous and different to your normal navy work, and could be a bit dangerous.'[27]

The pair were Lyon and Davidson, the former dressed in the kilt of the Gordon Highlanders. Jones was one of around 40 sailors from the base who responded to the approach, a number whittled down to 17 once each volunteer had been interviewed. 'They asked you all about your pre-war life and what you used to do and where you'd been during the navy,' recalled Jones. 'I think what probably interested them was that we used to do a lot of canoeing and boating on the Canning River in the younger days and perhaps a lot of swimming, and also the fact that I'd been up to Singapore on the [HMAS] *Manoora* and called into places like Indonesia and this sort of thing.'

Jones learned subsequently that he was also selected because Lyon had sized him up physically. 'I was nuggetty and not too big and hefty to go into a canoe,' said Jones. Not only was he the right fit, literally, for Operation *Jaywick*, but his natural colouring would come in handy. Swarthy in appearance, Jones would, in a sarong and with a splash of dye, resemble a local fisherman, should a Japanese aircraft spot the *Krait* en route to Singapore.

Jones had also assessed his assessor. 'I think he was a bit suicidal myself,' he said of Lyon. 'One of these chaps . . . "do or die", you know, and bugger the expense.'

The 17 volunteers were subjected to three weeks of rigorous physical training devised by Overell and Davidson. Nearly all were sailors in their late

Camp X, January 1943 (left to right): Major Francis Chester, Major Ivan Lyon, Capt Bill Reynolds, Lt Cmdr Donald Davidson and Sub Lieutenant Bert Overell. (AWM P01806.002)

teens and early 20s, but it was the 34-year-old Davidson who set the fastest time over the assault course, a feat that put an end to any lingering doubts about the durability of the 'funny-looking' Pom. As well as asking questions of the men's physical fitness, Davidson and Overell were also scrutinizing their mental suitability. 'The officers would take note during the training of how you got along with one another, whether you argued, whether you . . . were choosy about things,' said Jones.[28]

Three of the volunteers failed to stay the distance during the training, and were Returned to Unit (RTU'd). Those who came through were given eight days' leave and ordered to report to the Garden Island Naval Base on 6 September.

While the men rested their aching bodies, Lyon scouted for a suitable training camp for the unit, far from the madding crowd. It had to be remote, and rugged, offering a buffet of natural challenges that would test the men physically and mentally. He found his ideal spot on a clifftop overlooking Refuge Bay to the north of Sydney, 'amongst the very rough and wild hills that form the surroundings of the Hawkesbury River estuary'. Lyon christened it 'Camp X', and upon arrival the men were handed shovels and pickaxes.

'A week's hard work digging, breaking rock, and clearing scrub around the camp site and parade ground, was the prelude to long, and progressively longer, days and nights spent canoeing,' wrote Lyon. There were also plenty of route marches across the rocky hills, which 'consisted of point-to-point walking or scrambling, compass work, stalking and attacks'.[29]

Arthur Jones recalled Camp X was:

situated on top of a rocky area probably about a hundred feet above
the water and there were about eight or nine tents, [we were] all living
in tents, no electricity or running water or showers or anything like
that. You had a running stream that ran through the camp and
everybody had to bathe in that and there was a big waterfall that went
down to the beach and a big cave behind it. Our canoes and
explosives were kept there and after going out in canoe training we
used to just put the canoes in this big cave area behind the waterfall.

Sometimes the men would canoe north across Broken Bay to Gosford, a round
trip of approximately 26 miles; on other occasions they paddled south to Bobbin
Head and back, a distance of 17 miles. They also canoed in the dark, remembered
Jones, 'getting used to working of a night time, and approaching places like the
searchlight area of a night and working out the best way to keep them invisible
or as near as invisible as possible'.[30]

In a memo written by Lyon entitled 'X Training Camp: Notes and
Observations on Training', he outlined the physical and moral requirements of
the three months at Refuge Bay:

Physical:
a) To reach a state of perfect physical condition, capable of being maintained for
six months on 'hard tack' [a biscuit made of flour and water] under difficult
victualling and living conditions.
b) To be able to cover long distances over land and water: 50 miles a day on foot
over roads or tracks; 40 over rough trackless country; 30 by canoe on rivers,
estuaries and open seas; and 30 by land and water combined, were aimed at.

Moral:
a) Morale. To be capable of maintaining high morale under extremely trying
conditions. These are expected to be:
i) Cramped living conditions: 20 men in a 70ft trawler.
ii) North-east monsoon weather.
iii) Coasting by night in dangerous navigational waters, and lying up by day
in rivers and mangrove swamps, by islands and exposed coasts.
iv) Voyaging in enemy controlled waters, in the vicinity of, and often ashore
on, enemy occupied territory.

v) No contact, other than by W/T, with headquarters or with assistance for six months.

vi) Limited medical aid.

vii) Tropical climatic conditions.

b) Initiative and Alertness. To train each man to be capable of taking a lone hand if necessary in the execution of our intended operation; to be alert enough to take the initiative should events alter the execution of subsequent movements; and to be versatile enough to be able to make his way through enemy-controlled waters and lands to a friendly territory should separation from the main party overtake him.[31]

A typical day commenced with reveille at 0655, and then half an hour's PT before breakfast at 0805. Morning training was split into two sections; it might be two hours of small-arms instruction from 0900 to 1100, and then canoe maintenance from 1115 to 1315, or it could be four hours spent running, walking and canoeing across 10 miles of land and 4½ miles of sea. Lunch was an hour. The afternoon could be anything: a 14-mile run to White Horse Bay and back on one day; unarmed combat for a couple of hours followed by instruction in the 3-inch mortar the next; sometimes they scavenged for wood and on other days they carried out an attack on a local AA battery. Tea was at 1900. The day concluded with an hour's land stalking or canoe maintenance or night paddling. At 2200 it was lights out.

Jones recalled that the men all had a stick of gelignite hanging up in their tent to get used to the smell. 'Gelignite used to give you a bad headache when you handled it,' he explained. 'But if you were handling it every day you never got the recurrence of the headaches.'

The rivalry among the men was friendly; though they didn't know for what they were training – or that only a handful of them would actually be required to canoe – the awareness that they were an elite unit wove a tight mateship. They were also conscious that self-discipline had superseded the more rigid discipline of a ship's company; there was little in the way of saluting or shouting or parading, but there was a tacit understanding that if a man dropped beneath the standard of excellence expected by Lyon and Davidson he would be RTU'd. 'The discipline was pretty lax in the camp really,' said Jones. 'As long as you did your job all right and showed you were interested and that sort of thing.'[32]

Lyon had a keen sense of what he sought from the volunteers, which he committed to paper for Davidson's benefit. He knew he would be absent for periods because his presence was required in Melbourne, working with Francis

Chester in ensuring the logistical side of the operation ran smoothly. The task of Davidson and Overell was to shape the men for what lay ahead. 'Officers must study each individual minutely, and must arrange his attitude to, and his treatment of, each accordingly, if serious trouble is to be avoided,' Lyon wrote. 'Unobtrusiveness in this respect is of vital importance. The test of the correctness of the balance struck during the training period will come during the operation.'[33]

Lyon believed this goal was attainable provided the officers led by example: 'To arrive at strict discipline and a proper regard on the part of the ratings for their officers, it has been made an invariable rule that the latter try every new thing first, whether it is landing in a canoe in dangerous surf, or an endurance test, or the portaging of canoes and full packs overland.'

The men were also tested on elementary navigation, including chart-reading and tide tables, visual signalling with semaphore and Morse and the use of the prismatic compass on land and sea; they fired a variety of weapons, such as the Owen sub-machine gun, the Bren and the Lewis gun, with a view to shooting down enemy aircraft. They practised unarmed combat, became skilled in the safe handling and application of grenades, limpets and gelignite, and received lectures on ships' engines.

The most intensive training was done in a canoe. They practised under Davidson's tutelage on the standard British Army folboat, a collapsible canoe constructed of black rubberized canvas stretched over a wooden dowel frame that was 17 feet 9 inches long, 32 inches wide and had a cruising speed – in the hands of the Camp X men – of 4 knots. Even with a loading capacity of 800 pounds, it was found that they could paddle into creeks and shallows with a 4½-inch draught.

Roger Courtney, a British pre-war adventurer in Africa, who had canoed the length of the White Nile, had popularized the folboat on raising the Special Boat Section in 1940. 'They had a skin, which we could collapse the framework out of, and reassemble them,' recalled one of Z Special Unit recruits, Jack Mackay. 'It would collapse in the middle, and you could sort of turn it down, stick it in the bag, and stick the skin alongside it in the bag. Quite heavy but we did carry them overland quite a bit.'[34]

In its bag, which was 6 feet by 2 feet by 2 feet, the canoe weighed 68 pounds.

Davidson put a clock on the men to test their proficiency in dismantling and reassembling the canoes. Anyone who took longer than 15 minutes received a stare of disapproval. Arthur Jones said it was fairly simply to erect a canoe, a question of assembling the dowelling in the right order and remembering the nuts and butterfly screws on the gunnel. The end result was a 'reasonably rigid' canoe.

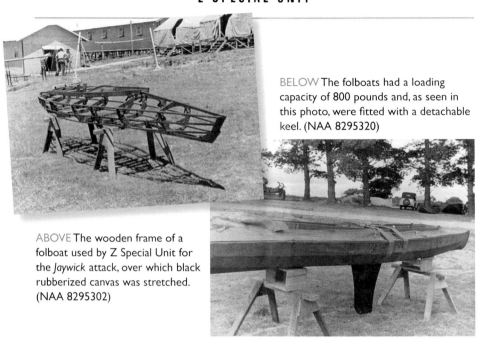

BELOW The folboats had a loading capacity of 800 pounds and, as seen in this photo, were fitted with a detachable keel. (NAA 8295320)

ABOVE The wooden frame of a folboat used by Z Special Unit for the *Jaywick* attack, over which black rubberized canvas was stretched. (NAA 8295302)

Sometimes the wooden framework broke, usually because of the wet rubberized canvas. Davidson therefore tested a few woods, and found that rattan was the most practical for their purpose.

The men's spraydecks, that covered the cockpit, were also made of canvas and were coated in beeswax.

Mackay teamed up with Fred Marsh on one of the many night exercises, which entailed paddling unseen to an Australian Navy vessel, climbing on board and leaving a calling card, or on occasion, pinching a souvenir. One flaw revealed by these exercises was the paddle. 'We had a choice of the double paddles or the single paddles, and all the paddles gave off a phosphorous,' said Mackay. 'Anyone standing high could see the wake of the canoes by virtue of the phosphorous sparks. So we had to wrap the canoes in a cloth to eliminate the phosphorous trail.' They also agreed that the single paddle emitted less phosphorus than a double, and they practised emergency stops to perfection, the point of the canoe facing their enemy, rendering them practically invisible to a lookout at night.

As for clothing, they experimented as they trained. A stipulation from the outset was that the men during training wear 'as little clothing as possible to allow the maximum of sun tanning'. Lyon was all right in this regard, bronzing rapidly and deeply, as did Jones, but others felt obliged to lie under the sun's rays during any down time in order to rid themselves of their Caucasian complexion.

On night schemes, the men wore 'giggle suits', the Australian fatigue uniform of khaki drill, and navy blue boiler suits. It was found that the former were more effective on land on moonlit or starlit nights; trouser legs should be tucked into one's socks to avoid brushing against foliage, but in truth the most practical apparel for moving silently at night through foliage and over rocks was a 'pair of sandshoes and socks and nothing else. The naked body makes none of the noises of clothing'. However, it was conceded that stalking an enemy wearing only sandshoes was psychologically awkward for men who from infancy had been taught that nudity was unnatural; so they wore a pair of tight bathing shorts as these made very little noise.

The blue or black boiler suits were best on the water. Burnt cork or boot polish was used to blacken all exposed skin, be it fair or dark. It was discovered that even black-clad men in black canoes were clearly visible against a sandy landing beach on a dark night, so the choice of their landing beach would have to be made with extreme caution. Furthermore, 'care should always be taken to land from a canoe in bare or stockinged feet, keeping the sand-shoe dry for stalking. Wet ones will squelch faintly for a long time after treading in water.' There was always the risk of coming ashore on a barnacled rock, but thick woollen socks were found to reduce much of the discomfort.

The outcome of the experimentation with clothing was an agreement by Lyon and Davidson that the ideal outfit for the operation proper was a 'navy Japara cotton suit of pyjama type with breast pockets and a pyjama string round the jacket waist as well as round the trouser top'.

Jones, like his comrades, had by now come to respect Davidson. 'He got on well with everybody and he knew what he was doing,' he recalled. 'Very athletic, and he was the sort of fellow that would go and do things first and then he would lead. He would go and do trips of a night time, he'd go and map out somewhere to go hill climbing and canoeing, and then the following night he'd lead everybody out on the job so you had a lot of confidence in him and he was good.'

Jones's pal was Able Seaman Fred Marsh, 'a real nuggetty young fellow and he had rather a big head to go with his nuggetty build so he got called "Boof".'[35] A cabinetmaker's apprentice in Brisbane when war broke out, the 18-year-old Marsh was a popular figure at Camp X. Short (5 feet 8 inches) and stocky, with a low centre of gravity, the agile and irrepressible Marsh was a handful in unarmed combat training. 'A most admirable type,' said Davidson, 'and a great lad to have behind you when things might be going wrong.'[36]

Marsh liked to wind up the 'old man' of the ranks, Able Seaman Walter Falls, nicknamed 'Poppa' on account of his grand old age of 23. Born in Aberdeen, the son of an Australian soldier and his Scottish wife, Falls had been a dairy farmer prior to enlisting. He was big in build and calm in temperament, but at Refuge Bay Marsh did his best to unsettle Falls's sangfroid. On one occasion he slipped a dead snake into Falls's bed, but the target of Marsh's practical joke was so tired he didn't notice on turning in. He did, however, discover the serpent the next morning, emitting a 'blood-curdling yell' and threatening blue murder when he discovered the prankster. Marsh thought it prudent to keep quiet, and in future he refrained from playing any more jokes on 'Poppa'.

By the start of 1943 the 17 men had been reduced to ten, the training having exposed flaws in the mental or physical make-up of seven volunteers. Jack Mackay failed to stay the distance because of an outbreak of septic carbuncles on his hips – caused by endless hours in a canoe – that was so debilitating he required a spell in hospital.

But on 17 January there arrived at Refuge Bay a new recruit that was cheered to the heavens by the men. It was the *Krait*.

CHAPTER 3
AN OLD *KRAIT*

The *Krait* had docked in Sydney Harbour on Christmas Day, and she ushered in 1943 in a repair yard, receiving substantial work on her hull and also undergoing modifications above and below deck to increase her storage capacity.

When the *Krait* hove into view in Refuge Bay she created wild excitement among the men in Camp X. 'One morning, this dirty looking craft came into our bay, and our skipper said, "Righto boys, go out and have a look at it, that's going to be your home for the next few months,"' recalled Moss Berryman. 'This turned out to be the old Japanese fishing boat, and dear, oh dear, what a craft … There was nothing on there at all. There were no beds. No bunks. No nothing. It was as plain as a baby's backside.'[37]

The *Krait*, her name emblazoned on two wooden planks hammered to the outside of the wheelhouse, was powered by a Deutz four-cylinder engine; she had a beam of 11 feet, a range of 8,000 miles and a maximum speed of 6½ knots. From afar the vessel wasn't much to look at, a 'herring-gutted beam' in the words of Davidson. She needed more than just a lick of paint, and her awnings had seen better days.

Before the men began transferring the folboats and equipment from Camp X to the *Krait,* Davidson had them assembled. The time had come to reveal the eight men chosen for the operation. 'He read out the names of those that were [in] and those that weren't, and apologised to them,' recalled Jones. 'They were sent back to the navy for general service. And the rest of us went and joined the *Krait.*'[38]

When they departed Refuge Bay early on 18 January there were 21 people on board – including Francis Chester and Ivan Lyon, and Taffy Morris's cat,

The *Krait* wasn't much to look at, but the boat was durable, and most importantly, innocuous, which was why Lyon wanted it for Operation *Jaywick*. (AWM 067338)

Cleopatra. It was, remembered Davidson, a bit of 'a scrum'. Oil, petrol and kerosene drums were lashed on deck, along with the seven canoes, while the holds below deck were piled high with more fuel drums, water, food, limpet mines and explosives, enough to last 20 men six months at sea. One hold had been set aside as the officers' mess, although its three bunks were strewn with equipment and there was also a wireless transmitter and receiver.

More stores had been stashed on top of the wheelhouse and wedged into the corners of the engine room. In short, there was not a nook or cranny on board the *Krait* that hadn't been filled by some essential piece of kit. Three hammocks above the engine room housing constituted the men's sleeping quarters, and the call of nature was answered by squatting over the stern where below there was a bucket on a rope. The *Queen Mary* she was not, but the men loved their vessel, their means of finally taking the war back to the Japanese.

From the moment the *Krait* left Refuge Bay she struggled, moving erratically and diffidently, like a drunk man leaving a public house. Not long after midday the engine began to play up. Reynolds repaired the problem, but it was only a temporary reprieve. They were soon being towed to Newcastle by a minesweeper, the sailors grouching at the ignominy of their situation. 'We wondered what the hell was going on and why all this wasn't done in the first place,' said Jones.

'Why would you put to sea for a long trip when you had a motor that was so broken down and worn out?'[39]

Operation *Jaywick* had got off to the worst possible start, a worrying omen for those of a superstitious bent. That wasn't Lyon. The vessel underwent running repairs, good enough for the *Krait* to limp to Brisbane, whereupon she was laid up for several weeks undergoing a complete refit. Lyon sent the men to Surfers Paradise, a coastal resort 50 miles south of Brisbane, to continue their fitness training, while he, Grey Egerton Mott and Jock Campbell studied the latest intelligence reports and sourced outstanding items of equipment required for the operation.

On 14 February Mott sent a report to SOE London on the progress of *Jaywick*. 'I have been through the plans Lyon has worked out in rather more detail than he gives them to you,' he wrote. 'I cannot say much, not knowing the islands of Singapore, but Lyon apparently knows them all well ... he certainly gives the impression of knowing what he is at, and seems very thorough in what he does: though I am sure no one wholly sane would conceive such a project.'

Mott then praised the support of Commander Rupert Long, the Director of Naval Intelligence, an 'indefatigable intriguer', who had used his political connections and influence to ward off those officers inimical to a 'private army' such as Z Special Unit.

Finally, Mott expressed his doubt that the operation would commence in April, but despite the setback with the engine, he was cautiously confident that *Jaywick* could succeed: 'Lyon and Campbell have really worked hard and, on the whole, carefully, so that I think they will start with every chance that thought and energy can give them ... if you get this in time and the Baker Street [SOE's London HQ] experts have anything to suggest, it can be done or said before they leave.'

That was to be Mott's final contribution to Operation *Jaywick*. Over the course of several months he had grown increasingly frustrated with the interference and general bloody-mindedness of certain staff officers within GHQ, notably Lieutenant-Colonel Caleb Roberts, Director of Military Intelligence at the Allied Intelligence Bureau (AIB). It was a familiar tale, one encountered by all special forces units during World War II, be they the Special Air Service, the Special Boat Section or the Long Range Desert Group; there was a certain type of staff officer – characterized by David Stirling of SAS fame as 'fossilized shits' – who could not get to grips with irregular warfare. Usually, as in Roberts's case, they were relics of a bygone age, men born in the previous century whose slow-moving minds were not agile enough to understand how inter-war advancements in transport, communication and weaponry had ushered in a new era of warfare. But a young generation of soldiers, far more independent-minded and intrepid than their fathers, grasped the significance.

The power, however, resided still with the staff officers, and on 17 February Mott was relieved of his command on the grounds he was 'recalcitrant', and replaced with an Australian, Major Arthur Oldham. There may have been a whiff of Anglophobia in the decision; many of General MacArthur's staff had an innate dislike of the British (believing that the undoubted arrogance of some senior British officers was applicable to all ranks of every service), and it was a hostility shared by some Australian officers. Before he left Australia Mott vented his anger in a letter to General Sir Thomas Blamey, but it was a futile missive. Indeed, when Ralph Bagnold had received permission from General Wavell to raise the Long Range Desert Group in June 1940, he flew to Palestine to ask Blamey, the then commander of the Australian Corps, if he would release a couple of hundred men to serve in the unit. Blamey refused. It had been decided by the Australian government that none of its soldiers would be siphoned off on eccentric British enterprises. Memories of Gallipoli had not faded.

Believing that some feathers needed smoothing over, London despatched Lieutenant-Colonel John Chapman-Walker to Australia in the wake of Mott's departure. A qualified solicitor, the 35-year-old had stood unsuccessfully as a Conservative parliamentary candidate in the 1929 general election and was experienced in deftly dealing with large and competing egos. By April 1943 a new organization had risen, the Services Reconnaissance Department (SRD), recruited from the ranks of SOA and available for operations within the South-East Asia Command. Significantly, SRD was autonomous, free from the financial control of the Americans.

Once in Australia Chapman-Walker reported to London that he found everyone 'most co-operative', but nonetheless the political squabbles and the *Krait*'s engine troubles had caused the postponement of *Jaywick* at a conference in Melbourne on 27 March. There was even doubt that it would ever go ahead, and in the spring Davidson and the Australian sailors were posted to HMAS *Assault*, a training centre in New South Wales.

It wasn't until the end of July 1943 that the personnel of *Jaywick* were reunited with the *Krait* minus Bill Reynolds, whose volatile character – he had punched a seaman – resulted in his departure from the operation.*

---

* Reynolds was recruited by the Americans as an intelligence agent, but in November 1943 he was captured shortly after arriving in southern Borneo in an attempt to contact Chinese agents. He was executed in August 1944.

The *Krait* had a new engine, a Gardener diesel 105 HP, and some new crew: James McDowell from Belfast, predictably nicknamed 'Paddy', a 36-year-old chain-smoking engineer. A former stoker in the Merchant Navy, McDowell had been living in Sydney when war broke out, but he re-enlisted and was signed on by Lyon in Brisbane. Another British-born volunteer was the new cook, Corporal Andrew Crilly, who had relocated to Ipswich, west of Brisbane, before the war and trained as a motor mechanic. He had seen action with the 24th Field Engineers in New Guinea the previous year, and subsequently joined the 2/14 Australian Infantry Battalion, but an old foot injury flared up in the summer of 1943 and he was posted to Wongabel staging camp as a general reinforcement. 'They were looking for another man for this "hush hush" job,' recalled Crilly. 'Lyon, of the Gordon Highlanders, told me there might be little chance of the chaps on the stunt coming back but I decided to have a go at it . . . Anything was better than staying at Wongabel because conditions were so bad at the camp.'[40]

There was one slight drawback, however, on Crilly's application, extracted by Lyon during his interview. He couldn't cook. 'When are you leaving, sir?' he asked Lyon. In a matter of days, came the reply. 'Oh, yes, I'll be able to cook by then,' Crilly assured the officer. Lyon bought him a cookbook in the hope it would provide inspiration.

The loss of Reynolds forced Lyon to look for a new navigator, and the man who got the job was the choice of Commander Rupert Long. He and Lieutenant Ted Carse went back 30 years to when the pair were teenage cadets at the Naval Training College in New South Wales. Long had remained in the navy ever since, but boredom and drink had got the better of Carse after World War I and he had quit the service in 1921. The years that followed were sad ones for Carse: a slow decline amid a succession of short-lived jobs that included prospecting for gold, factory cleaning and selling fake jewellery. He re-enlisted in the navy in 1942 aged 42, but by now he was a sorry specimen physically and temperamentally. But Long was loyal to his old chum and convinced – or perhaps forced – Lyon and Chapman-Walker to accept him as *Jaywick*'s navigator. Davidson was not impressed when he appeared on the *Krait*. 'Physically, he was not very strong,' he reflected. 'He was troubled with asthmatic and bronchitic coughing, and his eyes became steadily worse.'[41]

The new telegraphist was Leading Telegraphist Horace 'Horrie' Young, a 22-year-old from Perth whose love of the telegraph system had begun when he joined the Postmaster General's Department at the age of 14 as a messenger. He learned Morse code as part of his training and became interested in crystal sets, 'like most children of my age'.

Young's other passion was the navy and he joined the Royal Australian Naval Reserve as a cadet. On the outbreak of war he was mobilized into the Royal Australian Navy as a telegraphist and in July 1943 he crossed paths with Donald Davidson at HMAS *Assault*. On hearing that the telegraphist assigned to the *Krait*, Don Sharples, didn't much fancy going on a cruise into enemy territory, Young sought out Davidson with a request to take his place. Davidson told him he would sleep on the matter. 'When I went up the next day he shook me by the hand . . . "Well, Leading Telegraphist Young, we've decided to accept you into service with [the] reconnaissance department. While you work with us, we will pay you 50% over and above your base pay."'[42]

Davidson and the *Jaywick* commandos had been sent to HMAS *Assault* to teach the sailors unarmed combat. They had all volunteered for combined operations and many thought they had little else to learn. But Davidson and his team proved otherwise. 'These guys were really fair dinkum and they treated us to some displays of unarmed combat,' said Young. 'They were playing with arms and slashing at each other with these great stilettos and parangs [a Malayan machete]. They weren't mucking around either. You had to be quick to get out of the way.'

Accepted onto the team, Young began to get to know his new comrades as they travelled up to Cairns where the *Krait* was docked. Davidson, he described as 'always the showman, a wonderful fellow'. He was to many of the Australians unusual for a British officer in possessing not a jot of conceit or aloofness. 'He was such a human being [sic] and he'd never ever ask a bloke to do anything that he wasn't prepared to do himself,' said Young. 'He was greatly admired by this mob. They'd do anything for him, really. Just had that ability to relate to the guys.'[43]

Lyon was different. More self-contained and remote than Davidson, he was burdened not only by the political wrangling behind the scenes but also the uncertainty of what had befallen his wife and son. 'He was all right,' said Young. 'He used to speak to me now and again, but he never spoke a great deal . . . Davidson was always swashbuckling, a gung-ho type of guy. Lyon was the far more quieter of the two of them.'

Young considered Ted Carse another quiet man, but a popular one, who despite his vast experience 'never threw his weight around with the crew'. The other officer chosen for the final party of 14 was Lieutenant Bob Page, who had gone from studying medicine at Sydney University into the army. He was engaged to be married and he and his fiancée, Roma, agreed they would tie the knot as soon as he returned from his impending operation. Page had been

LEFT From Guildford, Western Australia, Arthur Jones was described by Davidson as a 'typical sailor, smart and trim, beer-loving and bawdy'. (AWM 045409)

BELOW Fred 'Boof' Marsh (left) and 'Tiny' Hage prepare to launch a canoe jokingly christened 'HMAS *Lyon*' at Refuge Bay in January 1943. (AWM P01806.008)

RIGHT Fred Marsh and 'Tiny' Hage in their canoe, 'HMAS *Lyon*', undergoing some training at Refuge Bay in January 1943. (AWM 067336A)

drafted in to replace Francis Chester, who had been assigned to an operation in North Borneo. Page was a 'decent' man, and very popular with everyone on the *Krait*.

Among his fellow sailors, Young considered Fred 'Boof' Marsh the 'larrikin of the team . . . [who] never took anything terribly seriously'. Able Seaman Moss Berryman was a 'good guy', as was Arthur Jones, who was 'very, very efficient'. 'Poppa' Falls was 'a dour Scot ... a very serious person and a very, very capable fellow, the sort of guy that would be handy if you were ever in a tight spot'. Of a similar character was Able Seaman Andrew Huston, nicknamed 'Happy' because he was anything but. 'I don't think I ever saw him laugh,' said Young of the 19-year-old Queenslander. 'Everything was a big deal. He was a very, very serious boy, but very efficient too.'[44]

In contrast, Crilly was 'one of the boys . . . a hell of a good bloke'. His cooking didn't match his personality, alas, but he had mastered the art of making a delicious pancake, so he was christened 'Pancake Andy'.

Leading Seaman Kevin 'Cobber' Cain, the bosun's mate, was a powerfully built sailor who kept himself to himself, unlike Taffy Morris, who, when he wasn't singing, was cheekily insulting his crewmates because a) they were Australians and b) they were sailors. The Aussies gave as good as they got, recalled Young: 'Taffy had a fairly loud voice. He'd be screeching out something from a song and the next thing you know a missile would come flying over at him and he'd have to duck to dodge it ... a very light-hearted fellow, very easy to get on with.'

If Young appreciated his new shipmates, the ship itself was a shock to his system. 'It looked so crook, it was terrible,' he recalled. 'She was dirty, untidy, full of cockroaches the like of which I've never seen in my life. They were monster big cockroaches. You could almost hear them walking around they were that noisy. I don't know whether you can find words to describe how it really looked.'[45]

The *Krait* chugged out of Cairns at one minute to midnight on 4 August 1943. The ship's log noted: '2359. Departed Cairns for Townsville, on completion of dockyard repairs and installation of new Gardiner Diesel engine (6 cylinder HP).'

The log recorded the name, rank and branch of service of the 14 crew, each of whom was praying that the *Krait* would this time prove seaworthy. Their destination was the submarine base at Exmouth Gulf, on the north-western corner of Australia, chosen, as Lieutenant-Colonel Chapman-Walker explained in a memo to London dated 30 August, because it was 'completely isolated' from the world.★

Chapman-Walker continued to say that Jock Campbell, who had been in Cairns delivering some last-minute supplies and messages, had sent him a 'most encouraging preliminary report on the general morale of the party'. He added: 'They expect to make the final departure on 2/9/43 . . . if all goes well the operation should take place on or about 30 Sept 43.'

★ In fact the location of Exmouth Base had been revealed a few weeks earlier by the Australian PM, John Curtin, while campaigning for re-election (he was successful), a gaffe that meant the 'submarine depot ship had to be moved in a great hurry!'

CHAPTER 4
'GOOD LUCK AND GOD'S SPEED'

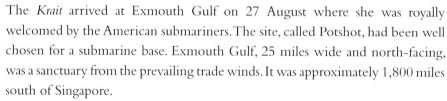

The *Krait* arrived at Exmouth Gulf on 27 August where she was royally welcomed by the American submariners. The site, called Potshot, had been well chosen for a submarine base. Exmouth Gulf, 25 miles wide and north-facing, was a sanctuary from the prevailing trade winds. It was approximately 1,800 miles south of Singapore.

The Americans, like the Australian sailors aboard the *Krait*, had no idea of the purpose of the 70-foot fishing vessel, but they were delighted to welcome a group of men who, judging from appearances, were evidently up to something out of the ordinary. 'We were made much of,' said Davidson. 'Loaded with kindness and presents in the most generous treatment we had ever received.' Particularly appreciated was the cornucopia of provisions lavished on the *Krait*: tinned meat and fish, orange juice, lime juice, sacks of rice, potatoes and flour, biscuits, sweets and dried fruit, and enough tea and coffee to keep them refreshed all the way to Singapore and back.

American sailors from the submarine repair ship, *Chanticleer*, painted the *Krait* grey, removed her name from the wheelhouse and installed a copper sheet to the vessel's hull to boost the efficacy of wireless communication.

The crew also took possession of their new canoes, 'beautiful compared with the old ones,' recalled Arthur Jones. 'The old ones were only 12 feet long and

these were 16 feet . . . so there was room for a third man if you needed it.' In fact, the four canoes weren't as pristine as Jones remembered.

Davidson had concluded that there were weaknesses in the folboats that they had used at Camp X, and consequently he asked for several adjustments. He was not impressed when he unloaded the modified canoes at Exmouth Gulf. The sloppy stitching and an ill-fitting dowelling on the new canoes meant they each had to be reconditioned by Davidson and some of the men. With that done, said Jones, 'we went and had a paddle around the bay and got used to them, that's all you could do'.[46]

The men wrote letters home, to mothers and fathers, wives and sweethearts. Lyon joked to his parents about his appearance, describing his tanned and leathery skin, and reflected that his life hitherto had been unusual but satisfying. His one regret was the absence of his wife and son.

Davidson wrestled with self-doubt, as soldiers throughout the centuries have done on the eve of battle. 'Our blood tingled at the thoughts our imaginations crowded on us,' he reflected. 'How would each of us, personally, bear whatever was in store for us? Could we meet it? Would some of us fall short of perfection?'[47]

The big day was 1 September. They received a message from Admiral Sir Guy Royle, wishing them 'Good hunting', and at 1400 hours Admiral Ralph

Aboard the *Krait*, en route to Singapore. Among the men in this photo are Ted Carse, far left, Moss Berryman (buttocks to camera), Bob Page (in wheelhouse), Andrew Crilly (in wheelhouse) and Ivan Lyon (foreground). (AWM 067336)

Left to right: Andrew Huston, Ivan Lyon, Kevin Cain and telegraphist Horace Young, on board the *Krait* prior to leaving Australia for Singapore. (AWM 045413)

Christie, commanding US submarine operations out of Australia, and the only American at Exmouth Gulf to know the *Krait*'s destination, came to the jetty to say his farewell. He had already asked Lyon 'to keep a look-out in Lombok Strait to see whether it was being patrolled or not because his subs wanted to use it'.

Then the *Krait*'s engines began to throb, and the 14 men on board waved goodbye to the Americans. They were on their way at last. Or so they assumed. 'We got half way out of the Bay at Exmouth and there was a hell of a bang,' recalled Horace Young.[48]

The *Krait*'s log recorded the cause of the bang: '1700. On moving off astern we sheared the coupling key of the intermediate propeller shafting. Dropped anchor and signalled for assistance.'

The embarrassment felt by the crew of the *Krait* at their misfortune must have been acute, for none more so than Ivan Lyon, who had invested so much of himself into Operation *Jaywick*. He knew that there was a small coterie of staff officers – British, Australian and American – who regarded the whole enterprise as a waste of time and resources. This was not how wars were won, in their view, by indisciplined renegades gallivanting into enemy territory.

There were no smirks from the Americans who towed them back to base. On the contrary, the engineers and mechanics from the *Chanticleer* worked tirelessly through the night. They repaired the propeller shafting by brazing, not welding, because of 'some metallurgic consideration'. Even so, the engineers told Lyon, 'their job was only very temporary . . . it might last some time with very tender care, but it might give at any moment'. Lyon assured them that they were going only as far as Perth, about 775 miles down the coast.

As they waited for the shafting to cool, they lunched with the Americans on 2 September, a copious meal of chicken, and then at 1400 hours they were off once more. This time they traversed the Gulf without incident, but more drama awaited on the open sea.

'Outside the Gulf we ran into a heavy swell and a confused sea from the South, with a fresh South wind,' ran the *Krait*'s log. 'We very nearly foundered, but just managed to carry on.'

The original plan of attack on Singapore had been to depart from Darwin, and to reach the target via the Timor Sea and Flores Sea. But when *Jaywick* was postponed in March, Lyon re-examined the plan and decided to go through the Lombok Strait. None of this was known to the men. It was on the third day that Lyon gathered the men to disclose the truth. 'He said, "Righto, do you know where we're going?"' remembered Jones. One or two of the men hazarded a guess. Jones suggested Surabaya in East Java. Then Lyon revealed their destination. 'They couldn't believe it when they were told they were going to Singapore "to blow up a few ships"', said Moss Berryman. Lyon could see one or two of the men were stunned at the thought of going so deep inside enemy territory. 'Nobody expected to be going that far and there was sort of talk about how dangerous it was,' said Jones.[49] Lyon reassured the men that wasn't the case. 'This is not a dangerous trip,' he said, 'it's an experience.'*

---

* The Long Range Desert Group adopted a similar philosophy in North Africa, believing that 'the further behind enemy lines that you went the safer you were. Fifty miles behind their lines there was activity but 500 miles behind it was quiet'.

But for anyone who didn't fancy it, Lyon said he understood and he would 'drop you off at the first island we come to and if you're there when we come back we'll pick you up'. It was a smart psychological ploy; he knew that no one would dare lose face in front of his mates by withdrawing. He stared at their faces and they returned his gaze. No one moved. They were all fully committed.

On 4 September the dawn broke clear and calm. The log noted that it was 'an uneventful day', other than the men began painting their bodies. 'Stain is very dark, more the colour of a New Guinea native than anything else. When thinned down to a medium brown it is hard to apply evenly. Tanned skins take it well.'

The dye was contained in tins; it was sticky and it stank. Lyon told them how to apply it. There was much guffawing and joking as the men lathered themselves in the dye. Somebody looked down at his crotch and wondered aloud if 'I have to dye the old fellow?' 'Of course, said Lyon, joining in the fun, how many natives have you seen with a white old fellow?' When Fred Marsh was fully togged up in dye and sarong, he began dancing the hula to the amusement of his shipmates.

Lyon instructed the men to wear their native sarongs and coolie hats so that to any passing Japanese pilot they would look like local fishermen.

The next day, 5 September, the log noted that the dye was not terribly effective. Sweat made it run, clothes rubbed it off, but from a distance it looked convincing.

To further aid the subterfuge, their blue ensign was removed and the Japanese ensign was run up the stern pole, but only after the pristine flag had been trampled and scuffed by the men in order to make it more in keeping with their decrepit vessel.

The plan was that if they were challenged by an aircraft or another ship, the four most naturally dark among them – Jones, Berryman, Huston and Lyon – were to dash to the foredeck and point frantically to the Japanese flag. The rest would remain hidden on the aft deck, which was covered by an awning, their fingers curled around the triggers of their machine guns.

On 6 September McDowell changed the engine to silencer, and instead of chugging it began purring. The next day they were about 80 miles south of the Lombok Strait and by 1700 hours on 8 September they were 20 miles south. They had seen no sign of the enemy, but nor had they experienced the 'very hazy' conditions promised them by intelligence reports. 'We therefore decided to ignore the threat of air reconnaissance and make a direct approach to the Strait entrance,' wrote Lyon. 'At sunset we set a course for the centre of the narrows and increased to our maximum revs.'[50]

The six kayakists on *Jaywick* christened this stretch of coast on Panjang the 'Bay of Otters', and it was here they rested before setting out to raid Singapore. (AWM 300920)

As they sailed north towards the Strait they were flanked by two imposing sentinels – the 10,000-foot volcano of Gunong Agoeng on Bali to the west, and the 12,000-foot volcano of Gunong Rindjani on Lombok to the east. Nearly 40 miles in length, the Strait is narrowest at the southern entrance, 12 miles, with the island of Nusa Bear an impediment, and it widens to 24 miles at the northern entrance.

A searchlight shimmied across the water from the south-east corner of Bali as the *Krait* increased its speed to 6½ knots. Lyon and Davidson joined Carse in the wheelhouse. By 2100 hours they were abeam of Nusa Bear; two hours later they were in more or less the same position. 'At times *Krait* was travelling backwards,' ran the log. 'Therefore the tidal stream must have reached 7 knots.'

McDowell kept a watchful eye in the engine room throughout the night as the *Krait* fought the tide. They made 6 miles between midnight and 0400 hours but the tide rip didn't slacken as dawn broke. 'We awoke to find ourselves right in the middle of the narrows between Bali and Lombok,' noted the log. The atmosphere among the officers in the wheelhouse was 'very tense', said Jones. 'They knew that there was an aerodrome on Lombok and there was an army garrison over there but it just depended where they were.'

Then the tide turned in their favour and the wind came to their assistance too, a fresh southerly of force 4. At 1000 hours on 9 September, Ted Carse wrote in his log: 'Thank Christ we are through the Strait, steering for Sekala, sixty-eight miles distant. After a clear morning the haze now at 1020 is increasing, although the Island of Bali is still clearly visible. Lombok is almost totally obscured . . . this war is certainly hard on the nervous system.'

Once the *Krait* was through the Lombok Strait she headed west through the Java Sea, only occasionally spotting in the distance a small island or a native fishing boat. They were alone, none more so than Ivan Lyon. 'Quite often he used to stay apart a little bit,' said Arthur Jones. 'He'd often be seen sitting up forward on his own, probably be thinking and working things out.'[51]

The officers took their turn at the wheel, while Fred Marsh was set to work in the engine room under the instruction of Paddy McDowell. Jones, Andrew Huston, Wally Falls and Moss Berryman were the lookouts, either from the cross-tree on the mast or atop the wheelhouse, on four-hour shifts. 'I spent a lot of the time at the top of the mast with binoculars looking out for any craft,' said Berryman. 'Occasionally, a Japanese float plane would fly over and we would stand in a circle pretending to unpick fishing lines.'[52]

Telegraphist Horace Young sat in front of his wireless station, sweating profusely in the sweltering heat below deck. 'The radio equipment was squeezed in behind the companionway that went down into the officers' accommodation,' he recalled. 'It was only very small, about 9 by 9 feet, barely enough to squeeze down there, and the cockroaches of course.'[53]

It was an AR-8 wireless, originally manufactured for Hudson bomber aircraft, with a 50-watt transmitter and an all-band receiver. 'I had to spend at least eight hours a day on certain channels that the navy had given me to monitor,' said Young. As a treat, he would sometimes tune in to Tokyo Rose, the

Posing in front of the *Krait*'s wheelhouse are (left to right) back row: Walter Falls, Kevin Cain, Ivan Lyon, Ted Carse and James McDowell. Front row: Andrew Huston, Moss Berryman and Horace Young. (AWM P00986.001)

Having a dip in the 'Bay of Otters' on Panjang Island are (left to right) Ivan Lyon, Andrew Huston, Bob Page, Wally Falls and Arthur Jones. Donald Davidson was behind the camera. (AWM 300919)

Japanese propaganda programme broadcast in English by several female presenters, which the men found amusing, and he also 'rigged up a speaker down aft so we could play a bit of the BBC'.

Life on board the *Krait* was cramped, particularly the sleeping quarters. The sailors took it in turns to sleep in one of the three hammocks above the engine room hatch with just a very thin mattress. Andrew Crilly, the cook, bedded down on top of the water tank, just opposite his little galley, and those in the engine room had a bunk to share.

There were two meals a day, breakfast and supper, while lunch consisted of a cup of lime juice and a couple of hardtack biscuits or a handful of raisins. 'Andy [Crilly] did a wonderful job with his pancakes and the other stuff,' said Young. 'He used to have to cook in seawater because he couldn't spend any of the fresh water.'[54] The highlight of the day was the tot of rum poured into the men's mugs after the evening meal.

Lyon was meticulous in ensuring that Crilly burned the labels of the food tins once he had cooked their contents. The tins themselves were punctured before being thrown overboard. Lyon was determined to leave no clues for the Japanese.

On 12 September the *Krait*'s log had little to report other than a low visibility due to the hazy conditions, and the fact the sea was 'a queer olive green'. The next day, however, as they sailed past the south-west corner of Borneo they spotted a number of sailing craft: three-masted junks and two- and one-masted prahus, the traditional Indonesian sailing boat.

More vessels were seen on 14 September as they sailed to within 50 miles of the Borneo coast, and that evening the wind freshened to force 5. It was a benevolent breeze, however, speeding them north towards the Lingga Archipelago. On 15 September the wind died and the rain arrived, the first deluge of the voyage.

On 16 September they were chugging up the Temiang Strait towards the island of Pompong, where 18 months earlier Bill Reynolds had rescued a group of evacuees from Singapore. He had reported that the island was uninhabited. Those on the *Krait* were looking for a secluded anchorage, where the *Krait* could lie up while the three canoes paddled into Singapore Harbour. It had to be hidden from any passing ship, and well away from any habitation.

The *Krait* arrived at Pompong in the early afternoon of 16 September, and spent a while cruising the island in search of a suitable anchorage. There was nothing. Lyon ordered Carse to take them to Bengku Island, a few miles south of Pompong. Once there, wrote Lyon, 'we lowered the dinghy and started taking soundings around the coastal reef, hoping to find a way by which the *Krait* could get close ashore.' An enemy single-float biplane flew overhead while Davidson was gauging the depth of the water, but the pilot took no interest in them.

The result of the soundings convinced Lyon and Carse that it would be foolhardy to take the *Krait* any closer. The vessel returned to Pompong, and that evening the officers had a conference. The upshot of their discussion was recorded in the boat's log: 'September 16th: … could not get into Bengku's bays and inlets on account of off-lying coral reefs. All the islands in the vicinity are similar. So the alternative of going over to the Sumatra mangroves and river mouths was dropped. Instead it was decided that *Krait* should return to Borneo, and keep moving, after landing the operational party.'

By daylight on 17 September a creeping apprehension had pervaded the crew of the *Krait*. A disturbing number of aircraft had passed overhead the previous day, and during the night there had been the reflection of searchlights on the sea. At 0700 hours two Japanese float planes flew past at no more than 2,000 feet. There was either a seaplane base in the vicinity or a warship at anchor. Lyon considered it an 'unhealthy area'.

It wasn't just aircraft they saw with increasing frequency. There were many sailing vessels, one of which, a kolek (a small Malayan boat), powered by three paddlers, made for Pompong. Lyon ordered Carse to lower the mast into its cradle and start the engine. 'We didn't know how the locals were going to treat you, whether they were going to dob you in or whether they were going to be friendly,' said Arthur Jones. 'We didn't know what the position was with the Japanese and whether they had planted a police station on the island and taken over, we didn't know what to expect.'[55]

The lack of intelligence was one of the formidable obstacles for *Jaywick* to overcome. In Occupied Europe it was straightforward (although still dangerous) for British agents to infiltrate enemy lines; even in North Africa, a relatively compact theatre of war that ebbed and flowed, the Allies (and the Axis forces) established good spy networks using European and Arab agents. In the Far East intelligence was much harder to come by, although by 1942 the US navy was decrypting Japanese naval messages.

The *Krait*'s hurried departure from Pompong forced Lyon to improvise. His intention was to reach Durian Island, 30 miles away, at nightfall, so to kill time they sailed north, then turned east, towards the island of Galang Bahru. Two miles from the shore they spotted an observation tower. Taut nerves tightened further. 'We cautiously altered course until heading as though bound from Sumatra to Singapore,' wrote Lyon.

North of Galang Bahru is the island of Panjang, approximately 25 miles south of Singapore. As the *Krait* passed its western shore Lyon noticed its sandy coves and its lack of habitation. It looked ideal for their purpose. Now was not the time for further investigation, not with an observation tower so close, but at nightfall the *Krait* returned. The log recorded their arrival:

> Panjang was reached shortly before midnight and we anchored in 3 fathoms off a small beach about two thirds the way down from the North end. A strong wind was blowing about force 6 from the Southward, bringing with it a considerable swell and breaking seas, and beating against the flood tide. Breaking surf was all round the island making it impossible to land our valuable gear in our flat-bottomed dinghy.

The wind eased in the early hours of 18 September, allowing Arthur Jones to row Donald Davidson ashore to reconnoitre the island. 'We had a good look around,' remembered Jones. 'We couldn't see any sign of any natives living there in any of the villages. So I went back to the *Krait*, paddled back to it, and told them everything was OK and it was a good spot. So then the work started.'

The work consisted of bringing ashore canoes, limpet mines and rations, which were tins of Australian Field Operation Rations. Inside each tin were three packets labelled breakfast, lunch and dinner. 'Two packs had little containers of dehydrated M & V [meat and vegetable] tablets, it was like an oily looking sawdust and you crushed these, soaked them in water and heated them up and you just more or less ate them like soup,' said Jones.[56] The third packet contained a tin of beef, and there were also tea tablets, salt tablets and a small tin of vegemite. They had water to last for 14 days at three quarts each a day.

The six-man canoe party comprised Lyon, Davidson, Bob Page, Andrew Huston, Wally Falls and Jones. Fred Marsh and Moss Berryman were the reservists, primed to step in if one of the others had fallen sick or picked up an injury. None had, to the disappointment of Berryman and Marsh, who continued to badger Lyon to join the operation right up to the last moment. 'We put on a bit of a turn,' admitted Berryman. 'We said, "We've done all the training, sir, why can't we be in it?" And he said, "nope, you two are going to be baby sitters and look after them."'[57]

Berryman ferried over the last batch of equipment in the dinghy at 0345 and then bade his comrades 'Good luck and God's Speed'. 'A shake of the hand all round, and we pushed the dinghy off,' said Davidson. 'A few strong pulls at the oars, and he was gone, swallowed up in the night.'[58]

The six men stood on the shore for a few more minutes, staring after the invisible Berryman. They heard the faint noise of the dinghy being lashed to the *Krait* and then they made out the silhouette of the vessel as it headed away to the south-east. It would return in a fortnight and collect the men, all being well.

CHAPTER 5
SINGAPORE STRUCK

When dawn broke on 18 September the six men on Panjang realized that they had company on the 40-yard stretch of beach. A family of nine otters played in the rocky pools, the cubs chasing each other in and out. The raiders christened it 'Bay of Otters' and embarked on a thorough reconnaissance, pushing through the thick jungle. Once the vines thinned, the ground dipped into a small valley and then climbed to form a short steep hill. On the other side of the hill was a village, but there was no track linking the two coasts and they judged they were safe from prying eyes. They also found a freshwater hole, a further stroke of luck. Now they could rest for a couple of days and, as Lyon told them, 'get our land legs back' without breaking into their water rations.

In a clearing among the jungle, about 25 yards from the beach, the men redistributed their stores, while one stood guard behind a tree with a view of the ocean. With that done, they bathed and slept and took pleasure in observing the monkeys and otters.

At dusk on 20 September they were good to go. They had food and water, charts, an Admiralty register of enemy shipping and 27 limpet mines, nine in each canoe in strings of three. These delayed-action magnetic mines would cling to a ship's hull like a barnacle to a rock. The 9 pounds of explosive were in a container with magnets in flexible sockets on either side. A detonator was attached to one end with a colour-coded time fuse, which ranged in duration from one to 48 hours. One limpet could rip a 3-foot hole in a hull but a cluster of three on the same side of the ship could roll her over.

The men had practised laying the mines myriad times. They could do it in their sleep. While the officer in the stern set the mines, using a 5-foot collapsible stick to attach them below the waterline of the target, the seaman in the bow of the canoe secured the craft to the hull with a holdfast, an instrument of two parallel bars festooned with several small strong magnets.

Loading the canoes with 700 pounds of arms and equipment took time, recalled Jones: 'The idea with the canoes, they were not very strong, so you've got to put your canoe into the water and then bring all your mines and equipment and everything, and stow it away up in the bows and down aft and midships.'

The limpets, which in each canoe weighed 100 pounds, were stashed between the legs of the officer in the stern of the canoe. They examined the rubberized canvas of their canoes, searching by sight and touch for any small defect, and paid similar diligence to their spraydecks.

They were loaded and ready to go on the evening of 20 September when they stiffened at a faint noise out to sea. 'We heard this diesel [boat] coming along the straits from Singapore so we had to back off into the mangroves and wait for it to go through,' said Jones.[59] It was a 70-foot Japanese launch, chugging through the islands, its crew no doubt bored with yet another tedious patrol.

When the night was once more still, the six men eased themselves into their canoes. Lyon was paired with Huston, Davidson with Falls, and Page and Jones were a team. 'We paddled out into deep water and carried out our normal routine of sinking all debris, such as tins, that might betray our presence,' said Lyon. 'Then with Davidson acting as navigator we paddled slowly to the North West in close arrowhead formation.'[60]

They soon discovered a flaw in their navy Japara pyjama suits as they paddled against a slight tide through the Riau Archipelago. 'There was no ventilation in the darned things,' reflected Jones.[61] 'They were buttoned up, and of course in that climate you sweated like the devil.' They stopped for five minutes an hour, an opportunity to wring the sweat from their suits and take a swig of water and eat a square of chocolate.

Just after midnight on 21 September they had covered 10 miles, and it was agreed they would push on for another 2 miles until they reached Pulau Bulat. The *Krait* had passed the island four days earlier when it was killing time before dropping anchor at Panjang, and it had looked suitable. So it proved after

Davidson and Falls conducted a reconnaissance. It was little more than an uninhabited knoll with a sandy beach and some thick mangroves in which they and their canoes could be concealed. 'Here we spent a pleasant day observing the passage of numerous small craft in and out of the [Bulan] Strait, under conditions of such safety that it was possible to allow bathing,' recorded Lyon.

At nightfall they paddled away from Pulau Bulat into the Bulan Strait, and into trouble. The narrow strait was crowded with small islands and numerous houseboats, from which hung a complex system of nets to trap the fish as they swam through the narrow strait. To entice the fish into the nets, the fishermen suspended kerosene lamps a few feet above the water.

The three canoes negotiated their way through the strait. It was slow and frustrating progress, and by dawn they had covered only 12 miles, obliging them to 'shelter in a sandfly infested swamp to avoid being caught out in daylight'.

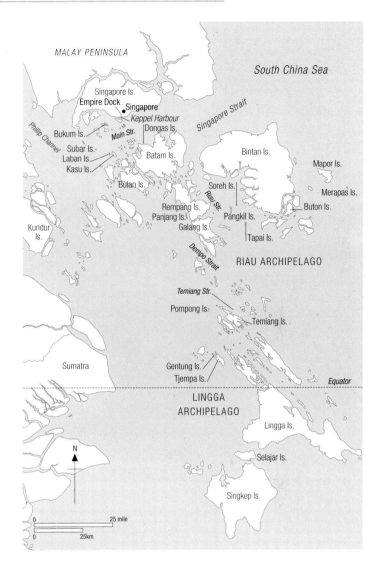

As they paddled towards land, on the Batam coast near the village of Sagilang, Page and Jones's canoe was seized by a tide race and as the pair tried to wrest back control they collided with the canoe containing Lyon and Huston. There was a 'sickening noise like splintering ribs' and everyone feared the worst. But the canoe had absorbed the blow without sustaining any serious damage.

They spent the daylight hours of 22 September slapping away the sandflies and trying to catch what sleep they could despite their antagonistic environment. A tropical storm swept in at midday and the rain fell in sheets, shielding the raiders from observation. They stood under the rain, letting it cleanse their bodies of salt water. At dusk they pushed off and powered north. 'We made

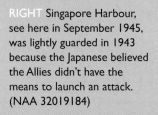

TOP This photo, taken in 1945, shows a folboat with an outboard motor and a spray cover similar to the one used on the *Jaywick* raid. (NAA 8295327)

ABOVE Although this folboat has an outboard motor, it is similar in shape and size to the ones used by the men of *Jaywick* on the Singapore raid. (NAA 8295323)

RIGHT Singapore Harbour, see here in September 1945, was lightly guarded in 1943 because the Japanese believed the Allies didn't have the means to launch an attack. (NAA 32019184)

excellent progress and, by 2030 hours, we had reached the end of the Strait and could see ahead of us the lights of Pulau Sambu, formerly a Dutch Oil Depot, five miles south of Singapore,' wrote Lyon.[62]

The island selected as the forward observation post was Dongas, off the north coast of Batam and 8 miles south-east of Singapore. Lyon had paid it a visit or two before the war when he had cruised the islands in the *Vinette* and his memory had served him correctly in believing it suitable.

Lyon and Davidson had proved themselves a highly effective team. There was no clash of personalities, or more specifically, egos. Lyon had the strength of character and the self-confidence to tacitly hand over command to Davidson when the operation required his expertise. 'Lyon was the senior officer and he was in charge and it was his operation,' said Jones. 'Davidson took over once we went into the canoes. He was more or less made the leader and led the way. He was in the first front canoe and he did all the scouting and Lyon said, "We'll follow Davidson from now on, whatever he says goes". But he was close behind him so naturally he could talk to Davidson.'[63]

Jones never heard a bad word pass between the pair. They complemented each other, brought out the best in one another, and more importantly, they inspired devotion from their men.

The first thing the raiders did on bringing the canoes ashore in the early hours of 23 September was sleep. They woke rejuvenated and explored the island. '[We] found that the high ground on the North side provided an excellent view of the Roads,' wrote Lyon. 'Drinking water was found in a disused well. The island, therefore, fulfilled our requirements.'

Dongas was uninhabited, save for some black and yellow-banded sea iguanas and two 6-foot crocodiles that fled at the approach of intruders.

The men spent the day sleeping or at the observation post squinting through the telescope at Singapore Harbour and occasionally glancing at the Admiralty register of Japanese shipping. The absence of patrol boats and the ease of access of native craft indicated the harbour was not mined.

Lyon noted down other sites of interest, and while 'there was no change to be seen in the general outline of the city', several wireless masts had been erected, including one of the roof of the Cathay Building.

When night fell the lights of Singapore shimmered over the water. They remarked that it was significant that there was no blackout imposed, an indication of the Japanese belief that they regarded Singapore as impregnable, 'with the war many thousands of miles away, and the almost impassable submarine barriers surrounding it'.

The intention was to launch the attack on the night of 25/26 September, but in the early afternoon of 24 September Lyon spotted something through his telescope that elicited a cluck of contentment. He dashed down the hill to inform Davidson that there were 'thirteen sizeable ships in the Roads, all with steam up, probably sailing in the morning, perhaps as a convoy'. Sixty-five thousand tons at anchor was too good an opportunity to let slip. Davidson agreed. They must bring the operation forward a night.

They left Dongas at 2000 hours, the limpet mines stowed in their canoes and a rubber cyanide pellet secreted on each man. The distribution of the pills had been one of the few moments on the operation when the bantering ceased. Young men, all in their own mind indestructible, suddenly understood the danger of their situation. 'I leave it up to yourselves to decide what you want to do,' Lyon told the men. 'But I can tell you now that if you get caught you won't have a very good time of it. They're not known for being gentlemen, the Japanese.' Don't delude yourselves in thinking you are tough enough to resist interrogation, added Lyon. 'You could be tortured enough to give away the whole story. You may not be able to do anything about it.'[64] Above all, they had to think of their mates on the *Krait*. If they fell into enemy hands, the Japanese would want to know how they arrived in Singapore.

They made good headway at first in their arrowhead formation, the only alarm caused by a lazy searchlight on the top of the Cathy Building that caught them in frame for a moment and then swept past. Then the capricious tide turned against them. They paddled defiantly for an hour longer, but at 0100 hours Lyon aborted the attack; they had run out of time to lay the mines.

Despondency sapped the men's mental strength as they paddled back towards Dongas. The tide taunted them, and in the darkness the three canoes became separated. When dawn broke on 25 September only Davidson and Falls and Page and Jones had made it back to the beach.

Lyon and Huston's canoe hadn't been holed in the collision a few days earlier, but something had gone awry and it was sluggish and temperamental, requiring greater effort to keep it on course.

The pair had come ashore on the southern coast of Dongas, and remained concealed among the boulders until nightfall when they paddled round the island to rejoin their comrades. It was agreed that they would launch a second attack on the following evening, 26/27 September, but from the island of Subar, approximately 6 miles due west of Dongas on the other side of the Bulan Strait. Lyon and Huston wolfed down a hot meal prepared by Davidson, and they then paddled to Subar, a small flat island strewn with rocks and bracken, arriving shortly before dawn on 26 September. They constructed a hide, about 15 feet wide, among the bracken and overhung with the branches of small trees. The day was spent in observing their target, 8 miles north. Those not on observation post duty were too excited to sleep as they lay among the bracken. They listened to Lyon describing some of his pre-war escapades. Then the talk 'got round to cool beer and hot barmaids'. When dusk began to darken the sky, Lyon led his men down to the beach. 'I think we were all confident,' recalled Jones. 'I was confident we could do the job but I was a bit doubtful about getting away.'[65]

The limpet mines had seven-hour fuses, so if all went to schedule they would detonate at 0500 hours on 27 September, not long before sunup. That would give them a few hours to paddle south to one of the islands and lie up among the rocks or mangroves. Reaching the rendezvous at Padang was the more daunting challenge; surely the Strait would be swarming with enemy patrol boats?

At 1900 hours the six men shook hands, wished each other luck, and pushed off for Singapore. The plan had been finalized during the afternoon: Davidson and Falls, Canoe 2, would paddle north to the shipping in Keppel Harbour, while Canoes 1 (Lyon and Huston) and 3 (Page and Jones) would head north-west to the shipping in Examination Anchorage, and the wharf at Pulau Bukom. Canoe 2, the strongest team, had the additional responsibility of going hell for leather to Pompong, to make the rendezvous with the *Krait* and hold it until the other canoes arrived.

'See you at Pompong,' said Lyon to Davidson, as the men paddled slowly away from the shore.

'Cheero, Ivan,' replied Davidson. 'Bye-bye, Bob, old man.'[66]

The three Australian sailors exchanged some banter. Falls wagered he'd bag more enemy shipping than Jones. 'Get to hell,' he was told. 'Won't believe a bloody thing you tell us, anyhow.'

Progress was slow for Donald Davidson and Wally Falls as they paddled north towards the Roads across the Main Strait. The flood tide was on the starboard, noted Davidson in his report, making the going hard. Their arms and shoulders were sore, their buttocks aching, and their palms raw from five previous nights of punishing paddling. They had slept for only a few hours in the past week, but their bodies were fuelled by adrenaline as they stared ahead at the bright lights of Singapore.

This photo of Ivan Lyon was taken on Dongas Island and shows the *Jaywick* leader beside his camouflaged canoe. (AWM 067335A)

They steered a course around an anchored ketch on the edge of the main channel, and continued between the islands of Blakang Mati and Tekukor. A searchlight on Blakang Mati suddenly pierced the darkness and for an awful moment Davidson thought it was seeking them out. But its beam swept the sky and Davidson and Falls resumed their paddling. A heavy rip tide helped the canoe keep to the water boat channel and soon they saw the pylons of the Keppel Harbour boom. They passed a big steam ferry heading out of the harbour before they reached the boom gates; the gates were open, and there was no boom patrol in attendance, so like a burglar taking advantage of an open window, Davidson and Falls slipped inside. 'Inside the boom against the east wharf were two ships but they were too small to be worthy of attack,' commented Davidson. There was no shipping at the main wharf, and nor was there a suitable target in the Empire Docks, which were also too well illuminated for their purpose. 'We turned back and crossed over the boom again, heading for the Roads,' said Davidson. 'Here there were many excellent targets . . . their bows were to the east, showing that the tide was now on the ebb and would be with us as we attacked, and as we retired afterwards.'[67]

The raiders selected a vessel, a 6,000-ton cargo ship, which was sitting low in the water, an indication it was heavily laden. The pair passed the vessel and then turned, making their approach under the stern. Davidson estimated the tide to be about half a knot, 'excellent for our purpose'.

It was no accident that the tide was benign; he and Lyon had studied the tides and calculated the best window for launching the attack.

They paddled down the port side of the vessel, away from the lights of Singapore, until they saw the waste water gushing from the engine room. 'Right, Falls,' said Davidson. 'On with the holdfast.'

Everything went as smoothly as they had rehearsed in Australia. Once Falls had attached the holdfast, Davidson set the fuse on the limpet and then slipped the first of the three clusters of mines onto the 5-foot wooden placing stick. The stick had a catch on the end on which the mine was placed and Davidson then poked it through the water at an angle until he felt the mine's row of magnets set in rubber snap against the ship's hull. Then he delicately disengaged the catch and pulled the stick out of the water. Without a word, Falls released the holdfast and they drifted down the length of the fuse and clamped the second cluster mine in place, a procedure they repeated on the same vessel a third time.

Their second vessel was also a 6,000-ton cargo vessel, and the third ship was of similar proportions, although this one had little in its hold. All the while a clock from somewhere in town proved a faithful timekeeper. It was 0115 hours when they attached the last of their nine limpets; they had nearly four hours before they went off, although the manufacturers had warned that their time fuses weren't entirely reliable.

It was time to depart. Davidson and Falls dumped the holdfast and the placing stick in the sea. Their canoe was now over 100 pounds lighter having dispensed of their mines and accoutrements, but they had the paddle of their lives ahead of them if they were to reach Pulau Nongsa.

They set off at a steady pace and covered about 5 miles in one hour and a half. Then they agreed to up the tempo. 'From then on the canoe's bow wave was a record,' said Davidson. 'For the next hour the only word spoken was now and again "change", when the arms started to ache, and it was time to paddle on the other side.'[68]

They could feel the wind stiffening from the east, ruffling the sea and cooling their perspiring bodies, but they were so utterly focused on their relentless rhythm that their pace didn't slow. But the tide now turned into their adversary, flooding to the west, and they agreed that Pulau Nongsa was beyond them this night. Instead they came ashore on a rocky stretch of coastline 6 miles west of their intended destination at 0430 hours, lifting their canoe out of the water and up a small beach among a jumble of jagged rocks. Falls had a quick scout around but there was no sign of habitation, only some coconut trees. They curled up on the sand behind the rocks and had just fallen asleep when Davidson sat up. 'Falls! Did you hear that?'

The other two canoes had found the going 'easy' on leaving Subar. The tide was running east to west, massaging them towards the target. For the first two hours they paddled together until, at 2130 hours they separated. Bob Page and Arthur Jones made for the wharves at Pulau Bukom. 'We were halfway across and a searchlight opened up on our port side, and it flamed down on the water and it came towards us,' said Jones. 'We headed the canoes into the light to cut down the silhouette and I slid underneath, down as low as I could get in the canoe, and Bob Page sat up on the back of the canoe and sort of just paddled with one paddle – we had single paddles – just paddled with one paddle like the fishermen do.'[69]

For a moment the canoe was captured in the harsh glare of the searchlight, 'and then suddenly it flipped up in the air, went across over our heads and then out.' Ten minutes later the light returned and Jones once more slid low in the canoe. The searchlight caught them, released them, and darted off into the sky. Jones said a silent prayer, exchanged a few whispered words with Page, and the pair then began working the water with their paddles.

At 2200 hours their canoe reached the target area. They glided the length of the wharf, a shark searching silently for some prey. They could see men working under the stern of a barge, welding amid a cauldron of steam, illuminated by the lights that ran parallel with the wharf, oblivious to the danger that lurked in the water.

They came to a tanker and paddled on, aware that such a gargantuan vessel was too big to be hurt by their explosives because of all the different compartments for the various types of oil and fuel.

Next they passed an old freighter with a funnel midship and the engine room at midships, not ideal, but in the absence of any other suitable target

Ivan Lyon observes the target from his OP on Dongas Island. It was from this island that the men unsuccessfully launched their first attempt on Singapore on 24 September. (AWM 067335)

better than nothing. 'So we paddled straight in and got right in alongside,' said Jones.[70] He clamped the holdfast to the hull and winced at the clang. It sounded like a hammer blow loud enough to wake Singapore. But Jones told himself that to anyone on the ship it was inaudible or at worst just another innocuous noise. Gripping the holdfast with one hand, Jones used the other to tuck the bow of the canoe into the hull so its stern jutted out, allowing Page to better manoeuvre the placing stick under the water and clamp the limpet mine. To activate the mines, Page turned a screw on the time fuse that broke the glass ferule inside which was the chemical that would eat through the fuse in just under six hours.★

Page tapped Jones on the shoulder when the mine was set. He released the holdfast and took up his paddle, guiding them slowly down the ship, while Page splayed out the detonating cord for the second of the three limpets. Jones felt another tap on his shoulder and repeated the procedure with the holdfast.

It was a little after 2300 hours when they finished attaching the first cluster of three mines. They had worked their way up the length of the ship to under the bow, and for a few moments they clung to the anchor chain and rewarded their efforts with some chocolate. As they savoured the treat, the pair observed a sentry walking up and down on the wharf, and beyond him some men working under lights on another ship. 'We back-paddled up to the centre of the ship where there was a bit of darkness,' recalled Jones. 'When you look out, "Oh God", and you see all that water and light, and you think no way can you get out again.' Steeling themselves, the pair paddled out of the protective darkness east towards Keppel Harbour. 'You don't know whether you're going to get a bullet in the back or what's going to happen,' said Jones. 'So you had to turn around and paddle out and just hope for the best until you hit that dark patch again.'[71]

They were paddling north, towards Examination Anchorage, and they could feel the tide had now turned and was running west to east. They spied their next target, a modern freighter with engines aft and three sets of goalpost masts. Jones and Page had a whispered discussion, agreeing that if there was any crew up on deck they would likely be on the port side, observing the work that was going on in the wharf area. 'So we went under the starboard side bow and we were just about to get ready to start putting the first limpet on and we looked up,' said Jones. There above them were several sailors leaning on the rail, dragging on cigarettes and gazing in the direction of Singapore, its lights obscured by a spit of land. Jones

---

★ Jones recalled that on each mine there was also a pencil time fuse of one minute's duration, so that in the event 'you got caught putting them on, you pressed it and it activated and the mines would go up'.

and Page back-paddled under the bow and round onto the port side. One limpet was clamped to the engine room and the other two to the hatches. 'We didn't look up the whole time we were doing this,' said Jones. 'Because sometimes your face would show or a movement would give you away.'

They hitched a lift on the tide to their third target, an old 6,000-ton freighter. 'This one was low down in the water, it was well loaded, obviously,' said Jones. 'We snuck up alongside up to the midship section.'[72] The hull was so rusty that Jones had trouble making the holdfast do its job. He could feel his heart thumping against his ribs. Unlike the other two vessels, this ship was compact, so compact that Jones reckoned if he stood in his canoe he could reach the upper deck. Should a sailor appear at the rail, they would be in trouble. Page worked fast and efficiently, and in a matter of minutes Jones had felt the familiar tap on his shoulder. He consigned the holdfast to the sea and Page let go of the placing stick. They had a piece of chocolate and then turned south-east towards Dongas.

After separating at 2130 hours from Page and Jones, Canoe 1, containing Ivan Lyon and Andrew Huston, continued towards Examination Harbour, the most northerly of the target areas. They reached their objective an hour later, but to their consternation discovered that all the shipping except tankers were blacked out and 'completely invisible against the background of hills'. Here there were no Singapore lights to illuminate their targets. With mounting frustration Lyon and Huston snaked through the water, trying to locate a victim. 'When my time limit was exhausted I decided to attack a tanker,' said Lyon, 'two of which I could clearly distinguish by the red light in place of the normal white anchor light.'[73] The limpets lacked the power to sink a tanker, but Operation *Jaywick* had always been in Lyon's eyes as much about inflicting psychological hurt on the Japanese as wreaking material damage. The canoe streaked through the dark water towards its prey from astern, and Lyon attached the first limpet to the propeller shaft. They drifted down the ship until they reached the engine room and Lyon applied the second mine. He reached out to tap the Australian on the shoulder, but saw that Huston had a finger raised to the sky. Lyon looked up and stared into the face of 'a man who was watching us intently from a porthole ten feet above'. For a second Lyon froze. The man gazed down, saying and doing nothing. Bluff it out, thought Lyon, and he tapped Huston on the shoulder. They glided a few feet further down and laid the last of the mines. The man continued to watch them impassively for a couple more minutes until 'he withdrew his head and lighted his bedside lamp'.

As they paddled away from the tanker they heard no alarm nor saw any activity on deck. The man had seen them, surely, but perhaps he mistook them for Japanese repairmen inspecting the ship, or even hungry locals searching the hull for barnacles. Evidently, never in his wildest dreams did he imagine that a Briton and an Australian, having travelled a vast distance from Exmouth in a decrepit 70-foot fishing boat, had paddled up to his tanker and laid three explosive devices just beneath his bed. 'He'll soon be dead,' Lyons whispered to Huston, as they set off for Dongas Island.

Peering out from behind the rocks Davidson and Falls stared north from their hiding place towards Singapore. Could the distant explosion really be the result of their handiwork? They had paddled 15 miles during the night and were physically and emotionally shattered, but the noise had them crackling with excitement. They heard another faint boom, and another, and another. 'So we had pulled it off!' reflected Davidson. 'All these months of training and waiting had not been in vain. We had breached the Japanese lines; had sailed nearly two thousand miles inside the lines to attack.' Davidson and Falls shook hands and settled down to a contented sleep.

In Singapore there was bedlam. The Japanese were ignorant as to the nature of the attack, they only knew that several ships were in varying states of ruin in Keppel Harbour, Examination Anchor and at Pulau Bukom wharves. Ships' sirens began wailing and 15 minutes after the first explosion, the lights on

This photo was taken from the observation post built among the bracken on Subar Island, and from there the raiders scouted the shipping in Singapore, 8 miles north. (AWM 300921)

Singapore and Sambu Island were extinguished. When dawn broke one ship was partially submerged in Examination Anchorage, its bow jutting out of the water, while thick black smoke billowed from the tanker, possibly the *Shosei Maru*, that had been targeted by Lyon and Huston. At 0615 hours the first flight of Japanese aircraft took off from Kallang airfield and headed west towards the Malacca Strait. Their orders were imprecise; after all, what or whom were they looking for? Had the attack originated from the air, the sea or the land? The aircraft returned two hours later having seen no trace of the enemy. They were sent up again, this time with orders to search the sea to the south.

When Davidson and Falls woke, it was nearly midday. They spent the rest of the day hidden and at 1900 hours paddled out into the Riau (also spelt Rhio) Strait, keeping tight to the eastern coastline of Batam until at 0430 hours they came ashore at Pulau Tanjong Sau. It was now 28 September, three days before the arranged rendezvous with the *Krait* on Pompong Island. They spent the day concealed and pushed their canoe once more into the water at 1900 hours. It was a hard night's paddling, recorded Davidson, but a satisfying one, the pair now powerfully in sync as they passed 'to the north of Pulau Lepang to Tanjong Piayu, thence to Pulau Anak Mati and down the channel between Pulau Renpang and Pulau Setoko'.

The brevity of Davidson's report concealed the tense hours they spent negotiating the narrow channel, only a quarter of a mile wide at some points. There was an abundance of fishermen, their lights illuminating the water for long stretches as the two bearded men in black outfits glided south on the tide. On occasion they came within 15 feet of a kolek, close enough to hear the fishermen talking as they attended to their nets. As they neared Panjang, from where they had parted from the *Krait* on 18 September, they suddenly heard a familiar sound, the pop-pop of that 'utterly damned patrol boat'. They paddled towards the island of Klinking as the enemy vessel headed north. It was only 50 yards off their starboard side; they could hear voices.

Once it had passed, Davidson and Falls paddled like fury to Panjang, dragging their canoe out of the water and onto the welcoming sand of Otter Bay. They slept well, their minds soothed by the familiarity of the beach. When they woke they located their supply dump and removed a tin of rations. After breakfast they bathed in fresh water, slept, lunched and gathered themselves mentally and physically for the final stage of their journey to Pompong. Before they departed at nightfall, Davidson wrote a note to Lyon detailing their progress and left it in the supply dump. Then they struck out for the coast of Great Abang and were soon in an agitated sea. When the storm broke the canoe was 4 miles from the coast. 'The screaming wind lashed the sea into a maelstrom of breaking waves and thrashing spray,' said Davidson. 'The thunder and lightning were magnificent. The lightning left one utterly blinded for nearly a minute at a time. Then came the rain.'[74]

The rain was ferocious. It stung the face and forced the pair to shut their eyes. They could do little else other than sit out the storm, keeping the canoe head onto the gale and the waves. For two hours they were buffeted by nature, 'steering by the feel of the wind on our cheeks'. They felt more exhilarated than frightened, confident that their canoe that had taken them so far would see the task through to the end.

They reached Abang Besar and came ashore by chance at a freshwater creek. The storm had thwarted their ambition of reaching Pompong that morning, but they knew their destination was deliciously close. The last leg of their epic journey was wearisome in both body and spirit; their adrenaline had nearly run dry, and the physical toll of the last fortnight was keenly felt in their arms and shoulders. They landed on the western coast of Pompong, at a stretch they christened the Bay of Rocks, purposely avoiding the northern shore, where nearly a fortnight earlier they had encountered the three fishermen.

When dawn broke on 1 October Davidson and Falls scouted the island's interior. Nothing appeared untoward. At dusk they paddled cautiously around the island to the rendezvous point on the northern beach. They sat down on the sand, wrapped a blanket around their shoulders, and waited. They shivered, feeling a mix of excitement, anticipation and a touch of anxiety. What if the *Krait* didn't show? What if Lyon and the others didn't show? What if they were the only ones still alive? They decided there was no point in both of them staying awake; one should sleep and the other stand guard. Falls offered to take the first shift. Davidson scooped out a hip-hole in the sand and was just drifting off when he was nudged awake. Falls pointed north into the darkness. There was a 'shapeless blur' edging towards the beach. They could hear nothing but they sensed it was the *Krait*. Jumping into the canoe, they paddled noiselessly towards the blur until they were almost within touching distance. Then a voice shattered the stillness, that of Davidson in a vaudeville Japanese accent: 'Poop 'em up, you white bastards! It's a hold-up! Surrender or die!'

CHAPTER 6

THE WIZARDS OF OZ

When the *Krait* had sailed from Pompong in the early hours of 18 September the atmosphere on board was maudlin. 'We had a feeling that what they were going to try and do was almost mission impossible,' recalled Horace Young, the vessel's telegraphist. 'We didn't think we'd ever see them again.'[75]

As dawn broke on 18 September, the crew of the *Krait* were focused on their own survival, almost as precarious as that of the six men they had seen off a few hours earlier. They spent most of the day in the Temiang Strait, chugging towards the greater safety of the open sea, and that evening Ted Carse wrote in his log: 'All the crew are feeling the strain of long hours and ceaseless watching. Unless we get a quiet time soon I will have to issue Benzedrine.'*

The men slept well over the next 24 hours and by 21 September Carse was feeling more confident. 'Still good weather, still no sightings,' he wrote in the log. In fact, his main gripe was now the food. In the galley, Crilly was fully justifying his nickname of 'Pancake Andy'. 'When the cruise commenced pancakes were one of my favourites,' remarked Carse. 'At the present rate if I ever look at one again I shall be sick.'

---

* Benzedrine was an amphetamine first issued to Allied troops in 1942, and which became increasingly common in the next three years, particularly among special forces units, including the SAS and the SBS.

On the night of 22 September they passed through an electric storm, but for the next week they sailed serenely among the islands off the south-west coast of Borneo, catching only the odd glimpse of a vessel. With a depleted crew there was plenty to keep the eight men occupied. 'I had to close down the wireless watches and help out with the normal deck watches because they were so short of crew,' remembered Young. 'So in addition to doing the lookout duties, I had to try and squeeze in a bit of time on the radio as well because we weren't too sure whether the canoes had been successful or not. If they had been caught, we could have been going back into some sort of ambush. So it was pretty important to try and get some sort of information.'[76]

Young tuned into the Japanese radio on 25 September hoping to hear a clue that might indicate the raiders had been successful. There was nothing, nor was there on the next day. The men told each other that no news was good news, that at least there was no crowing broadcast about the capture of six enemy guerrillas. But the doubts began to gnaw at the men as the days passed. 'We are all filled with anxiety as we have had no news at all of the party and this does not seem too good to us,' wrote Carse in his log on 28 September.

Two days later his entry ran: 'Another day gone. Tomorrow night we should know our fate, for if we make contact safely the job is almost done.'

The weather was ungracious to the *Krait* as it headed to Pompong on the evening of 1 October, a strong tide holding them up. 'We were a little bit late getting to the rendezvous,' said Young. 'That had put us back . . . from our rendezvous time, which was supposed to be round about the midnight.' In fact they were only a few minutes late, and the men were on edge as they stole towards Pompong. 'We weren't too sure what the hell we were going into,' said Young. They gave thanks to a moonless night as they peered into the darkness, every sense straining for an unusual sound that might signal an enemy preparing to spring an ambush. 'Carse went in and [we] dropped the anchor, and everybody was waiting there with the fingers on the Owen gun triggers and the Brens,' recalled Young.[77]

They were 100 yards from the shore when Moss Berryman suddenly pointed. A movement. On the beach. He was sure. Taffy Morris squinted in the direction of Berryman's outstretched hand. Now he saw it. Was it someone launching a boat? The men's fingers curled around their triggers as they watched sparks of phosphorus thrown up by paddles. They still couldn't make out what was approaching and so they trained their weapons on whatever it was. And they heard the whispered challenge: 'Poop 'em up, you white bastards! It's a hold-up! Surrender or die!' The next moment, said Young, 'Davo slipped over the stern and [was] closely followed by Falls. Naturally we were more than delighted to see them. But boy, they were really beat.'[78]

Davidson and Falls were showered with rations, and pancakes, and as they ate they told a tale that riveted the crew of the *Krait*. Mission accomplished. They remained at anchor off Pompong until shortly before dawn, in the hope that the other two canoes would show. When they didn't, the *Krait* recommenced its cruise, heading into the Temiang Strait once more in the direction of Borneo.★

Both Young and Berryman had been present on the *Krait* on 18 September when Lyon had issued his final instructions to Carse, which Berryman remembered as: 'On the 14th night [2 October], come back, pick us up and we'll go home, and if we're not there, go without us, because we've been caught, or drowned or something.'[79]

Ivan Lyon and Andrew Huston had reached Dongas Island at 0515 hours on 27 September, minutes after the first explosions had shattered the pre-dawn stillness. Arthur Jones and Bob Page paddled ashore as Lyon and Huston were still congratulating each other on their success. 'Dawn was breaking,' recalled Lyon, 'and the natives had been roused by the activity in the harbour.' Lyon watched through his telescope as villagers on the adjacent island of Patam jumped with joy and hugged one another. Finally, someone had struck back at their hated oppressor.

From a hide inside the mangroves the quartet of raiders peered south but, apart from the aircraft they observed taking off, they saw no Japanese activity on the water.

At 1100 hours they slipped out from the mangroves and paddled around Dongas to the north shore, where they had camped a few days earlier. They climbed the hill to the observation post and stared south. 'All you could see was

---

★ In *Deadly Secrets,* the Australian historian Lynette Silver alleges that Carse's 'nerve had failed' and he wanted to leave at once for Exmouth Gulf. But Davidson, 'with the assistance of a well-positioned pistol', ordered the navigator to spend the day cruising the islands before returning the following night. No mention of this incident is made in the official *Jaywick* report, or in *Winning Hazard*, the book published in 1944 by Davidson's wife, Nancy, under the nom de plume Noel Wynyard, and with which Davidson co-operated. In a 2003 interview Young denied that Davidson had to threaten Carse with a pistol, saying: 'This person claims that Carse had to be persuaded to come back. It was nothing like that at all . . . It wasn't in Carse's nature to start with. Not in the slightest.' Young added that this allegation was attributed post-war to Taffy Morris, but that at the 50th anniversary reunion of the raid, in 1993, the Welshman vehemently denied having said such a thing, and was 'stricken' at the suggestion he could have traduced Carse.

a lot of smoke going over the harbour so one of the oil tanker's holds must have been caught alight,' said Jones. They had heard several explosions, and deduced that Davidson and Falls must have accomplished their task without detection. 'Everybody shook hands all around, a good job well done,' said Jones. 'But when we looked around from this Dongas Island and the view across the harbour you realized you were only a little island stuck there. If they sent out patrols looking around they could have easily searched that island.'[80]

It was a tense day for the quartet as they waited for the long daylight hours to pass. Finally, at 1900 hours, they pushed off from Dongas. Surely the next few days would be the most dangerous of the whole operation? The enemy had been complacent until 0500 hours that morning; now they were enraged, and out for revenge. 'We expected to encounter difficulties in the form of searchlights and patrols around Sambu, but found that everything was normal,' recorded Lyon. There was a small steamship at anchor at the north entrance to the Bulan Strait, but no one appeared to be on guard detail. 'So we just took our paddles out of the water and let ourselves drift with the current until we got past,' said Jones. 'I could have reached out and touched the anchor rope that it had out at the stern.'[81]

By early on the morning of 30 September they were back at Otter Bay in Panjang. None could believe how easy it had been. Where were the Japanese? They rested for the day, but in the late afternoon heavy cloud began banking in the skies to the west. Lyon knew the region well enough to appreciate that was a harbinger of a gathering storm. He had been caught in a few such storms during his pre-war cruising days in the *Vinette*. Lyon had to make a choice, both of which were fraught with risk: take to the water tonight and paddle through the storm, or sit it out on dry land and try to cover the 28 miles to Pompong the following day? He settled on the latter. 'To risk a day passage of 28 miles was a serious decision,' admitted Lyon. 'But it was amply justified by the violence that later developed.'

Davidson and Falls came through the storm unscathed, but they were superior paddlers and their canoe was flawless; Lyon and Huston, in their sluggish and unresponsive vessel, which sapped the strength from their bodies with every stroke, would have struggled to survive.

The canoes left Panjang at first light on 1 October, an hour's delay between departures with Page and Jones the first to strike out. There was a strong headwind and the men had to draw on their dwindling reserves of strength as they stuck to their routine of one hour's hard paddling, and then a five-minute break when they took a swig of water and bit into a hardtack biscuit.

On their return to Australia, the *Krait* was buzzed by a Japanese patrol boat in the Lombok Strait, seen here from a satellite image, but the enemy vessel took it for a fishing vessel. (Getty Gallo Images / Contributor)

'By lunchtime we made an island probably about half way to where we were going,' said Jones. 'It was just a bit of sand out of the water with a couple of trees on it. So we pulled in there and had a drink . . . Lyon and Huston caught up with us, so we had a little break there'. Neither pair had anything untoward to report. No sightings of enemy vessels and only a few Japanese aircraft in the sky, none of which had spotted the canoes in the turbulent seas.

The canoes reached Pompong at 0300 hours on 2 October, just within the agreed rendezvous time slot of between dusk and dawn on 1/2 October. They paddled around the island but saw no sign of either the *Krait* or Davidson and Falls. The emptiness of the island drained the men's morale and the physical exhaustion that had been kept at bay for days suddenly overwhelmed them. 'We were completely exhausted,' said Jones. 'We just flaked out on the beach and pulled up our canoes when dawn came.'[82]

Just as they completed this task they spotted a vessel a couple of miles out to sea heading towards the Temiang Strait. They would have recognized its shape anywhere: it was the *Krait*. Misery momentarily swept over each man as they realized that 'such had been our fatigue on the previous night we had paddled to and fro in the anchorage without being able to see the ship'.

Doubts began to crowd them like mosquitoes at dusk. 'We sort of hid up behind the mangroves,' said Jones. 'There was a little bit of talk, "well, what if she doesn't come back, what are we going to do? What is the best thing to do?"' Someone pointed out that they had nearly exhausted their rations. Lyon sensed the incipient panic. Don't worry, he told the Australians, if the *Krait* didn't return they would paddle back to Panjang, to the supply dump, stock up on rations and water. Then, recalled Jones, Lyon coolly explained that 'we would capture ourselves a junk of some sort and . . . head towards Ceylon. He'd done a trip before, when the fall of Singapore happened, so he knew what he was about.'[83]

Lyon's breezy confidence allayed the anxiety of his three companions and they settled down to wait for nightfall. At 2200 hours the *Krait* returned and the four men climbed aboard, trying desperately to appear as nonchalant as possible. Crilly had a celebratory supper on the stove, one which mercifully didn't consist solely of pancakes. Rather, they tucked into a bully beef stew, dehydrated mutton and tinned vegetables. Food had never tasted so good. As they gorged on the feast Lyon asked Davidson to fetch a bottle of rum he'd secreted in the hold. 'Everyone had a little tot,' said Jones. 'And then we got in our hammocks and slept for 24 hours.'[84]

The *Krait* reached Exmouth Gulf on 19 October, 47 days and 4,000 miles after its departure. The return had been for the most part uneventful until heading through the Lombok Strait when they were buzzed by a Japanese patrol boat that guarded the northern narrows. Moss Berryman had been asleep on deck when he was shaken awake and told to 'Get your machine gun, we've got a visitor . . . keep your head down low.' Berryman peered into the darkness and saw the enemy vessel almost on top of them. 'He sat there for quite a few minutes, looking at us in the dark,' remembered Berryman. 'He never put a light on us, and he never challenged us in any way – and then he just turned and zoomed off into the distance, and we thought, "oh beauty, he's gone."'[85]

There was scant fanfare for the men upon their arrival at Potshot submarine base. Secrecy was paramount. Only Admiral Christie knew where they had been, and he was in awe of their feat. He hosted Lyon and Page to dinner in his quarters, and wrote in his diary of their 'almost single-handed endeavour of extremely bold pattern. My hat is off to them'.

Stoker James McDowell watches as Wally Falls and Moss Berryman clean and check their Owen sub-machine guns on board the *Krait*. (AWM P00986.002)

The *Jaywick* raiders in Brisbane, 11 November 1943. Back row: Berryman, Marsh, Jones, Huston. Centre: Crilly, Cain, McDowell, Young, Falls, Morris. Front: Carse, Davidson, Lyon, Jock Campbell (non-operational), Page. (NAA 8295615)

Lyon and Page then flew to Darwin for a debrief, and the former wrote citations for a clutch of medals, including Distinguished Service Medals to Paddy McDowell, Wally Falls, Arthur Jones and Andrew Huston. Lyon, Page and Davidson were rewarded with the Distinguished Service Order, and Ron 'Taffy' Morris and Andrew Crilly received Military Medals.

The first chance the men of Operation *Jaywick* had to toast their success was in Brisbane when Major Jock Campbell laid on a party for them all on 11 November. Then they went off on leave for a month, which for Arthur Jones meant a flight home to Perth. He went to the pub, had a couple of beers, and kept his mouth shut. 'You couldn't tell anyone where you'd been and what you'd been doing or anything,' he said. Those were the implicit instructions from Lyon. 'He said, "If any of you get talking . . . there is a penalty, you could be shot or put in jail probably for the rest of the war and kept isolated. You've only got to talk to somebody and it could upset a future operation."'[86]

Following the debriefing of Lyon and Page, Lieutenant-Colonel John Chapman-Walker sent a memorandum to London on 3 November, summarizing the achievement of Operation *Jaywick*. Seven vessels, 37,000 tons of shipping,* had been either sunk or badly damaged, and furthermore useful intelligence

---

* This claim has been queried in recent years and some sources believe that the limpet mines on one unidentified vessel failed to explode, resulting in damage to six ships, of 26,000 tons.

about Singapore had been harvested by the raiders. In his covering letter, Chapman-Walker wrote:

> I cannot tell you what a tremendous fillip it has given to everyone of this Organisation. It is difficult to express what a magnificent performance this party has put up. We are naturally preserving the greatest secrecy about the results but I am glad to say each of the few high ranking officers outside the Organisation who know the details have been equally enthusiastic in their appreciation.[87]

Referring to Lyon as the 'party leader', Chapman-Walker explained that Lyon had recounted the story of the raid in person to General Blamey, who adjudged it a 'great success', and was so taken with the audacity of the raid that he took Lyon to Brisbane and presented him to General Douglas MacArthur, 'who was equally enthusiastic and most kind in his remarks to the Party Leader'.

What most delighted senior command was the fact that the Japanese had no clue as to who had perpetrated the attack, and how they had done it. Allied intelligence intercepted Japanese messages that expressed ignorance and outrage. The senior command decided to keep them in the dark; there would be no triumphant press reports or taunting communiqués about the raid. That way they opened the possibility of launching similar attacks on other Japanese targets. In doing so, however, the Allies deprived themselves of the opportunity of lauding it over their enemy. Some extravagant press reports on the daring raid would not only have caused much humiliation to the Japanese, they would have been a cause for celebration for those living under their yoke, particularly the Chinese and resistance groups in the Far East.

So who had carried out the raid? That was the question the Japanese were determined to answer.

On 10 October – a date that subsequently became known as the 'Double Tenth Massacre' – the Japanese Kempeitai, the military police of the Imperial Army, arrived at the Changi Prison in Singapore and read out a list of civilian names. These men were taken away for interrogation, torture and in several cases, death. Over the course of the next six months around 50 Europeans and Australians suffered a brutal inquisition. They were beaten with knotted ropes, given electric shocks, had nails driven into their feet, cigarettes burned into

Toasting the success of *Jaywick* back in Australia are (left to right): Wally Falls, Donald Davidson, Andrew Huston, Ivan Lyon, Arthur Jones and Bob Page. (AWM 134349)

their genitals and water forced down their throats. In total, 16 died as a result of their treatment. Yet nothing that passed between the broken teeth and split lips shed any light on the attack.

The Malays and Chinese suffered far worse. After their torture and fruitless interrogation, they were executed and their severed heads displayed on posts around Singapore.

After six months of torture and murder, the Kempeitai tentatively filed a report speculating that the raid had been carried out by 'two Chinese and one Malay'. They didn't really believe it, and nor did their superiors.

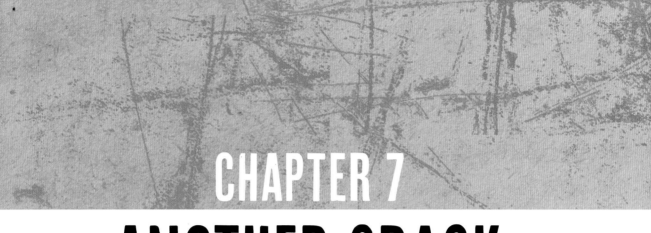

CHAPTER 7
ANOTHER CRACK

Harold Robert Ross, 'Bobby' as he preferred, had not enjoyed a spectacular war. On graduating from Cambridge University in June 1939 with a first-class honours degree in Anthropology, he passed his Colonial Service exam and in July 1940 sailed from England for the Far East. En route to Malaya he corresponded with his younger sister, Mary Rose, an actress whom he called 'Rosebud'. 'Never never go to bed with anybody unless you are in love with each other,' he advised in response to his sister's relationship problems. Ross told his sister she could always seek counsel from his girlfriend, Peggie, whom he hoped to marry upon his return.[88]

On landing at Singapore in the first week of September, Ross reported to the Malayan Establishment Office, and for the next year he was stationed in Kuala Pilah on the west coast of the country, enlisting in the Malay State Volunteers. When war came to the Far East, Ross was attached to the 88th Field Regiment, and the fall of Singapore left him 'sickened'. His battery had surrendered on the afternoon of 15 February, with only Ross and six others prepared to risk an escape attempt on the open sea. On 16 February they had rowed from Singapore to a small junk and for the next few days they 'picked up a good wind to the coast of Sumatra and made for the Indragiri River . . . where we left the junk and found an organization to deal with survivors.'

The 'organization' was the one run by Bill Reynolds at Rengat, and Ross may have briefly encountered Ivan Lyon and Taffy Morris at this time, as they made their way up the Indragiri River from their staging post at Pulau Durian.

Ross was taken overland by bus to Padang and from there he sailed by cruiser to Colombo and from there to Bombay.

Given a choice of returning to England to a commission in the British Army, or joining the Indian Army, Ross chose the latter, but to his chagrin found himself posted as a District Officer to a colonial backwater – Eket in the south-east corner of Nigeria. For more than a year Ross languished, his only pleasure exploring the region's rivers and estuaries. 'I am getting pretty dried up both in mind and body, and seem, morally speaking, to have lost a lot and gained absolutely nothing except a certain indifference to people and things,' he wrote to his sister in November 1943. 'Good heavens, this is frightful. It must be the gin. I will go to bed and see if I can't write more cheerfully in the morning.'

A few weeks later Ross returned to England on leave, and after visiting his parents at their home in Sussex, he travelled to London in search of a posting that offered more excitement. 'I seem to have seen a lot of useless people and can get little information at least of an encouraging kind,' he told his parents in a letter dated 1 March 1944. 'I gather that I am free to resign now, but I'm not likely to get in on the European war. On the other hand I shall certainly be wanted for something in the Far East.'

He went up to Cambridge to visit some old haunts, dined with one of his former professors, and returned to London to find a summons to an interview at room 238 in the Victoria Hotel on Northumberland Avenue on 31 March. Ross was greeted by Major Grey Egerton Mott of SOE and another officer, Flight-Lieutenant Mailer. No doubt Ross described his escape from Singapore, the courage and initiative he had displayed in making his way to Sumatra, and he also surely expanded on his wretched time in Nigeria, including his adventures exploring the coastline in a canoe.

He was given a questionnaire to complete, in which he outlined his technical knowledge of anthropology, elementary engineering and map-making. Asked if he was interested in office or administrative work, he replied in the negative. He sought outdoor work abroad. Ross listed the many countries he had visited and he explained that he knew no country as well as Malaya where, during his 18 months, he had done a lot of independent travelling, learning the language and the customs of the local people.

On 17 May Ross wrote to his sister to tell her: 'Everything seems to be moving in the right direction as far as I am concerned ... I am to go off tomorrow on some kind of training course. I have to be at a certain place at 10.30, and will then be told where and when to go on.' Ross then informed his sister that he had been briefed

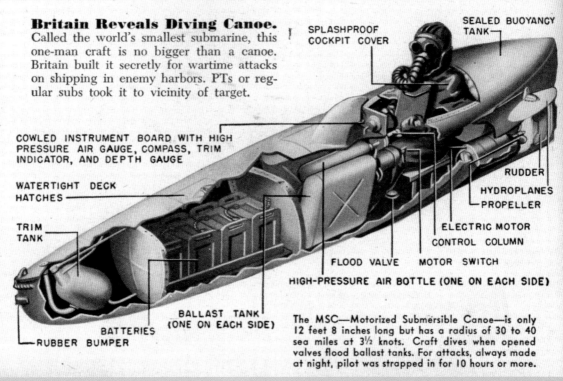

Britain Reveals Diving Canoe.

Called the world's smallest submarine, this one-man craft is no bigger than a canoe. Britain built it secretly for wartime attacks on shipping in enemy harbors. PTs or regular subs took it to vicinity of target.

SPLASHPROOF COCKPIT COVER

SEALED BUOYANCY TANK

COWLED INSTRUMENT BOARD WITH HIGH PRESSURE AIR GAUGE, COMPASS, TRIM INDICATOR, AND DEPTH GAUGE

WATERTIGHT DECK HATCHES

TRIM TANK

RUBBER BUMPER

BATTERIES

BALLAST TANK (ONE ON EACH SIDE)

FLOOD VALVE

HIGH-PRESSURE AIR BOTTLE (ONE ON EACH SIDE)

MOTOR SWITCH

ELECTRIC MOTOR

CONTROL COLUMN

RUDDER

HYDROPLANES

PROPELLER

The MSC—Motorized Submersible Canoe—is only 12 feet 8 inches long but has a radius of 30 to 40 sea miles at 3½ knots. Craft dives when opened valves flood ballast tanks. For attacks, always made at night, pilot was strapped in for 10 hours or more.

BELOW Bobby Ross's last telegram to his parents in Sussex: 'Can't return home. Letter follows. Loving Goodbye.' (Author's Collection - Courtesy of the Ross Family)

ABOVE Dubbed the 'Sleeping Beauty', the submersible canoe was a top-secret innovation that the British had high hopes for in 1944. (Author's Collection)

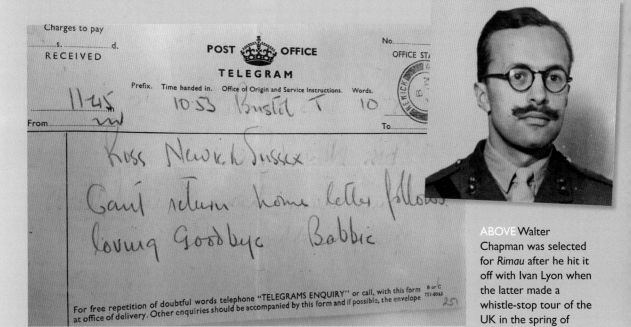

ABOVE Walter Chapman was selected for *Rimau* after he hit it off with Ivan Lyon when the latter made a whistle-stop tour of the UK in the spring of 1944. (Author's Collection - Courtesy of Jeremy Chapman)

on what he was training for, and he had 'accepted it'. It was classified information, of course, so he could not elaborate, but in his usual self-deprecating manner, Ross cast doubt on whether he would make the grade: 'I gather that one has to be pretty efficient ever to be employed in the real thing, and many fall by the way. However, it is definitely what I want and I am prepared to go all out for it.'

Eight days before Ross's interview at the Victoria Hotel, Ivan Lyon had arrived in London from Australia. Operation *Jaywick* was still unknown to all but a small cabal within the British military, but those who knew the details were eager to meet the mastermind. They weren't disappointed. On 6 April the Admiralty cabled Lieutenant-Colonel John Chapman-Walker in Melbourne, stating: 'Lyon has been great success with everybody. He had most satisfactory interview with First Sea Lord [Andrew Cunningham] who now takes personal interest in *Hornbill* and is determined the project should take place if humanly possible.'

Hornbill was the successor to *Jaywick*, a plan that had been germinating for several weeks in Australia with the encouragement of Admiral Lord Louis Mountbatten, Supreme Allied Commander South-East Asia. Britain and Australia lacked the resources of America to be able to make a similar contribution materially to the war in the Far East, but they could to a degree compensate for this deficiency with their flair for unorthodox warfare. Earlier in 1943 Orde Wingate's Chindits had penetrated deep behind Japanese lines in Burma and waged a guerrilla war for two months. In terms of material damage inflicted on the Japanese, the Chindits' success was modest, but after 18 months of defeat and humiliation at the hands of an enemy some Allied soldiers believed 'invincible', what Wingate's men accomplished was a psychological victory. 'One of the greatest guerrilla operations ever undertaken,' declared the Reuters correspondent. Winston Churchill was so tickled with the eccentric Wingate that he brought him to the Quebec Conference in August 1943. Wingate so impressed President Roosevelt and his staff with his vision of a 'conquest of Burma north of the 23rd Parallel' that FDR ordered the formation of an American special air unit★ to support the Chindits and a new command structure was agreed,

---

★ 5307th Composite Unit (Provisional), better known as Merrill's Marauders, after their CO, General Frank Merrill.

the Allied Operational South-East Asia Command with Admiral Lord Louis Mountbatten as its supreme commander.

Jaywick was another feather in the cap for the British in the Far East, one which had even impressed the peppery General MacArthur, and Mountbatten desired a second operation that would showcase the bold innovation of the British fighting man.

The result was *Hornbill*, outlined as three operations within one, namely:

a) Establishment of a base on the Natuna Islands, an Indonesian archipelago on the west side of the South China Sea.
b) A strike at enemy shipping in Singapore Harbour.
c) Intelligence and sabotage launched from the Natuna base.

Operation *Hornbill* would comprise three phases, starting in March 1944 and culminating in December 1944. The object, stated the memo, was 'to establish and maintain secret bases in the South China Sea from which surface craft can operate. The unit shall be mobile and change its base as the situation may dictate. Operations will be planned and executed under the direction of Major Lyon acting under the direction of S.O.A.'[89]

The initial plan was ambitious in the extreme: a base would be established on one of the islands from which raiding parties would attack enemy targets. Additionally, a coast-watching network would gather intelligence and agents would set up an escape route for POWs and train and supply arms to local guerrilla units. Submarines would transport the personnel to the region, but Lyon and his men would carry out their work in 'country craft' vessels, fishing trawlers converted to resemble native fishing boats.

In fact the construction of the 'country craft' boats was delayed by several months, explained Rear Admiral Taylor of the Naval Intelligence Division in a memo, owing to problems in obtaining suitable engines and industrial action by dockworkers in Australia. There was also a recognition that the initial plan was too grandiose and required paring down. The result was that *Hornbill* was cleaved in two becoming Operation *Kookaburra*, which was the reconnaissance of the Natuna Islands, and Operation *Rimau*, an attack on enemy shipping in Singapore. In his memo Rear Admiral Taylor wrote that the only alterations to the *Rimau* plan in light of the cancellation of *Hornbill* were:

a) an advanced temporary base was to be established on Merapas Island in the Rhio Archipelago.

b) a junk was to be captured and used for the transport of the men and stores from the point where they left the submarine to a point near Singapore.

The submarine allocated to the mission by Lord Mountbatten was the Porpoise and the man chosen to lead the attack was Ivan Lyon. The *Rimau* codename was Lyon's idea; it was the Malayan word for 'tiger', the beast he had tattooed across his chest.

When Lyon arrived in Britain on 22 March 1944 it was the first time he had been home for seven years. London must have looked unrecognizable to Lyon as he scuttled between the Admiralty and SOE Headquarters, past buildings that had been flattened in the Blitz.

There was much for Lyon to do in the short time he had allotted himself in England. He must pay a visit to his family in Surrey, but his first priority was the organization for *Rimau*. He wished to inspect Porpoise, recruit one or two officers to the mission and, above all, he wanted to pick the brains of SOE about the latest in kit and equipment.

At the Baker Street HQ, Lyon was introduced to Major Walter Chapman, a Londoner who had just celebrated his 29th birthday. An architect before the war, and a territorial major in the Royal Engineers, Chapman had served with that regiment in the Middle East in 1941 before being posted to northern India, where he was struck down by a wasting disease. After a lengthy spell in hospital in South Africa, Chapman returned to the UK in 1942 and was soon recruited by SOE in January 1943 for his technical expertise. He was sent to work at the organization's research station at Aston House in Knebworth as a technical staff officer. In his SOE file Chapman was described as 'very conscientious and reliable . . . he has a quiet but pleasant personality and would make a good regimental officer as well as a Technical Staff Officer'.[90]

Chapman looked what he was: a 'boffin', a gentle and sensitive man, who wore spectacles and sported a handlebar moustache. He had been sent on a parachute course in 1943, as all SOE personnel were, regardless of whether they were staff officers or operatives, but had broken a leg.

Chapman was not a combat officer; his strengths lay in other areas, but when Ivan Lyon walked into his office there was an immediate affinity. They were thinkers and innovators, their minds attuned to the technical side of war, and both had a streak of eccentricity.

Lyon told Chapman about *Jaywick* and about *Rimau*, emphasizing that his intention was to cause greater damage to Japanese shipping this time around,

Sub-Lieutenant Grigor Riggs, Lieutenant Richard Cox and Lieutenant Bobby Ross at Sinaloa, a Mexican restaurant in San Francisco, 15 July 1944, en route to Australia. (Author's Collection)

but more sophisticated equipment was required to achieve that ambition. On *Jaywick* their potency had been limited by weight and space. According to Chapman the ensuing conversation began when he suggested using 'Sleeping Beauties':

'What on earth are they?' replied Lyon.
Submersible metal canoes, explained Chapman, designed by Major Quentin Reeves. He continued:
'We have only two or three test models at the moment but they are just what you need. Battery-driven with a range of 20–30 miles. The operator has a skin-diving suit, breathes from air bottles and can flood the thing so that his head is just out of the water or can take it down to twenty or thirty feet in an emergency.'[91]

Chapman boasted that he had seen a test model in action, and it was a sight to behold. It could bank like a Spitfire and one of the pilots had even done a loop the loop. But best of all, stressed Chapman, 'you could carry your limpet mines on the foredeck and stick them against your targets underwater'.

The man who had looped the loop was Sub-Lieutenant Grigor Riggs★ during a series of trials the previous autumn at Staines Reservoir. SOE had

---

★ Some histories spell it 'Gregor', but on completing his SOE form Riggs spelt it 'Grigor'.

been most impressed, and the Commanding Officer of their Station IX weapons factory at Welwyn, Colonel John Dolphin, had sent Riggs a memo in order to 'congratulate you on the very fine performance you put up on the recent trials …at great discomfort to yourself you have proved the admirable seaworthiness of the craft and its endurance in rough weather'.

In another Admiralty memo, this one not for the attention of Riggs, the 20-year-old sub-lieutenant was described as 'a first class Naval man with any amount of courage, ability and confidence in carrying out his orders on all trials …he is quick to appreciate a situation and in taking appropriate action without instructions'.

Born in Inverness in June 1923, Riggs's parents farmed on the Black Isle, and he had gone straight from Inverness Royal Academy to university before joining the Navy in January 1942. On the surface he didn't have much to recommend him for special operations. He didn't run, box, ski or even sail a boat; nor did he have any knowledge of map reading or wireless communications. At 5 feet 9 inches and 10½ stone he was not an impressive physical specimen, but Riggs had something about him that perhaps but for the war would have lain dormant. He had the temperament for high-pressure situations; where other men panicked he stayed calm, able to think clearly and swiftly in dangerous situations.

On 18 March 1943 Riggs was attached to SOE (and awarded 'special Danger Pay' of nine shillings per day gross) and by June that year he was embarked on the 'Welman Course', learning to pilot the SOE's one-man midget submarine that carried a 425-pound warhead.

After completing the obligatory parachute course in September, Riggs started to trial the Sleeping Beauty. He also found time to fall in love with a local girl, Didi Brown, and the pair were engaged to be married.

Grigor Riggs was a test pilot for the 'Sleeping Beauty', and owed his inclusion in *Rimau* to his skill at the controls. (Author's Collection)

With his experience, Riggs was well placed to school Ivan Lyon in the Sleeping Beauty (SB) when he arrived at Staines Reservoir. First, he explained the machine's capabilities: its three speeds – cruising speed ahead, full speed ahead and full speed astern; its range, 40 sea miles at 3 knots cruising on the surface and 27 sea miles at 2 knots cruising submerged; its maximum depth of 50 feet; its maximum load of 12 2½-pound magnetic or other type charges as well as a small storage locker behind the pilot's head for small quantities of rations and personal kit. As for its dimensions, the SB was

12 feet 8 inches in length with a beam of 27 inches and it weighed 625 pounds with batteries and was powered by a .5 HP electric motor.

There was one other feature, which Lyon discovered on Staines Reservoir; namely that the SB, which was constructed from steel and aluminium, could also be used as a conventional boat on the surface with a paddle or a sail.

Impressed with the initial demonstration, Lyon asked to see how they fared in less benign water. Riggs had already tested an SB off the Sussex coast the previous October, spending ten hours in the Channel in a wind that reached force 5 at one point. The SB had handled well in what Riggs described as a 'rather rough' sea. He and Lyon put an SB through its paces in Portsmouth Harbour; Lyon was thrilled with the result and emerged from the water convinced this was the means of inflicting serious sabotage on the Japanese.

There was one obstacle, other than persuading SOE to give him a dozen or more SBs, and that was how to transport them to within range of Singapore? It was far too dangerous for the Porpoise to carry them inside, as the submarine would have to surface deep inside enemy territory for a considerable time in order to launch the SBs. After Lyon and Walter Chapman visited the 1,800-ton Porpoise on the Clyde they agreed the most practical method would be to store the SBs in mine-laying casing that ran the length of the Porpoise's hull, an innovation that had first been used by submarines to re-supply Malta.

Back in London Lyon used his strong character to great effect in opening Admiralty doors. It helped that he had the confidence that came with his background: an illustrious military fame and an education at one of Britain's most prestigious schools. He didn't care how many, or whose, feathers he ruffled in obtaining what he required for Operation *Rimau*. 'It was entirely due to Ivan's methods,' recalled Chapman. 'He would go around talking to people, raising the "ante" every time, saying "so-and-so has agreed to this", "someone else has agreed to that", and the thing gradually became an ascending spiral.'[92]

By now Lyon was required back in Australia to establish the training base. With time in England running out, he and Chapman contacted the Directorate of Naval Construction in Bath and, over the telephone, described the specifications for the containers. Lyon also enlisted the help of the Royal Marines, who were delighted to be asked to test out the full complement of SBs when they came off the production line later in the summer.

Next he turned his attention to securing the release of Grigor Riggs for the operation, in which he succeeded, and he also endorsed the selection of Bobby Ross on the recommendation of Major Mott, recognizing that a fluent Malay speaker and an experienced canoeist, not forgetting Ross's intimate knowledge of Singapore and the surrounding islands, could be invaluable.

Lyon also believed that Walter Chapman would be an asset on the operation, his technical expertise and his military connections relieving some of the workload that would otherwise fall on his shoulders. Chapman accepted the invitation once Lyon had found someone to fill his position at SOE.

Before Lyon left England on 2 May he visited his family at their home in Farnham, Surrey. He had last seen his father and mother seven years ago, and there was much to catch up on, not least the fact that the Lyons now had a French daughter-in-law and a young grandson, Clive. Lyon's recently widowed sister, Ann, was present and she found that her brother had 'become more expansive and sociable, less buttoned-up'.[93] At some point in the day Lyon – probably out of earshot of his mother and sister – told his father a brief outline of what he had planned. He informed his father that 'he had been making a study of living alone in the jungle', perhaps a consequence of Operation *Jaywick* during which he realized his knowledge of jungle survival was inadequate. Lyon also told his father he was confident of success but 'that he did not intend under any circumstances to be taken prisoner by the Japanese'.[94]

Bobby Ross and Grigor Riggs followed Lyon to Australia two months later, flying from England to Newfoundland on the first leg of an arduous journey that included a train journey across the USA. On the eve of his departure, Ross wrote to his parents from the Grand Hotel in Bristol informing them that he and Riggs 'had the devil of a rush to get our papers complete yesterday but it was worth it to get here in comfort'. He concluded: 'Well, my darling parents, thank you for all you have done during the past five months. If all goes well on this trip I may be home earlier than the threatened five years'.

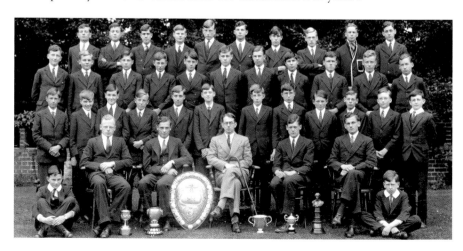

Wellington College, 1932: Bobby Ross stands on the far right of the second row in this photo of Lynedoch House. (Author's Collection - Courtesy of Wellington College Archive)

CHAPTER 8
SLEEPING BEAUTIES

The months after the exhilaration of *Jaywick* had been a bitter anti-climax for Arthur Jones. He had spent a month on leave and when he returned to Z Special Unit it was to a new commando school on Fraser Island, off the coast of Queensland. The school had opened in October 1943 under the command of Major Jock Campbell (he was succeeded by Donald Davidson in January 1944) and offered its students a variety of terrain ideal for guerrilla training. But Jones spent a lot of time running errands, going to the mainland to pick up supplies or collect the mail. He was bored. So, too, was Moss Berryman. Together they went to see Donald Davidson. 'Lyon by this time was over in England, we didn't know what he was doing,' recalled Jones. Davidson told the pair Lyon would be back shortly but he couldn't shed any light on future operations. 'I told him that we were going back to the navy,' said Jones. Davidson tried to persuade Jones and Berryman to be patient, but both were frustrated at the inertia on Fraser Island. Reluctantly, Davidson granted the pair's request and Jones was transferred to HMAS *Lonsdale* in Melbourne, the Royal Australian Navy's training base. 'I was doing guard duty and this was all I was doing,' said Jones. 'It was winter time and raining like hell and I thought "Oh no". So I rang Davidson up at the headquarters.'[95]

Jones begged to come back and Davidson, having first admonished him for his 'silly' mistake in leaving Fraser Island, promised to have a word with Lyon, not long returned from England. Davidson mentioned that 'there is another operation on' and told Jones to call back in a couple of days. He did, but it wasn't good news. Lyon had found someone to replace Jones.

He was welcome to return to Z Special Unit, but there was no place for him on the next operation. Jones declined the offer. If he couldn't be back with the *Jaywick* boys, he preferred to stay in Melbourne.

The loss of Jones and Berryman was a disappointment to Lyon, but when he arrived at Fraser Island he was greeted by several familiar faces; as well as Davidson, there was Bob Page (now a captain), Andrew Huston, Wally Falls and Fred Marsh.

Captain Page was now a married man, having wed Roma Prowse in Canberra on 1 November 1943. She was good friends with Davidson's wife, Nancy, who was an intelligence officer in Australia and had just begun to write an account of the *Jaywick* raid having been involved in the early stages of its planning. 'We were sharing a lovely old house in South Yarra [a suburb of Melbourne] with the Davidsons, which had been converted into self-contained flats,' recalled Roma Page. For several months the two women had enjoyed the company of their men, but the return of Ivan Lyon shattered the harmony. 'When Bob told me they were going out again I asked him if it was dangerous,' said Roma Page. 'But he said it was only to drop some supplies or something similar, and that it would not take long and there was no great risk.'[96]

Nancy Davidson knew all the details of the *Jaywick* raid; it has been a brilliant success, but they had been blessed with good fortune from the off. Surely lady luck wouldn't be such a loyal companion on a second audacious foray into enemy territory? 'Nancy Davidson had more knowledge than me and she was most unhappy about the second operation,' said Roma Page. 'She certainly was able to learn enough about the first operation to make her realise the dangers involved, and she did ask me to persuade Bob not to volunteer for the second mission.'

Neither man, however, wanted to let down Lyon.

By the time Lyon returned from the UK, training was well underway and Davidson had already culled several men from the 60 or so who had volunteered for Z Special Unit in January. 'There was pretty rigorous physical training, unarmed combat, a lot of lectures on tactics and things, outlining what we might be doing,'[97] recalled Ross Bradbury, who joined the Unit too late to be considered for *Rimau*. The men paddled across to the mainland, up the Mary River to the town of Maryborough, where there was a railway marshalling yard. Their challenge was to plant dummy limpet mines on an engine without being detected. There were also timed runs in full kit to Lake McKenzie and back, and swimming tests in the lake itself. Beached on the east side of the island was the wreck of the *Maheno*, a New Zealand liner, that ran aground in 1935, and this was used by the commandos to practise attaching limpet mines to the hull of a ship.

At the start of July the men vacated Fraser Island and travelled by train across Australia to a new training base at Careening Bay on Garden Island, approximately 12 miles south of Fremantle.

Many of the volunteers selected by Davidson were Australian soldiers who had distinguished themselves as commandos in fighting in the Solomons and New Guinea. Among their number was Private Doug Warne, a muscular former station hand from New South Wales with a pencil moustache, who had caught Davidson's eye while teaching unarmed combat in a jungle camp in Queensland. Another volunteer with an imposing physique was Warrant Officer Jeffrey Willersdorf of Victoria, while Corporal Pat Campbell was a tough, sinewy ex-jackaroo who had been wounded fighting at El Alamein in 1942. He was impressed with Ivan Lyon, whom he called 'the most wonderful man I have ever met'.[98]

Corporal Roland Fletcher had been born in Dublin and raised in Liverpool by an English father and an Irish mother. His parents were both theatrical, not always in regular employment, and with seven children they struggled to feed and clothe them. Consequently, in 1929 the 13-year-old Roland and two of his brothers emigrated to Western Australia as part of the Child Emigration Scheme. On leaving school, Fletcher worked for three years on a farm, then as a storekeeper, while studying commercial art in a correspondence school. In 1937 he changed direction again, joining the merchant marine, where he remained for four years, until he enlisted in the Australian infantry.

Another volunteer who had a touch of the unconventional about him was 30-year-old Lieutenant Walter Carey. Raised as one of six children by a single mum, Walter had joined her in the family corner store upon leaving school. He had the Irish gift of the gab, a handsome charmer with a ready smile, and he became involved with one of the customers, a music teacher called Winifred. A child was born from their union, but Walter denied it was his. Winifred took him to court, and won, but when Walter refused to accept the judgment he was jailed. His mother – who accepted Jean Anne as her granddaughter – bailed out her son.

That furore, and the bankruptcy of the family business in the Great Depression, prompted Walter to start afresh in Papua New Guinea. He ran a

TOP One of the submersible canoes, dubbed 'Sleeping Beauties', is unloaded at Careening Bay camp, Garden Island. Note the folboat in the background. (NAA 8295525)

ABOVE An unidentified member of Z Special Unit dives a 'Sleeping Beauty' as part of their training on Garden Island. (NAA 8295524)

RIGHT Walter Carey, a 30-year-old lieutenant, boasted a colourful and intrepid background and was to prove an invaluable member of the *Rimau* party. (AWM P05790.002) trade store on the far north-west coast and fathered a second daughter, Anne, with a local woman. Walter recognized this child but the war broke the familial bond and he enlisted in the Australian Imperial Force (AIF) in 1940, volunteering for special service in China with Mission 204. Walter's brother, Sam, was also a member of Z Special Unit and in 1943 he and a small team (including Bob Page) had infiltrated Townsville Harbour in canoes and embarrassed the Australian Navy by festooning several of their ships with dummy limpet mines.

A latecomer to the party was Major Reggie Ingleton, whose background could not have been more different to Carey's and Fletcher's. Born in West Ham, London, the 17-stone Ingleton was large in every sense, remembered as a 'a very big athletic young man with an extrovert personality'.[99] Educated privately in Gloucestershire, where he excelled at sport and amateur dramatics, Ingleton became an articled pupil in his grandfather's firm of architects in 1936, and on the outbreak of war he joined the Royal Marines where he was posted to the Corps' Armoured Support Group. Initially his howitzer battery was tasked with defending the Dover coastline from invasion, but when that threat receded he remained in England with the 32nd Howitzer Battery at Wimborne Minster. For much of 1942 and 1943 Ingleton, along with two other Marine officers, Peskett and Mabbott, invented an accurate fire-control system for the battery's 95mm-gun howitzers that were mounted on Centaur tanks, a system known as the 'PIM Board' after the initials of its three innovators.[*] Ingleton was conflicted when 1944 dawned. He was married and the proud father of a baby daughter, but professionally he felt unfulfilled; after nearly five years of service he still hadn't fired a shot in anger at the enemy. Then in the spring he met Ivan Lyon and Grigor Riggs when they came to Portsmouth Harbour to test the SBs and Lyon was impressed by Ingleton's 'technical expertise'. Not long after, the Royal Marine volunteered for 'hazardous duties' and was posted to Ceylon as part of an amphibious Special Operations Group codenamed Detachment 385. Shortly after Ingleton arrived in Ceylon to begin a training programme under Colonel Herbert 'Blondie' Hasler, one of the 'Cockleshell Heroes', his presence was requested in Australia by Ivan Lyon. The Royal Marines agreed to his release because they were keen to use the SBs in future operations, and Ingleton's presence on *Rimau* would be a fact-finding mission for them.

Lyon and his men began training with the five SBs they had at that stage in mid-July. By the 21st of that month eight men had been RTU'd: a couple had

---

[*] The Royal Marines' Armoured Support Group subsequently was in the first wave to land on Gold and Sword beaches on D-Day.

Some of Z Special Unit undergoing training in Careening Bay on Garden Island, 12 miles south of Fremantle, Western Australia. (Author's Collection)

a history of tuberculosis in their family, one had poor night sight and another was rejected because his false teeth made it impossible to grip the breathing apparatus when the SB submerged. A Private Mckee, 'requested to leave in sympathy with others'.

Ross Bradbury trained on an SB later in the year at Garden Island with Z Special Unit and recalled the experience: 'The operator sits in it and then he floods the tanks – tank aft – and it slowly submerges and when the SB sinks you open the valve till the nose dips down and then you turn the battery power on and away you go . . . you have your oxygen and mask on, and you put to dive and you go down – you don't go terribly deep – and when you want to come up you put the hydrofoil to rise and your head comes up and you look around, and then put to dive. So you go like a porpoise.'

Once the men had familiarized themselves with the basics they went out into the harbour at night to practise laying dummy mines on anchored vessels. 'These SBs had a mind of their own at times,' said Bradbury. 'For some reason I went into a bit of a dive and the next thing I am under the ship . . . I look up and it is a flat bottom and my head hit the bottom of a ship. I thought "this is not too good." Being night I could see lights on either side, and fortunately I was able to get into another dive and I got out on the other side.'[100]

Donald Davidson had been keeping a journal since the unit's arrival in Garden Island, and on 25 July he described the day's training, conducted in two groups, and jotted down some observations:

Ingleton successful but very big

Willersdorf now very good

Davidson had a peculiar 'turn' when static diving. Came to the surface weak & faint; tried again but had to come out and rest. Promoted Lt-Cd [Lieutenant Commander].[101]

The promotion had been championed by Rear Admiral Hugh Taylor, Assistant Director (Navy) with SOE, who in a memorandum on 10 July had written of Davidson: '*Jaywick* was about as thorough a test of this officer's qualities as a man, a seaman and a leader as anyone could want.'

Davidson's funny turn was a cause for concern; Lyon leaned on his second-in-command both logistically and emotionally and were he to be forced off the operation it would be a heavy blow. On 26 July Davidson went down again, and wrote later in his journal: 'Perfectly all right today. Very peculiar.'

The next day Walter Chapman arrived at Garden Island and Davidson remarked that training was 'proceeding very satisfactorily'. On 1 August Lyon gave an 'explanatory talk' after dinner to the officers and men about the purpose of their training, which included an 'outline of the plans'. Three days later Lyon and Davidson had selected their list of 'probables', the 15 men who would pilot the SBs into Singapore Harbour. One surprise omission was Andrew 'Happy' Huston, who had been Lyon's paddle partner during *Jaywick*; he had found submersible canoes harder to master. Also missing from the list was Reggie Ingleton, whose considerable bulk was not conducive to this type of warfare. Instead Ingleton – who had been nicknamed 'Otto' by the Australians – was appointed leader of the five-strong Maintenance Party, whose prime job was to hijack a junk in the South China Sea and sail them to within range of Singapore.

On 5 August Davidson led four men on a night exercise in their SBs. It was a disaster. All but Davidson were forced to abort the mission because of problems with their machines, and even he did not have enough power left to dive. Lessons learnt, he wrote in his journal:

1. Test bilge pumps (this is usually overlooked since the SBs start dry inside).
2. A head sea and wind of about force 3 to 4 slows down SBs to no more than 1 knot of cruising speed and is too rough for full speed.[102]

It was fortuitous that two days later Grigor Riggs and Bobby Ross arrived from the USA, along with Lieutenant Richard Cox, a skilled navigator who had been among the crew of the *Sederhana Djohanes* when she crossed from Sumatra to Ceylon in March 1942. No one knew SBs better than Riggs and on 8 August he took his first demonstration. 'Riggs did some very expert diving,' wrote Davidson in his journal. 'Pretty to watch.'[103]

By now it had been decided what colour to paint the SBs. Lyon, with the assistance of a professor of natural history at the University of Perth, had spent a couple days experimenting with various hues until both agreed that neutral dark green was the hardest to detect in the water. The SBs were already this colour when they arrived so their conclusion saved a lot of brushwork. On 10 August the Porpoise arrived under the command of Lieutenant-Commander Hubert Marsham, but of the containers for the SBs there was no sight. Or rather there was, at Fremantle on the deck of a merchant ship that had docked from Colombo. Unfortunately for Lyon the ship's captain was an insufferable pedant, and he refused to disembark the containers – even when Lyon pleaded with him – because on his manifest their final destination was listed as Melbourne. So the containers sailed on to Melbourne. They finally arrived on 30 August, a day that should have been a cause for celebration for Lyon, but his mood darkened when he saw the state of the containers. The axles and the wheels on which the containers were fitted had rusted and in general they were of a poor design. Marsham came to their rescue: why not load the SBs into the torpedo reload compartment of Porpoise? His mission was to deliver the *Rimau* men to their drop-off point, not attack enemy shipping, so there was space in these compartments. Furthermore, an Australian engineer called Alf Warren suggested welding the now redundant containers onto the mine casing as extra storage space. Among the 14½ tons of stores loaded onto Porpoise were: four radio transmitter/receivers, six hand-held radio transceivers, known as 'walkie-talkies', two PIAT anti-tank weapons, 124 blankets, six silent Sten sub-machine guns, 12 water conversion shakers, two folboats, 350 pounds of rations, 108 sets of three limpet mines, 80 single limpet mines, 22 rubber water bags and 11 two-man 'boat units', which each contained among other items: a two-man folboat, single paddles (x2) jungle hammock (x2), prismatic compass (x2), 10 cent piece (x250), condoms (x12), a Douglas Protractor, a Medical Pack B, skin dye, a sharpening stone and a commando cooker. The men were also issued with their personnel kit, such as cutlery, field dressings and sweat towels, and their uniform was green shirt and trousers, jungle boots of green leather and a black beret.

Lyon and Davidson had attended a final planning conference with SOA and the Royal Australian Navy in Perth on 6 July at which they submitted their final operational plan for *Rimau*. It was a comprehensive scheme. They had calculated that at a speed of 110 miles per day Porpoise would reach the forward area in 16 days. One day was allocated for a reconnaissance of the base, the island of Merapas, the most easterly island in the Riau Archipelago, 'a small, thickly wooded island about 1 mile in length, half a mile across, some 70 miles from Singapore . . . probably uninhabited.'[104]

Assuming Merapas was deemed satisfactory for their base, the *Rimau* party would cache sufficient stores to sustain 30 men for two months, along with a wireless receiver and a sum of money.

That was Phase 1 of the plan. Phase 2 would entail seizing a junk in the area of Pedjantan, a mountainous island carpeted in jungle. Lyon estimated it would take 36 hours to transfer the stores from the Porpoise to the junk. The submarine would then return to Australia while the junk would sail the 250 miles to the target area via the Temiang Strait at an average speed of 1.8 knots, a voyage Lyon reckoned would take six days.

As for the attack, the intention 'is to damage as many ships as possible by use of single limpets. 15 SBs each carrying 6 limpets, will be used.' In all 15 minutes would be allowed for attacking each target in the case of dispersed anchorages, and ten minutes when the vessels were alongside wharves. Lyon had worked out a timetable: at 1900 hours the SBs would commence unloading from the junk, and at 2130 the unloading would be complete. The first SBs would reach the objective at 2300 and the last at 2345. The first SB would reach the rendezvous at 0245 and the last at 0415. At 0500 the explosions would commence. Lyon had scheduled two weeks for the raiders to reach Merapas. Splitting into five parties, they would paddle on average 5 miles each night, and the route would be decided by the leader of each party.

Among the people consulted by Lyon was Captain H. J Ahgers of the Netherlands Naval HQ, who had spent 30 years in the South China Sea. His advice had been sought on native junks – where they might hijack one and how to sail one – and wind conditions in the South China Sea.

Also discussed at the conference was the attack itself, and 'in particular the pros and cons of doing a small amount of damage to a large number of ships, as against doing considerably more damage to, and perhaps sinking, a smaller amount'. The navy suggested that the charges would be most effective if placed against the propeller shafting, but Davidson pointed out this 'was not feasible owing to the thickness of the metal involved'.[105]

Eventually, it was decided that the raiders should follow the same modus operandi as on *Jaywick*, each SB operative using two clusters of three limpets to target heavily laden merchant ships.

Item No. 5 on the agenda was 'cover story', described in the conference minutes as a 'complicated' subject. Commander Rupert Long, the Director of Naval Intelligence, spoke frankly and 'took the view that, if captured, men were in any case liable to divulge all that they knew, consequently the only true form of security was to make absolutely certain that no one knew more than necessary'.

The last item of the conference was 'signals for pick up operation', which would be arranged before the departure of the party. Lyon rejected the idea of using the standard cipher keys and tables as a means of communication and instead arranged what he considered a more secure method with SOA's cipher clerk, Staff-Sergeant Mary Ellis. Each with a copy of the same book, they formulated a one-off code from a particular page by eliminating every third word and numbering the letters that remained. If Lyon sent a message using this code the numbers could be deciphered by Ellis by referring to her copy of the book.

Call signs were arranged for *Rimau* and for the base station in Darwin, and in a memo dated 12 August the radio frequencies were outlined along with the procedure for sending and receiving messages. In the event of an emergency a message sent by *Rimau* to Darwin could be forwarded to the RAAF, who in conjunction with the Netherlands Forces Intelligence Service had set up a network of collection points in the former Dutch East Indies to which flying boats could land to pick up air crew who had baled out during missions.

The plan was forwarded to SOA HQ in Melbourne and on 21 August Lyon received word that *Rimau* had been approved.

On 3 September Davidson listed the 15 SB operators in his journal, along with the names of their Sleeping Beauty. His was called *Sea Eagle* and Lyon's *Sea Nymph*; Bob Page's was *Sea Goddess* and Bobby Ross's was *Sea Horse*; Riggs had *Sea Urchin*, Jeffrey Willersdorf *Sea Leopard*, Wally Falls the *Sea Hawk* and Ron Fletcher's machine was christened *Sea Snake*. The rest of the machines were named using a similar theme.

Both Andrew Huston and Fred Marsh had missed out on selection, but Lyon, recognizing their worth, included them in a group of five under the command of Major Ingleton; their job was to board the junk in the event of 'resistance'.

On the same day he learned he was one of the 15 SB operators, Bobby Ross wrote home to his parents. He started off by describing Garden Island's spring flowers, particularly the freesias, and then he mentioned some of their training in the vaguest terms. 'Both the officers and men that I am with are a first-class lot,' he continued. 'All individualists in their way, and we don't suffer from too much heavy-handed regimentation . . . the work has been going well and whatever happens, I have no regrets.'

The last few days on Garden Island dragged. The men trained some more on the SBs and rehearsed the procedure for unloading the stores from the submarine and from a vessel that deputized for the junk they intended to seize.

The busier the men were, the less time they had to think. Unlike with *Jaywick*, when Lyon didn't reveal the exact nature of the operation until the

Krait had left Exmouth Gulf, this time he had fully briefed them, even constructing a sand and cement model of Singapore Harbour. It was another bold operation of Lyon's and he had been thorough in his planning. The men trusted him to be as meticulous in its execution, but if *Rimau* was to succeed it would require the same luck as *Jaywick* had enjoyed.

On 9 September the 23 men finished loading the SBs onto Porpoise, and the submarine sailed for Fremantle to 'top up, store and victual'. There was little to do therefore on 10 September, the eve of their departure. Ivan Lyon went to Fremantle for a final consultation with Lieutenant-Colonel John Chapman-Walker, but he was back by the early evening. '*Rimau* operators on a pre-embarkation spree,' wrote Davidson in his journal. 'Breaking training to the tune of much beer and spirits in all the messes.'[106]

It was quite a party. Personnel from Garden Island naval base helped the men drink their booze, as did the girls from a nearby searchlight battery. Everyone was in high spirits. The *Rimau* party particularly. The alcohol blunted the edge of their apprehension and strengthened the bonds that bound them together. Whatever the future held, they would meet it together.

The entry on 11 September was brief: '1100. Porpoise returned from Fremantle. *Rimau* personnel embarked and sailed at 1220.'

Sam Carey, brother of Walter, was also a member of Z Special Unit and in 1943 embarrassed the Australian Navy by infiltrating Townsville Harbour in a canoe in a mock attack. (Author's Collection - Courtesy of Harley Carey)

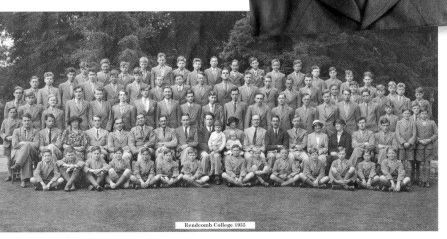

Rendcomb College 1935

Royal Marine officer Reggie Ingleton was a big man, as seen here from his school photo of 1935. Ingleton sits on the far left of the second row. (Author's Collection - Courtesy of Rendcomb College)

CHAPTER 9
PIRATES AND PORPOISE

'The whole business,' wrote Lieutenant-Commander Hubert Marsham, 'smacks of the days of Drake and Hawkins, an ambitious daredevil scheme proposed by a band of very gallant gentlemen; support and backing from high places and senior officers afloat but hopelessly marred by muddle and inefficiency, self-seeking and obstruction from those locally for the supply and transport of stores and equipment.'

It was hardly an effusive endorsement of Operation *Rimau*, but morale inside the Porpoise was high as she sailed north. It was cramped because of the extra personnel so to ease the overcrowding Marsham had the soldiers double up on watch with the submarine's crew. Other than that duty, Lyon and his men had little to do but sleep, read and play cards.

For Marsham the patrol was more than just a drop-off job. The Porpoise would be the first submarine of the Eighth Flotilla to penetrate inside the Malay Barrier 'and her experience of passing through Lombok Strait was therefore awaited with considerable interest'. At its narrowest the Strait has a permanent south-flowing current of about 6 knots so Marsham entered at night on the surface at a speed of 7 knots. He, Lyon and Davidson were on the bridge, getting a thorough drenching from the cross waves, while down below the sailors celebrated becoming the first British submarine to enter Japanese-controlled waters.

'On 19th September off Solembo Island [he meant Salembau Island, now known as Masalembu] dived three times for aircraft,' wrote Marsham. 'Otherwise the passage across the Java Sea was uneventful.' The next day three enemy merchant ships were sighted, a tempting target, but one Marsham resisted in order 'not to disclose his presence in the Karimata Strait'.[107]

There were 'anxious days' on 22 and 23 September for Porpoise because a surface trail was observed. Upon investigation it was traced to a leak in No. 2 starboard oil fuel group. Marsham had the fuel transferred to another group, but leaks in two more tanks caused further concern. 'Cured,' he wrote, 'by shutting the HP Tankside blow.'

The Porpoise reached Merapas Island on the same day that Marsham cured his leakage, 23 September, and circled the island at periscope depth at a distance of 1 mile. In shape it resembled a boot with a coconut plantation on the south side and the more rugged northern coast was covered with ficus and cactus palms. The only habitation that Lyon could see as he peered through the periscope were two huts on the western side and a couple of koleks on the beach.

It was decided that Davidson and Corporal Clair Stewart would go ashore at nightfall to conduct a thorough reconnaissance of Merapas. Stewart was unusual among the Australian soldiers in that he was married and, at 35, considerably older than his mates. A railwayman before the war, Stewart could have avoided enlistment as his was a reserved occupation, but he was determined to serve his country and, after being rejected by the air force, he joined the Australian Army, becoming a skilled signaller.

As the Porpoise loitered under the surface waiting for the daylight to draw to a close, Marsham spotted an 8,000-ton tanker steering south-east. It was unescorted and asking to be sunk, but Marsham let it pass 'in order not to compromise the special missions which it can only be hoped will justify such wasted opportunities'.

At dark Davidson and Stewart paddled ashore from the Porpoise. It took them 1½ hours to cover the 1½ miles. 'Made a difficult landing halfway down Northern shore,' wrote Davidson in his journal. 'Coast here very steep to and rocky to about 100 feet up. Good close cover. Slung hammocks between two fallen trees.'

He named the spot 'Hammock Tree' and he and Stewart settled into their new abode. Neither slept well. 'The change from close quarters in Porpoise to the scented peace of this island was too abrupt for sleep,' wrote Davidson. 'The scents of the flowering trees and lily palms was more delicate than any that ever came out of Paris. The sigh of welcome.'[108]

RIGHT Hubert Marsham, commander of the Porpoise, hoists the Japanese flag on his submarine, as they enter Japanese waters en route to Merapas. (Author's Collection - Courtesy of Jeremy Chapman)

FAR RIGHT Walter Chapman took this photograph of an unidentified vessel from the deck of the *Tantalus* in November 1944. (Author's Collection - Courtesy of Jeremy Chapman)

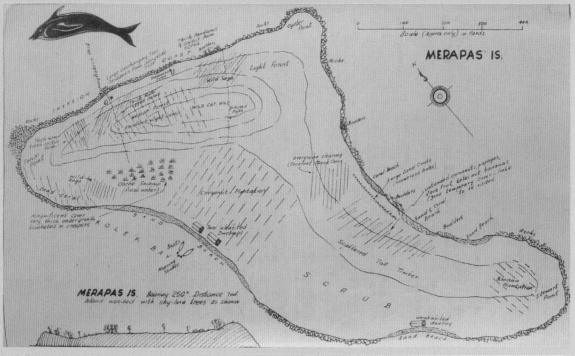

ABOVE Marked on Davidson's detailed map of Merapas is Hammock Tree on the north shore, where he and Stewart paddled ashore on their reconnaissance. (Author's Collection)

RIGHT Incorrectly dated 23 August instead of 23 September, this Davidson sketch shows Merapas, with Wild Cat Hill on the right (north). (Author's Collection)

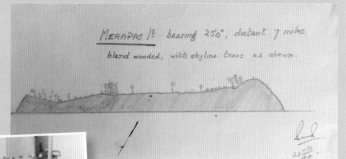

LEFT Taken by Walter Chapman, this photograph shows the crew of the submarine Porpoise en route to Merapas. (Author's Collection - Courtesy of Jeremy Chapman)

At dawn the pair struck out for the island's interior, exploring the eastern half in the morning and the western half in the afternoon. Their most exciting find was two lumps of rubber washed up on the beach. Davidson and Stewart agreed that they should each take one back to Australia where they reckoned they would fetch up to £20. They saw plenty of wildlife, including dozens of land crabs on the eastern beach, a wild cat of the 'stumpy-tailed type' and several flying foxes, one of which was seized by a sea eagle.

Back on the Porpoise on the evening of 24 September, Davidson made out his report along with a detailed sketch of the island. Merapas was 'quite a safe base with excellent cover never likely to be visited by man. Good water. Well placed for coast watching, a shipping route passing within view. Presence of villagers should not matter. They most likely only visit the island now and again for tending the coconut plantations.'

Lyon revised the plan on learning that the island was occasionally inhabited; he couldn't risk a local stumbling upon their supply dump. Lieutenant Walter Carey was selected to remain behind on Merapas as a guard, armed with one of the silent Sten guns. 'Lonely job, which I don't envy him, in the least,' Davidson recorded in his journal. 'Good man for it, though, and took to it with eagerness.'[109]

The men now began transferring their stores from the J containers, which were welded to the Porpoise, to Merapas on two folding engineers' boats under the increasingly fretful gaze of Marsham. He felt his submarine vulnerable and urged the commandos to make greater haste. Even Davidson considered the transference was 'disappointingly slow', although through no fault of their own; Lyon and seven men had remained on board the Porpoise in case they were forced to dive and leave the area. In such an event he and his companions would seize a junk and return in it to Merapas to continue the mission to Singapore as planned.

After three hours they still had not completed half of the operation, but eventually, at approximately 0200 hours on 25 September, Marsham flashed a red torch at the shore party to order them back as Porpoise's batteries were running low. By now the 5 tons of stores had been brought ashore, most in parcels weighing no more than 20 pounds, and all that remained was to carry these over the boulders, up the hill and to the site next to the freshwater swamp selected by Davidson for the supply dump.

Davidson and the rest of the shore party shook hands with Carey and wished him luck. He knew his instructions; once he had humped the supplies to the dump he was to gather as much intelligence as possible about enemy shipping and aircraft that passed his way; but from the evening of 15 October, the earliest arrival date of the SBs, he was to maintain a vigil each night at Hammock Tree on the north coast.

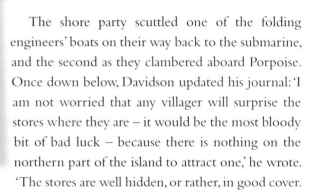

The shore party scuttled one of the folding engineers' boats on their way back to the submarine, and the second as they clambered aboard Porpoise. Once down below, Davidson updated his journal: 'I am not worried that any villager will surprise the stores where they are – it would be the most bloody bit of bad luck – because there is nothing on the northern part of the island to attract one,' he wrote. 'The stores are well hidden, or rather, in good cover. What worries me is the time Carey on his own will take to secure all the stores in the swamp. Three of four days, most likely. Thus increasing the risk of tell tale tracks over a long period. This risk I don't consider grave enough to warrant taking the men ashore again tonight. Carey can well cope with the problem, poor blighter.'[110]

Others among the *Rimau* party were also scribbling as the Porpoise headed east in the direction of Borneo. Lieutenant Bobby Ross had been meaning to write to his sister for weeks but had never found the time. Now was the moment. The departure of the Porpoise had emphasized to Ross their isolation. Here they were, 23 of them, many hundreds of miles behind enemy lines. It brought into focus the love he felt for his family, and for Peggie, the girl he wanted to marry. He had come a long way, figuratively and literally, and there were times Ross still found it hard to believe that six months ago he had been kicking his heels in England, wondering if it was his fate to remain in the wings of the war for its duration. Now he had a part to play. Taking a sheet of plain paper he wrote in pencil to his sister:

> I meant to leave letter writing until after our present occupation is over. I am not allowed to say anything about the work, and since nothing else in life matters at the moment this is therefore going to be awfully dull. But somehow I couldn't bear not to write to you before we go any further. I am full of optimism. This is all just what I wanted. The top, in fact. It gives one a feeling of tranquillity and peace of mind, which I haven't had for a very long time – indeed, which I have never had before. At the same time if anything goes wrong it will be your unenviable job to prevent a) false hope and b) outward display among the family. It was my choice & I don't regret it, & there's an end of it. Also, I would like you to write to Peggie after an interval. It seems stupid to write like this because this is the wrong spirit & as I say, I feel very optimistic. All the same there is something to be said for thinking in realities . . . well, bless you, Rosebud. Nothing remains but to send you all my love.

On 26 September the Porpoise sighted the island of Pedjantan, approximately 170 miles east of Merapas. Lyon had the steep and thickly jungled island in mind as a possible site to transfer the SBs from the submarine to the junk. A periscope reconnaissance appeared to support his idea.

What they didn't spot on this day was a junk, nor indeed on the next day. 'Alone on the sea's face,' wrote Davidson in his journal, no doubt mindful that it was one year to the day since they had raided Singapore. Walter Chapman, whose wisecracks had kept them entertained since leaving Australia, took it upon himself to carve a miniature idol from a piece of carbon. Wrapping it in Lyon's lucky scarf and inserting Donaldson's monocle into one of the idol's eyes, Chapman summoned the officers in the evening and had them each place a finger on the deity's head. In unison they began to chant: 'Find me a junk, get me a junk, witchery, witchery, bring me a junk.' The idol was then, recorded Davidson, 'cast into the deep with a rotary twist to start him on his long and important journey'.[111] As the idol sank into the sea someone asked Chapman if it understood English.

Evidently the idol did, for on 28 September they saw several junks. The one they decided to seize was at anchor near the island of Padang Tikar. It was a 40-ton and 60-foot two-masted junk, the *Mustika*, its Malay crew terrified

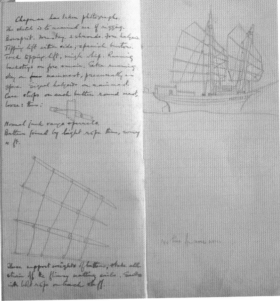

RIGHT The final entry of Donald Davidson's diary, written in pencil on the right-hand page: 'No time for more now'. (Author's Collection)

ABOVE This photo shows the submarine Porpoise alongside the *Mustika*, the junk hijacked by the *Rimau* party off Padang Tikar on 28 September. (NAA 8295619)

when the sea erupted and, amid the broiling water, a submarine surfaced. The first man the Malays saw emerge from the conning tower was Bobby Ross, who waved and smiled and in fluent Malay reassured the sailors that they had nothing to fear. They grabbed the lines hurled from Porpoise and within 12 minutes the submarine had vanished once more, leaving Ross, Lyon, Davidson, Ingleton and three Australians on board the *Mustika* with its crew of nine.

With his soft features and neat side-parting Ross was not an intimidating specimen, and his genuine interest and affection for the world's different ethnicities made him an ideal interpreter. He quickly won the confidence of the crew, skippered by Mohamed Juni bin Haji, who told Ross how much they loathed the brutal Japanese. Life had grown considerably worse and the *Mustika*, which pre-war had traded in timber and sugar, now transported only sub-standard wood. Ross explained that they needed the junk but the crew would be taken to Australia in the submarine and well looked after. The Malays thought this a great idea, explaining that most of them were related and the junk's owner, their uncle, was an unprincipled scoundrel who willingly collaborated with the Japanese and paid them a pittance. They then set about giving Lyon and the others a crash course in how to sail a junk. She handled well. The trick was to set the lateen sails correctly. Once that was done she cruised at 6 knots.

The Porpoise returned at nightfall on 28 September and towed the junk through the night to Pedjantan. It dived at dawn the next day and the two vessels reached their destination under their own steam, the *Mustika* anchoring

Walter Chapman took this photo from the conning tower of the Porpoise as it returned to Australia. (Author's Collection - Courtesy of Jeremy Chapman)

in a sheltered bay on the northern shore of the island. During the afternoon of 29 September the machinery necessary to carry out the transference had been assembled on the deck of the junk under the direction of Reggie Ingleton. At midnight the Porpoise surfaced and edged as close as Marsham dared to the beach. Four of the SBs were on the forward casing and half of the remaining supplies were also ready for swift disembarkation. Marsham signalled that he was ready to begin unloading the first of the SBs, but someone on the junk noticed that the purchase for the derrick was missing. Marsham lost his temper and vented his anger in a string of salty oaths. The genial Ingleton, ultimately responsible for the derrick, told everyone not to panic, that it wasn't lost, simply mislaid. He suggested it was down below in the Porpoise, which it was.

The *Rimau* party now put into practice the unloading procedure that they had rehearsed countless times on Garden Island, and before dawn on 30 September seven of the SBs were on board the *Mustika*. The submarine put out to sea again to recharge her batteries while Lyon and his men checked and stacked the stores and equipment. Some of the men undertook a reconnoitre of the island, recounted Davidson in his journal. 'Shore reconnaissance found Pedjantan entirely deserted. One old fish trap on northern side. Old coconut plantation (dated about 1900) had remains of old railway. Entirely abandoned and no sign of habitation. Coconuts good. Gathered a lot of coconuts for Porpoise.'[112]

Once Lyon was satisfied that all the stores had been checked and stashed, there was nothing to do but wait for the return of the Porpoise at dusk for the final unloading. Walter Chapman acted the tourist, taking several photographs of the *Rimau* party and their surrounds, including the crabs, fish and sharks that

The *Mustika*, the junk seized by the men of Operation *Rimau*, as sketched by Walter Chapman. (Author's Collection - Courtesy of Jeremy Chapman)

they saw in the water. Later he sat on the beach with Lyon, who was brimming with bonhomie, and confident that success was within their grasp. According to the Malays they were two days' sailing from the Strait of Singapore, which put them two days ahead of schedule, and gave the men the luxury of 48 hours' rest and recuperation on Pedjantan before setting out for their objective. Lyon's lucky scarf was working its magic once more. His sole twinge of apprehension was whether the Japanese had stepped up security in the Singapore Strait after the *Jaywick* humiliation.

At dusk the Malays,★ who had swapped their singlets and sarongs for jungle-green army uniform, hosted their new British and Australian friends to a beach party, cooking a delicious curry from some of the soldiers' rations. Donald Davidson took the opportunity to add a final entry to his journal. He described the events of the day and then spent several minutes sketching some of the junk's rigging as a reminder for future reference. 'Battens joined by light rope

★ The Malays spent the rest of the war in Australia as free men and were repatriated after the war. The junk's owner sought compensation for the junk but SRD refused to accept any liability because 'at the time of seizure [it] was employed in Japanese service.'

One of the two folding engineers' boats that were welded to the Porpoise and used to transport stores from the submarine to Merapas. (Author's Collection - Courtesy of Jeremy Chapman)

thus, swing 4 ft,' he wrote underneath one diagram. He made another sketch and annotated: 'These support weight of battens, and take all strain off the flimsy matting sails. Sails with bolt rope on leach and luff.'

He had just finished a pencil drawing of the *Mustika* when the silhouette of the Porpoise was spotted approaching the beach. 'No time for more now,'[113] wrote Davidson, and he closed his journal.

CHAPTER 10
TIGER HUNTING

From the forward casing of the Porpoise, Lieutenant-Commander Hubert Marsham and the men on watch gave three cheers for the 22 figures standing on the beach. Walter Chapman also saluted the *Rimau* party, the journal of Davidson clutched in his hand. A few minutes earlier, just before 2200 hours on 30 September, he had shaken hands with Lyon and wished him good luck. 'See you at Merapas,' he added. Lyon had laughed and said: 'Don't forget that Hammock Tree.'[114]

The agreement with Marsham was that the Porpoise would rendezvous at the Hammock Tree on the northern shore of Merapas on the evening of 7/8 November and every night thereafter until 7 December with communication by way of their 'walkie-talkies'. This recent innovation was battery-operated and had a communication range of 1 mile over land and 3 miles over salt water.

In the event of an emergency Lyon would use their wireless to contact SOA's cipher clerk, Staff-Sergeant Mary Ellis, using the one-off code they had arranged. Lyon had left his copy of the book in Melbourne having almost certainly transcribed the important passages onto a piece of paper, carbon copies of which he gave to the two signallers, Craft and Stewart.

By dawn on 1 October Lyon had altered the operational plan. He was uncomfortable at the thought of Walter Carey standing guard alone over their supplies. Reinforcements were required to ease the burden on the Australian. Merapas was in the general direction of their target so the *Mustika* made a

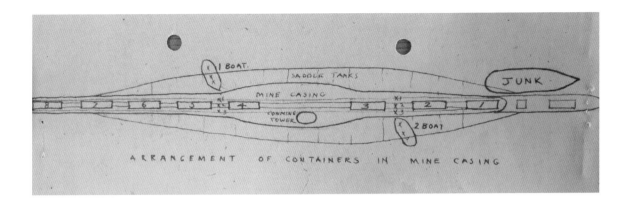

ARRANGEMENT OF CONTAINERS IN MINE CASING

detour and to Carey's undoubted delight dropped anchor on 4 October. The three men selected to join Carey were Alf Warren, the engineer who had come up with the suggestion for welding the containers onto the mine casing as extra storage space, and Corporal Hugo Pace, a 31-year-old French-Egyptian. An extrovert and an athlete with exotic good looks, Pace, who was born in Port Said, had emigrated to Australia in 1934, finding employment at a Queensland outback station. He had enlisted in 1941 and seen action in North Africa and New Guinea.

The third man was Sergeant Colin Cameron. Like Warren, Cameron was a dab hand with most things mechanical and before joining SOA had served in the Light Aid Detachment.* Having deposited the three men on Merapas, the *Mustika* continued towards its target. On board, the men had applied the skin dye and the most dark-skinned among them had donned the sarongs and singlets taken from the junk's former crew, now on their way back to Australia in the Porpoise. Most of the time they stayed below deck while the officers busied themselves by recording anything they saw of interest. Ingleton, deploying his architect's drafting skills, sketched several vessels they passed as well as the bauxite mines visible on the southern coast of Bintan Island.

On the evening of 9 October they anchored off Kepala Jernih at the south end of the Phillip Channel, and two folboats were launched, one containing Bobby Ross and Andrew Huston, the other Bob Page and Pat Campbell. Together they paddled 7 miles to the island of Pulau Labon and, after a reconnoitre that confirmed it was a safe place to unload the Sleeping Beauties,

This sketch of the Porpoise details how Alf Warren, the engineer, welded the containers onto the mine casing of the submarine for valuable extra storage space. (Author's Collection)

---

* The composition of the four men left on Merapas is disputed. Carey and Warren were definitely part of the group, but some sources cite Cameron and Pace as the other two and others Craft and Cameron. Neither Cameron nor Pace had been selected as SB operators, but Craft had, so it seems unlikely that Lyon would have left Craft on Merapas as it would have left him one trained operator short.

Page and Campbell returned to the *Mustika*. Ross and Huston carried on to the island of Subar, from where one year earlier Huston and his five companions had set out to raid Singapore on Operation *Jaywick*. It was another 7 miles for the pair and they were tired by the time they dragged their folboat ashore in the early hours of 10 October. Their job was to spend the day observing shipping in Singapore Harbour and then rendezvous with the rest of the party the following evening at Pulau Labon, from where the tigers of *Rimau* would strike at the Japanese.

In the afternoon of 10 October Bobby Ross and Andrew Huston spotted a vessel approaching from the south. But it was not the *Mustika*. As it drew closer to the shore it was identifiable as one of the folding engineers' boats of the type they had used to transfer stores from the Porpoise to Merapas. The men in the boat were paddling hard. Sharing the field glasses, Ross and Huston listed the faces they recognized: Ivan Lyon, Donald Davidson, Pat Campbell, Doug Warne and Clair Stewart.

Ross and Huston scrambled down to the shore from their observation post to greet their comrades. They were met with a tale of woe. Ivan Lyon's luck had finally run out. Dawn had broken that morning to reveal Singapore Strait crowded with Japanese naval ships on manoeuvres (preparatory to leaving for the Philippines). They would have to exercise extreme caution in approaching the target, not just for fear of being challenged but from the bow waves thrown up by the huge ships, Lyon steered a course north-west, the *Mustika* threading its way through the innumerable small islands off Batam. As usual there were three men on deck, their skin dyed and their bodies wrapped in sarongs. The rest were below, checking weapons and explosives, giving the SBs a final once-over. It was as they neared the island of Kasu at 1530 hours that disaster struck. Coming from the south they hadn't seen the village until they rounded a tree-clad cape. Suddenly they were in full view of a bustling village, the houses on stilts above the water and a jetty lined with boats. Someone on shore, probably one of the policemen, had seen them. From that distance, no more than 70 or 80 feet, the dye would have fooled no one with a pair of binoculars.

They saw several men jump into a motor launch. Then it started to rain, a torrential tropical downpour. If only the rain had come five minutes earlier they might have been left unmolested. As the launch sped towards them, Lyon issued the codeword for action stations, 'Patroller'. Below deck the men shuffled over to the firing loops with their weapons levelled at the approaching vessel. One man, the only one not in uniform, stood in the bow of the boat. He looked frightened and agitated. No one spoke, either on the launch or on the junk. The man in the bow had animal instincts. He sensed terrible danger and flung himself off the bow and into the water just a moment before someone on the junk opened fire. His comrades joined in, raking the wooden launch with a maelstrom of machine-gun bullets, until all movement ceased.

In the mistaken belief that the police department on Kasu had a radio transmitter with which to alert Singapore, Lyon barked instructions. *Rimau* was no more. He reeled off 12 names and ordered them to paddle to Merapas in the folboats. It was 85 miles due east. They probably had a few hours before the Japanese learned of the attack. Good luck. Davidson handed Bob Page one of the *Mustika*'s two Japanese flags. It might come in handy if they commandeered a local junk.

Lyon gathered Davidson, Campbell, Warne and Stewart, the strongest canoeists, and told them they would rendezvous with Ross and Huston on Subar and then carry out the raid that night on Singapore. Assembling the engineer boat, the five men loaded it with the three remaining folboats, a rubber raft, rations and dozens of limpet mines. The last act was to activate the fuse on one of the limpets that had been left behind on the *Mustika*.★ As the men paddled away the mine detonated. All that effort, all that training, consigned to the bottom of the South China Sea. But there was not a backward glance from Lyon and his four men as they struck out for Subar, 7 miles north.

Having given Ross and Huston a potted account of their misfortune, Lyon turned to the future: the attack would go ahead, but in the style of the *Jaywick* raid. They had four folboats and many limpets, enough to inflict another blow to Japanese pride. They paired off, the three officers each with an Australian soldier. Doug Warne had a folboat to himself; Lyon had faith in his mental and physical strength. Ross briefed his comrades on the shipping he and Huston had identified in Keppel Harbour. They divided targets between them and when it was dark they paddled towards Singapore.

At dawn on 11 October Singapore Harbour once more reverberated to the sound of violent explosions as the limpet mines exploded. Lyon and his six men watched the smoke drift across the city from their vantage point on Dongas Island.

★ At least one historian has claimed that the junk was scuttled by opening the sea-cocks, but this seems unlikely as Lyon would have wanted to destroy as many of the SBs as possible.

It wasn't until 13 October that the Japanese connected the destruction of the motor launch at Kasu to the attack of at least three ships in Singapore. In fact two men had survived the confrontation with the *Mustika* on the afternoon of 10 October. One was the civilian who had leapt from the bow seconds before the firing began, a Singaporean Chinese called Ati. He had been press-ganged by the police as the only English speaker on the island. The other was Sidek bin Safar, the police chief, who had tumbled into the water and sheltered behind the stern during the firestorm from the junk. Life had been agreeable for bin Safar for much of the war, and his first contact with the enemy had left three of his men dead. Shaken, he travelled by boat a couple of miles east to his police HQ on the island of Belakang Padang to make out his report. The next 48 hours were spent in a fruitless salvage operation on the sunken junk. On 13 October the police on Belakang Padang reported the incident at Kasu to the Japanese in Singapore, identifying the assailants as white men.

The Japanese had probably assumed that the raid on their shipping had been carried out from guerrillas based on the mainland – as they believed *Jaywick* had – and it wasn't until the report from Belakang Padang that they realized their error.

On 15 October the Japanese Navy in Singapore sent a message, stating, 'about twenty people including Caucasians have been engaged in a defensive stand in the northern part of the Riau Archipelago since October 10 . . . and are continuing to infiltrate into every part of the Riau Archipelago. The penetration into Pangkil, four miles east of Karus, has been confirmed. Even though the Army is at present searching them out, maintain strict watch in Riau Archipelago and Bulan Straits.'[115]

Pangkil was approximately 45 miles south-east of Dongas Island and it was an odd destination for Lyon and his men. Shaped like a dog's bone, it was certainly not the quickest way to Merapas, but it was remote and thick with jungle. As Lyon had told his father, he had been schooling himself in the art of jungle survival and at least two of the men with him – Davidson and Ross – also felt confident in the environment. Ross also had his fluent Malay, perhaps their most crucial weapon of all, and it was Lyon's intention to make their way cautiously from island to island, relying if need be on the kindness of strangers to feed them. Time was on their side. It was 15 October and the cut-off date for making the rendezvous at Merapas was 7 December. The men's confidence was high, their morale intact. Five days after being compromised by the police patrol launch, they had seen no sign of pursuers despite the raid on the harbour. Lyon may have been contemplating another attack on enemy shipping, using what remained of their limpets.

At dusk on 15 October Lyon, Bobby Ross and Clair Stewart left Pangkil and paddled 3 miles north-east to the nearby island of Soreh. Furnished with sweets and cigarettes they wished to glean information from the locals about the safest route to Merapas, and the island also offered a good view north to the Riau Anchorage if Lyon really was serious about hitting the enemy shipping a second time.

In their absence a Malay on Pangkil arrived at the men's hideout to warn them that their presence had been reported to the Japanese by a local informant. Davidson ordered Huston and Warne to take a folboat and tow the rubber raft with their remaining provisions a few miles south-east to Tapai Island. He and Campbell pushed the fourth folboat into the water an hour before dawn on 16 October and paddled hard for Soreh. His intention was undoubtedly to alert Lyon, Ross and Stewart to the danger and together rendezvous with Huston and Warne on Tapai.

The Japanese informant, a man called Raja Mun, had observed the commandos and then taken a boat to Bintan Island where he collected a handsome reward for his information about the white men on Pangkil. On 16 October a detachment of 100 men under the command of Major Hajime Fujita, an ardent Imperialist, was despatched to hunt for the renegades. The major split his force, leading a detachment in two motorized landing barges to Pangkil. Another landing barge containing around 45 Heibo, a local militia force of mainly conscripted Malays, led by some Japanese Kempeitai, had orders to scour the neighbouring islands.

When Davidson and Campbell reached Soreh they had little trouble locating their comrades on the small flat atoll, which was one-third of a mile at its widest point. But on hearing the news, Lyon decided to stay put rather than risk paddling the 7 odd miles south to Tapai. The one place they did not want to be found was on the open ocean in daylight. The Japanese believed they were at Pangkil so they would go there first, and on finding no trace of them would probably head south. At nightfall Lyon and his party would paddle to Tapai, pick up Huston and Warne, and then strike out for Merapas. The Japanese would never search for them there. That was Lyon's reasoning.

Lyon and his men approached the sole inhabitants on Soreh, the young manager of the coconut plantation, who lived in a hut with his wife and young child. Bobby Ross, who was dressed in a jungle green uniform with a weapon slung over his shoulder, asked the man if he would be kind enough to give them some coconuts.

Their breakfast over, the men selected the best position from which to defend their island in the unlikely event a Japanese search party arrived. There was scant cover for them but, assuming the enemy would land on the main beach on the north-west corner, close to the manager's hut, Lyon directed Campbell and Davidson to a dip in the ground on the western side. Stewart was a little way off in a shallow ditch armed with a bag of hand grenades.

Lyon and Ross climbed among the slender branches of a tall ru tree, one of the few intruders among the palm trees. It was around 0900 hours. The men waited. Ross and Lyon were at least shaded from the sun. The only sound, apart from bird song, was that of the manager hard at work splicing coconuts so he and his wife could extract their oil. Davidson and Campbell, tired after their night paddle, may have dozed while Stewart scanned the horizon. Lyon and Ross may have exchanged a few words from their vantage point. Perhaps the Japanese wouldn't search this island. They may have wondered how Huston and Warne were. They had plenty of time to think. Ross's head must have been crowded with thoughts of the people and places he loved: of Cambridge, and the Sussex countryside, his parents, Peggie, his sweetheart, with whom he wished to grow old, and his vivacious sister Rosebud, who idolized her big brother. Nearly a year ago he had written to her from Nigeria to express his fear he was 'getting pretty dried up both in mind and body'. He had yearned for a change, for some excitement, and he had found it thanks to the man beside him in the branches of the ru tree.

It was mid-afternoon when Ross and Lyon spotted the vessel heading their way. They heard the distant hum of its engine and identified it as a motorized barge as it approached the beach on the north-western corner of Soreh. The manager of the coconut plantation heard it too, and emerged from his house as the barge beached. Soldiers began disembarking, striding up the beach in his direction, rifles hanging from their shoulders. The world then erupted.

The manager ducked back inside his hut, terrified at the ear-splitting sound of exploding grenades. Several Japanese were killed in the first moments of the ambush; they'd been caught unprepared. Soreh wasn't the first island they'd visited, and there was nothing to suggest this sparse atoll would be hiding their prey.

The survivors threw themselves onto the beach and scrambled for whatever cover there was. Small fountains of sand burst from the beach as bullets hit the ground, but the Japanese soldiers could hear no sound of enemy fire. The men firing the silent Stens turned their attention to the landing barge. Bullets drummed against the hull as the soldiers inside cowered.

There was sporadic firing for the next couple of hours. Japanese soldiers crabbed across the beach, from cover to cover, trying to locate the hidden enemy. Wounded men pressed themselves into the sand or crawled slowly back to the landing barge. The plantation manager was seized and at around 1700 hours, the Japanese departed.

The defenders of Soreh emerged from their positions once the barge had disappeared from sight. Bobby Ross and Clair Stewart were unscathed and Lyon had sustained a minor flesh wound. But Davidson had been shot in the chest and Campbell had taken a bullet in his shoulder. Much blood had been lost. They received some morphine and Lyon made a quick assessment of their predicament. The Japanese would be back with reinforcements, but not before sundown in two hours. They had a few hours' respite. They could all try and make a dash to Huston and Warne on Tapai, but the Japanese would surely catch up with them once they realized they had withdrawn from Soreh. The goal was to have as many men as possible reach the rendezvous at Merapas. Lyon made up his mind. At nightfall Davidson and Campbell would paddle the 7½ miles south to Tapai. He, Ross and Stewart would fight a rearguard on Soreh, long enough, hopefully, for Davidson and Campbell to collect Huston and Warne and continue onto Merapas.

A little before 1900 hours the five men assembled on the beach. If Lyon and Davidson exchanged any words they would have been brief. Neither was the sort for heartfelt goodbyes. Together they had come far, in every sense. They'd dared much and won much, but their good fortune had run out. It was the end of their adventure and they knew it. In his last conversation with his father in the garden of his Surrey home, Lyon had said he would not let himself be taken alive; Davidson may have had a similar exchange with his wife, or he might have told her, in his whimsical way, that he was too clever to be caught by the Japanese. But now they both faced a bitter reality.

Not long after Davidson and Campbell paddled painfully away, the Japanese returned in force. Soldiers sprinted from the landing barges up the beach, but this time there was no furious resistance. Just an intimidating silence. Cautiously, they rose and moved forward, eyes straining through the dark, darting from one tree to another. Lyon and Ross had climbed into the branches of another ru tree, this one further inland and well away from the manager's hut where his wife and child huddled. Stewart and a bag bulging with grenades was in a ditch to the right of his comrades. He would spring the ambush with a grenade and then Lyon and Ross would open fire with their silent Stens.

The first Japanese to die never knew what hit them. Those that were wounded, and their comrades who dived for cover, were aware only that they were under attack from grenades and small-arms fire. But there was no rat-a-tat from the enemy's guns. They were up against silent assassins. For nearly four hours the three men held off dozens of Japanese. Officers screamed at their men to locate the enemy, but those brave enough to advance towards the trees were cut down. Lyon dosed himself with morphine at regular intervals, and during lulls in fighting, redressed his wound.

More reinforcements arrived and finally someone on the beach spotted the muzzle flashes of the silent Stens. Soreh was now carpeted with Japanese bodies, but at least one soldier crawled through the dead and the dying, close enough to hurl a grenade at the tree containing Lyon and Ross. The pair were blown out of their nest and when the Japanese reached them they were already dead. Clair Stewart, probably out of grenades, slunk silently away, deeper into the island.

The rearguard of Lyon, Ross and Stewart had not been in vain. It had given Donald Davidson and Pat Campbell the time to reach Tapai. It had been an extraordinary effort, given their wounds, a testament to their physical and mental fortitude. But it had stripped them of their stamina, and their spirits sank further when they found no trace of Huston and Warne. It was the early hours of 17 October and Davidson and Campbell were in a hopeless situation. They had drained themselves paddling from Soreh to Tapai, and neither was in a fit state to continue his escape. They had no rations and between them one grenade and a few rounds in their pistols. What they did have was their potassium cyanide capsules.

On Soreh, Clair Stewart faced a similar choice when dawn broke on 17 October. The Japanese had departed, leaving behind the corpses of Lyon and Ross for the animals and insects, but taking the folboats. Stewart was marooned.

So, too, were Davidson and Campbell. They made an unlikely couple. One a monocled upper middle-class English naval officer, the son of a vicar, and the other, a jackaroo from Queensland, more than a decade younger. They had dragged their bleeding bodies to a large rock well above the waterline and spent many hours contemplating the world and their place within. At some point during the night of 17/18 October they fished out the capsules that had been given to them by a Royal Marines medical officer on Garden Island. Don't swallow them, he had advised, it can take five minutes to die. Break the capsule between your teeth. You'll be dead in a matter of seconds.

The Japanese arrived not long after daybreak on 18 October. From their vessel they saw two white men side by side, their backs against a large rock. They seemed to be asleep. Neither reacted to their warnings or the sound of the boat. They hadn't been dead long. Their bodies were still warm and a smell of bitter almonds hung in the air. The Japanese stripped the pair for souvenirs but left their bodies to nature.

CHAPTER 11

'A BLOW TO US ALL'

HMS Porpoise reached Fremantle on 11 October. In his patrol report Lieutenant-Commander Hubert Marsham wrote that their 'passage was uneventful' and their special mission was 'successfully completed'. The 39-year-old Marsham listed four defects of the Porpoise but omitted his own flaw, a war-weariness brought on by nearly six years of continual patrolling. He needed a rest.

It was decided to send in place of Porpoise the British submarine Tantalus, commanded by Lieutenant-Commander Hugh Mackenzie, DSO, known among his crew of 60 on the T-Class submarine as 'Rufus'.★

One of its officers was a 22-year-old Lieutenant called Michael Tibbs, an experienced sailor who had joined the Tantalus in August 1943 after three years' service on cruisers and destroyers in the Mediterranean, Atlantic and Arctic. In a letter written to his parents that month he had said Mackenzie 'seems very understanding and I like him very much'.[116]

The Tantalus had conducted two Far East patrols already in 1944, the second in May and June, which included a brief part in an SOE Force 136 operation. Carrying two agents, Major James Hislop and Lieutenant-Colonel Innes

---

★ *Tantalus* brought Hubert Marsham back to Britain in 1945 and he described it as 'the happiest boat he had been in'.

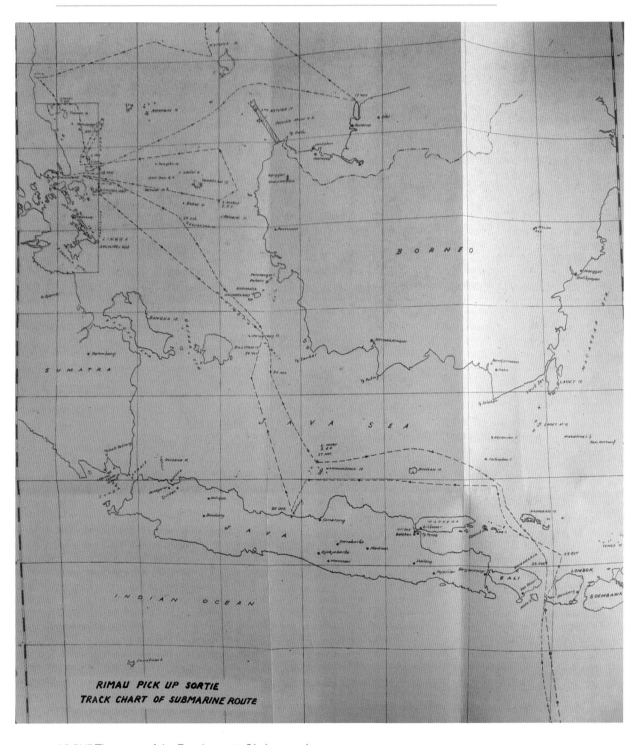

RIMAU PICK UP SORTIE
TRACK CHART OF SUBMARINE ROUTE

ABOVE The route of the *Tantalus* on its 51-day patrol that covered 11,600 miles but failed to collect any of the *Rimau* party. (Author's Collection)

HMS *Tantalus*, seen here in Plymouth Sound in 1948, was named after the mythological Tantalus, son of Zeus. (Author's Collection)

Tremlett, who was the Head of the Malayan Country Section, the Tantalus had instructions to rendezvous with an anchored junk; the junk was there but its signal lights were inaccurate and Mackenzie 'decided that he could not risk making any further contact'.

Mackenzie was a robust and charismatic character, a man of physical and intellectual strength, who considered dropping off secret agents an irksome distraction to his primary job of sending enemy ships to the bottom of the ocean. He had been awarded a DSO in 1942 after sinking 40,000 tons of enemy shipping while commanding HMS Thrasher. He was welcoming to new officers, but he expected nothing but the highest standards on his submarine. Away from duty, however, he could be good fun and even a little rumbustious. In August 1944 he required medical attention for two badly bruised ribs after a particularly lively mess party.

Lieutenant Tibbs had spent most of September enjoying Perth while the Tantalus was undergoing a maintenance check. On 10 October he returned to the submarine and five days later he wrote a letter home, in which he said: 'We are all rushing around at the moment, [and] as forecast I am neither Navigator nor Torps [torpedoes]. I am everything that no one else wants to do, such as confidential clerk, signals, correspondence, ASDIC, ciphers, but I am back in the boat which is the great thing . . . it is Sunday today so the ship is full of visitors – exactly like Navy Week.'

The next day Tibbs wrote again, 'in great haste', to warn his parents that 'you won't hear for a bit'.

A few hours later the Tantalus left Fremantle on its sixth war patrol. The operational order of Mackenzie was to sink enemy shipping with the submarine's 17 torpedoes and collect members of the *Rimau* party. The order, signed by L. M. Shadwell, Captain, Eighth Submarine Flotilla, stated: 'the operational party will be ready to embark in Tantalus from the eighth night 8th/9th November 1944 onwards'.★ Two charts of Merapas were supplied, one an Admiralty Chart and the other Dutch Chart No. 44, and a detailed description was furnished of the 'Hammock Tree', where the *Rimau* lookout would be stationed.

★ Some accounts of the *Rimau* operation, notably *Kill the Tiger* by Peter Thompson and Robert Macklin (Hodder Australia, 2002), claimed that the pick-up window began on 7/8 November, but Shadwell's orders stipulated 8/9 November as the first night of the rendezvous period.

But Mackenzie's orders were unambiguous:

The commanding officer HMS Tantalus is responsible for the safety of the submarine which is to be his first consideration and has discretion to cancel or postpone the operation at any time.

a) Subject to patrol requirements HMS Tantalus will leave her patrol at dark on 7th November and proceed to the vicinity of Merapas Island . . .

e) In the event of the pick up party and the *Rimau* party failing to keep the rendezvous for the embarkation, the greatest caution is to be exercised by Tantalus, who should not hesitate to abandon the operation if contact is not re-established, or if he has some reason to suspect that the operation is compromised.

f) Should the Tantalus owing to unforeseen circumstances, be unable to keep the above programme, the same programme is to be carried out on subsequent nights.[117]

Hugh 'Rufus' Mackenzie, commander of HMS Tantalus, seen here during the war, was a charismatic officer who inspired his crew. (IWM A 10254)

With Tantalus as she headed north was Walter Chapman, who found 'an attractive air of cheery efficiency' on board the submarine. He had with him still his camera and he roamed the submarine taking photographs. Tibbs enjoyed his company. 'He was not one to observe all the regulations,' he recalled, and he was a willing participant in the officers' Good Morning quiz and the evening card game of Racing Demon. Accompanying Chapman for the task of going ashore to Merapas to contact the *Rimau* party was Corporal Ron Croton, a member of Z Special Unit who had completed the Garden Island training but failed to win selection on the initial operation.

The Tantalus cleared the Lombok Strait at 0500 hours on 25 October, and the next day they rendezvoused with HM Submarine Stoic about 10 miles off the north coast of Java. On 27 October they passed Pajantan Island and Mackenzie noted in his log that the sea was dead calm, the visibility excellent and plenty of timber and coconuts could be seen on the surface. Meanwhile, recalled Tibbs,

Chapman had described the outline of *Rimau* to his new shipmates. 'Though we were never told the full details it was fairly obvious that Singapore must be the target,' said Tibbs.

The top of the hill ('Wild Cat Hill', as christened by Donald Davidson) of Merapas Island was sighted on the horizon on the morning of 28 October, recorded Mackenzie in the log. At 0800 hours they dived when two aircraft were spotted heading in a north-west direction. 'Surfaced at 0900,' wrote Walter Chapman in his intelligence report. 'Forced to dive again by a 2-engined bomber which was diving to investigate us. No bombs were dropped and she must have lost contact. Decided to stay dived for the rest of the day as the frequency of aircraft patrols were not known at this time.'[118]

Mackenzie must have asked Walter Chapman about the frequency of the aircraft, and the soldier would have replied that there was a marked increase in air activity from the previous month. They had hardly seen any during the unloading of the stores from the Porpoise to Merapas, or later when they transferred the Sleeping Beauties from the submarine to the junk at Pedjantan.

With more than a week until the earliest rendezvous date with the *Rimau* party, Mackenzie took Tantalus east towards Borneo, and on 2 November they sank a 3,000-ton freighter, the *Amagi Maru,* one of seven ships in a convoy that promised rich pickings. But the next day the submarine 'received a signal ordering us to proceed to the entrance of the Singapore Strait to do air sea rescue duties on the surface for the proposed raid on Singapore by B.29s on 5th November.'

Chapman, no doubt reflecting the thoughts of Mackenzie, wrote in his report: 'This was rather annoying as it meant going west at full speed to get there in time and leaving the convoy unmolested.'

The Tantalus spent 5 November on the surface 35 miles from Singapore Strait but saw no trace of downed B-29 aircrew, and they were still engaged on lookout duties two days later. Eventually, in the early afternoon of 7 November, Mackenzie resumed his aggressive patrolling, heading north towards Pulau Tioman, approximately 100 miles north of Singapore off the east coast of Malaya. They soon saw a convoy of three ships and Mackenzie 'went to diving stations and started the attack'. Just as they closed for the kill on the 5,000-ton vessel, the Tantalus was picked up by the ASDIC of the two escort destroyers. For the next two hours the submarine, on the continental

On 11 November the Tantalus launched a surface attack against the *Pahang Maru* and captured nine crew and a Japanese soldier. (Author's Collection - Courtesy of Jeremy Chapman)

shelf at a depth of only 50 feet, was hunted by its two prey. 'This was the worst amount of depth charging I ever went through,' said Tibbs. 'Everything was shut off and the atmosphere was stifling, as the destroyers came in, sounding like an express train going through a station.'

Walter Chapman on Merapas as photographed by Ron Croton, a picture probably taken from the east coast looking west, with Wild Cat Hill in the background. (Author's Collection - Courtesy of Jeremy Chapman)

The crew of the Tantalus heard the 'ping' of the depth charges being fired, and for a few awful seconds all they could do was say a silent prayer and wait for the 'woof' as it exploded. Once or twice the submarine shuddered, but apart from some glass items shattering there was no damage inflicted. At one moment the two destroyers were so close Tibbs and his crewmates 'could hear their Asdic transmissions quite clearly through the water' and then later, one of the enemy vessels ran right over the Tantalus firing depth charges all the time. Only Mackenzie's cool skill saved them. 'I thought it was the end,' said Tibbs. 'But thanks to Rufus, it was not.' Mackenzie barked orders with cool precision so that the submarine kept just ahead of the falling charges.

The one man on board the Tantalus who appeared unperturbed by their predicament was Walter Chapman. 'All this time,' remembered Tibbs, 'Chapman had been creeping through the boat with his cine camera, photographing paint coming off the bulkheads, light bulbs bursting and the wardroom lamp shade with its scantily clad ladies whizzing round and round as there were explosions all around us.'

Mackenzie and his crew were not unduly unnerved by their narrow escape. As soon as the destroyers departed, the Tantalus gave chase but called off the hunt when the convoy entered an area marked on Royal Navy charts as an enemy minefield. That evening, 7 November, Mackenzie and Chapman discussed the rendezvous on Merapas. Tibbs said that his commander considered 'his primary duty was to carry out an aggressive patrol [and] in any case the *Rimau* party had been told they would be picked up any time within a month of the initial date, 8th November, so therefore Rufus and Chapman agreed that the pick-up could be postponed.' The decision was radioed to HQ at Fremantle, 'who concurred'.

The Tantalus prowled the Malayan coast for several more days, sinking a coaster on 11 November and rescuing its crew of Malays, Chinese and one Japanese. That success prompted Mackenzie to further postpone the pick-up of the *Rimau* party from 10/11 November as 'it was decided the most useful thing the submarine could do would be to continue her patrol until the remaining torpedoes had been used up.'

Mackenzie was within his rights to delay the pick-up. His orders stated that he was to use his 'discretion' to cancel or postpone the rendezvous at any time, and the main purpose of the patrol was to sink enemy shipping. So far he had despatched two vessels and he was hungry for more. But to his consternation he received another signal on 15 November to return to the Singapore Strait to search for any shot-down bomber crew, what Chapman described in the report as 'life guard duties'. They remained in the Strait until 20 November, when Mackenzie ordered the Tantalus to head east to Merapas to effect the pick-up. It was a tense voyage and four times they were forced to dive by approaching aircraft.

Tibbs's 23rd birthday was on 21 November and for his present he asked Mackenzie if he could land on Merapas with Chapman and Croton. His commander agreed, as did the two soldiers. Chapman briefed him on the procedure. 'I had to remove all badges of rank, all identity disks and everything like that and wear something very dark,' remembered Tibbs, who complied with the instructions, cutting off an end of his scarf to use as a cap comforter. Chapman even gave Tibbs a cyanide capsule, for use 'to avoid you being captured and questioned'.

Michael Tibbs, seen here in 1940, served on HMS Tantalus and took part in the search for the *Rimau* party. (Michael Tibbs Collection)

It may have been the talk of suicide pills that changed Mackenzie's mind because just prior to their arrival off Merapas on the morning of 21 November he told Tibbs he couldn't let him go ashore because 'the risk was not justifiable'.

Tantalus spent 21 November reconnoitring Merapas from below the surface, coming in as close as 1,000 yards. 'Nothing suspicious was seen but there were no signs of the party,' wrote Mackenzie in his report. Chapman shared the periscope with the commander and saw nothing untoward. Merapas looked pretty much as it had seven weeks earlier. There were three or four Malays near the hut on the coconut plantation, just as there had been in September. That evening Chapman and Croton went ashore in a folboat, carrying some compo rations and a silent Sten gun each. They came ashore on the north-west tip of the island, at Punai Point, and experienced great difficulty in negotiating the rocks that were smooth, slippery and numerous.

Having seen the two men off, the Tantalus dived and spent the next 24 hours out at sea.

The arrangement was that the submarine would return for them at 1930 hours the following night, 22 November. There was a disquieting amount of enemy activity in the area. They dived when they spotted a destroyer bearing towards them, and shortly after surfacing the Tantalus was obliged to dive again when a float plane appeared, the same kind as they had seen the previous day. 'It looked as though there was some kind of search on,' said Tibbs. Nonetheless, there was an air of eager anticipation on the afternoon of 22 November when the Tantalus approached Merapas. 'One of the things we had done was to put up a false nose rack in the wardroom because we knew that we were going to be absolutely swamped by these officers with their strange kit,' said Tibbs. 'And we couldn't imagine any kind of spy not wearing false noses.'

A heavy swell impeded Walter Chapman and Ron Croton as they paddled their way back to the submarine from Merapas. When they finally scrambled on board their faces told their own story. Merapas was empty of soldiers. Yet they had been there, of that there was no doubt, and Chapman described finding the camp by the water hole. An elaborate and large lean-to had been constructed from palm leaves and there were half-eaten tins of food and discarded chocolate wrappers. Hanging from one branch they had found a bandage and a rag and they had also discovered a couple of empty packets of Three Castles cigarettes, the brand taken onto the Porpoise. Further on they came across eight individual lean-tos and outside each one a commando cooker on which were tins of congealed and rotting food. Also found was a can of oil that belonged to a Sleeping Beauty submersible and Davidson's small rake, a favourite toy of his, with which he had taught the men to erase their footprints.

What most troubled Chapman was the discovery of a large iron bowl, nothing to do with the *Rimau* party, and close by a tree on which had been carved in Japanese the word 'Japan'.

What they didn't find was the main supply dump or any sign of a fight or a struggle. It was, as Chapman told Tibbs, 'like the ship *Mary Celeste*', the American merchant vessel, discovered adrift in the Atlantic in 1872 having been hurriedly abandoned for no apparent reason.

Having reported to Mackenzie, Chapman and the commander had a brief consultation. 'We agreed that nothing would be gained by remaining any longer in the vicinity and trying again at some later date so Tantalus proceeded clear and set course to return to Fremantle,' wrote Mackenzie in his report. His decision was understandable. Since arriving in the vicinity of Merapas they had experienced much enemy activity in the air and on the water. It was not a healthy spot in which to loiter.

'It was a very bitter disappointment for Major Chapman, and a blow to us all,' continued Mackenzie. 'It is to be hoped that the delay in carrying out the operation was not the cause for the loss of this gallant party, but it is, unfortunately, very possible.'[119]

In the wardroom, Michael Tibbs removed the false nose rack.

HMS Tantalus reached Fremantle on 6 December, 51 days after her departure and having covered 11,600 miles, what Walter Chapman noted was an 'endurance record for British submarines'. It took a while for Chapman to recover his land legs; since 11 September he had been cooped up in submarines for all but five days. Within a week he submitted his report on what he titled the 'Attempted Pickup of *Rimau* Party'. He posited several theories as to what might have happened, but in his opinion the most likely explanation was: 'Lieut. [Walter] Carey★ was taken off the island by the enemy, his presence having been given away by the Malays, before the main party started arriving. The main party was then picked up individually as they arrived on the island. The enemy removed the stores at the same time as removing Lieut. Carey.'[120]

On 23 December Chapman attended a meeting in the presence of representatives from SOA and Naval Intelligence. His belief was stated and various other alternatives were then discussed. 'It was finally decided that the only point which could be definitely established upon the evidence available was that the *Rimau* Party, or part of it, had returned to Base A [Merapas] at some stage, and had departed either of their own volition, or in captivity,' stated the meeting's minutes. It was also agreed that another sortie should be sent to look for the missing men.

The other mystery was whether they had succeeded in raiding Singapore. Then on 1 January 1945 a memo passed between SOE and the War Office in London in which they referenced the Allied Land Forces SEA (South-East Asia)

★ Chapman did not know that Lyon had dropped three more men on Merapas after Chapman and the Porpoise had sailed for home.

An unidentified junk, photographed by Walter Chapman, from the deck of the Tantalus. (Author's Collection - Courtesy of Jeremy Chapman)

Weekly Intelligence Review No. 10. Excellent photographs taken over Singapore during the air raid of 5 November (for which Tantalus had been asked to look out for downed aircrew) showed 'no sign of any sunken shipping, [so] it can only be presumed that the operation was not successful'.[121]

But there was a footnote at the bottom of the memo, which stated: 'Since writing the above, telegram 214 has come from Melbourne which says in the final paragraph, "India report secret Royal Air Force information shows damage in area intended for [*Rimau*] strike so it may have taken place."'

CHAPTER 12
JUNGLE CHALLENGE

It was obvious as 1945 arrived that the Japanese were doomed to defeat in the Far East. It was also apparent, however, that they would cling tenaciously to every inch of land between Java and China.

In early February 1945 the Commander-in-Chief, Allied Forces South-West Pacific Area, General Douglas MacArthur, ordered his staff to begin planning the invasion of Borneo.

It was no easy task. The third-largest island in the world, covering approximately 287,000 square miles, Borneo has a hot, wet climate, the incubator of an unimaginable array of exotic creatures and flora. Towering peaks, like the 13,455-foot Mount Kinabalu, rise out of dense jungle.

A Christian missionary called Edwin H. Gomes had spent 17 years living among the people of Borneo at the turn of the 20th century, and subsequently turned his experience into a book. 'The Bornean jungles are immense tracts of country – covered by gigantic trees, in the midst of which are mountains clothed in evergreen foliage, their barren cliffs buried beneath a network of creepers and ferns,' he wrote. 'The striking features are the size of the enormous forest trees and the closeness of their growth, rather than their loveliness or brilliancy of colour. In the tropical forests few bright-coloured flowers relieve the monotony of dark green leaves and dark brown trunks.'

On the outbreak of war, Borneo was divided into five territories, four in the north administered by the British but the bulk of the island under the control of the Dutch East Indies. The colonial powers kept largely to the coastal towns; the only white people to set up home in the interior were missionaries like Gomes, who held the usual colonial attitudes towards local customs. 'These regions are still inhabited by half clad men and women, living quaint lives in their strange houses, observing weird ceremonies, and cherishing strange superstitions and curious customs, delighting in games and feasts, and repeating ancient legends of their gods and heroes,' he had written in 1911. 'But in a few years all these things will be forgotten; for in Borneo, as elsewhere, civilization is coming.'[122]

On 16 December 1941 the Japanese came to Borneo, invading the island for its oil. By 1944, Borneo provided the Japanese empire with 40 per cent of its fuel oil and more than a quarter of its crude and heavy oils. Borneo was therefore of strategic importance from the outset of the war in the Far East, but gathering intelligence presented a challenge because of the cultural, geographical and linguistic obstacles to be overcome. Then someone in SOE remembered Francis Chester, now a major, the man nicknamed 'Gort'.

Chester had joined the organization in 1942 and, at the request of Ivan Lyon, he was posted to Fraser Island in 1943 as part of Operation *Jaywick*. A few weeks before the *Krait* departed, Chester was pulled from the operation and instead of heading towards Singapore he was sent to North Borneo, leading Operation *Python*, the objectives of which were stated as:

To gather intelligence
To 'soften up' the native population
To prepare R.Vs and D.Zs and, if possible, to organise guerrillas.[123]

Chester was 44 but categorized as A1 in health. He stood 5 feet 11 inches and weighed nearly 14 stone and radiated power and vitality. Only the hair on his head had been diminished by Father Time. He was forceful but good-humoured, possessed of the unorthodoxy that characterized the officers in Z Special Unit.

Colonel Jack Finlay of SRD headquarters in Melbourne said that Chester could 'cut his way through close jungle quicker than almost any man alive', but when back in civilization he would rather hail a taxicab than walk 100 yards down the street.[124]

He had been selected to lead the operation codenamed *Python* because he had spent 20 years in the country as a rubber planter and was fluent in Malay and Dusun.

Among the five men Chester had led into Borneo was an Australian sergeant called Lawrence Cottee. 'Gort Chester was a very wild type, swore a lot,' recalled Cottee. 'He was keen to get back out here, to get back to Borneo.'[125]

Python had not been much of a success, as an SOE review compiled by Finlay explained. 'After he had been there some time he asked for 5,000lbs of stores, arms, medicines, etc, which he specified in a signal.' Chester received 7,000 pounds of supplies, most of which weren't the stores he had requested. 'He was therefore saddled with a number of useless things, as a consequence of which he had to cancel a prolonged tour of the West Coast that he had planned.'

A second supply drop by submarine was arranged, but two days before the submarine was scheduled to leave, SOA radioed Chester advising him of a new rendezvous. Chester replied that this new location, an island, was 'dangerous'. SOA retorted that 'unless he could appreciate the difficulties that S.O.A. H.Q. had, he would have to be relieved'. Chester's *Python I* party reluctantly fulfilled the rendezvous, but it was attacked by the Japanese and with some difficulty managed to withdraw without sustaining casualties.

Nonetheless, by the start of 1944 Chester, drawing on his pre-war contacts, had established a coast-watching and intelligence-gathering network that stretched from Jesselton on the west of North Boreno to Sandakan on the east coast. On 20 January a party of six Z Special Unit operatives, led by Major Bill Jinkins and codenamed *Python II*, arrived in a submarine off the eastern coast. Chester's party welcomed them, dined with the American submarine commander, and then gratefully unloaded their stores.

The next day *Python II* began its mission, which was to train and organize guerrilla bands in the north-east of Borneo. Immediately it ran into problems. Z Special Force had undergone extensive bush and survival training in Australia, but the Borneo jungle was like nothing it had ever experienced. The three sergeants of *Python II* had become disorientated on a reconnaissance and one, William Brandis, vanished. Sergeant Donald McKenzie and Lieutenant Alfred Rudwick, both of *Python II*, fell into enemy hands a few weeks later and were reunited with the incarcerated Brandis. The trio were charged with espionage, even though they were dressed in Australian Army jungle greens but, like all Z Special men inserting into Borneo, before departure they had removed rank and identification, and were issued with a silk map of their operating area, a small compass and a cyanide capsule. The three prisoners had their skulls fractured during interrogation and they were hanged on 30 December 1944.

On his return to Australia Chester made plain his anger with SOA. Their blasé attitude to resupply was symptomatic of desk wallahs who had no appreciation of – or interest in – the perilous nature of operating behind enemy lines in one of the most hostile terrains on earth. Chester told SOA he 'did not expect it to happen again'. Chester was put up for a Distinguished Service Order, but this award was rejected and he was instead appointed an Officer of the Order of the British Empire.

Chester was back in North Borneo on 3 March 1945, along with six other members of Z Special Unit, on a mission codenamed Operation *Agas*, the Malayan for sandfly. Landed by submarine between two Japanese outposts at Tegahang and Pura, just 3 miles apart, Chester's instructions were to a) obtain military intelligence for future operations, which was to be radioed to Australia, b) raise a local guerrilla force to harass the enemy and destroy his resources and c) organize the native population to deny the Japanese essential local food and labour.

Upon landing in North Borneo, Chester discovered that his last stay on the island had made an impression on the Japanese. Posters were plastered in settlements 'bearing his portrait and offering a reward of 15,000 dollars for him, dead or alive'. As a result, Chester encountered hostility among the coastal villages and he was forced, over the course of several nights, to travel 250 miles by canoe to reach a friendly contact. Once established inland, however, among mangrove and nipa, Chester and *Agas* became highly effective. They raised a 150-strong guerrilla force among the natives, and were credited with indirectly killing 600 Japanese by directed air strikes. For his leadership of *Agas* Chester was awarded a DSO.★

To complement Operation *Agas*, the Allies planned a simultaneous operation further south and west between Sarawak and Brunei, codenamed *Semut* (the Malayan word for 'ant'). The British had been deliberating about a guerrilla campaign in Borneo since late 1941 and the idea had been changed and amended ever since without ever coming to fruition. One of the contributors had been Tom Harrisson, a precocious, driven, headstrong and courageous man who had in his 33 years accomplished much and alienated many. His path had briefly crossed Ivan Lyon's at Harrow School, although being four years Lyon's senior it's unlikely Harrisson had encountered the younger pupil. Harrisson had

---

★ *Agas* and Operation *Semut* did not coordinate their guerrilla campaign because they were separated by a formidable terrain and a lack of rivers down which to travel.

RIGHT Lt-Colonel Francis Chester, second from left, with some of the guerrillas he recruited in Borneo, an island he knew well from before the war. (NAA 8295560)

BELOW Tom Harrisson was obnoxious and unpopular as an officer, but his knowledge of Borneo and its people proved crucial. (Getty Images Tunbridge / Stringer)

RIGHT Two unidentified members of Z Special Unit on Operation *Agas*, at their watch tower camp, near Tagahan. (NAA 8295566)

ABOVE Some of the Australians on Operation *Agas* schooling guerrillas in the art of irregular warfare. (NAA 8295588)

been 'dumped' at Harrow by his parents when they emigrated to Argentina, an abandonment that left him with a lifelong insecurity. In contrast Lyon was close to his parents and was motivated in life by a sense of adventure not a visceral need to prove himself as was the case with Harrisson.

While Lyon's schoolboy hobby was sailing, for Harrisson it was ornithology and at the age of 19 his first book was published: *Birds of the Harrow District 1925–1930*. From Harrow he went up to Cambridge, and on leaving university he went on expeditions to Lapland, Borneo and the New Hebrides, the fruit of which was another book, the anthropological *Savage Civilisation*. 'Placed in any part of the world, he would apparently have the capacity to discover something new,' said a contemporary of Harrisson, who didn't restrict his anthropology to distant lands. In 1937 he and two colleagues launched Mass-Observation, a social research organization that chronicled the lives of Britons from across the class spectrum.

In the middle of 1944 Harrisson was in London when he was summoned to 'one of those mysterious interviews in a half-lit hotel★ off the Embankment.'[126] Major Egerton Mott explained that what was required from Harrisson was his expertise; he had spent months in Sarawak in 1932, and was familiar with the natives, their language and customs. Few Westerners had his knowledge and that meant the 'intelligence map was blank'. So would he mind awfully returning to Borneo and 'help them fill in the blanks'?

Harrisson agreed, and 'within a few days I found myself going through a course of subversive training. Next thing I was being whirled across the world priority one, in a plane to Australia. There I met Carter and Sochon.'

Major Toby Carter was a 34-year-old New Zealander who had worked as a surveyor for an oil company in Borneo before the war and spoke the language. He was, in Harrisson's opinion, 'remarkably relaxed . . . tall, tough, but gentle to look at'.[127]

Bill Sochon was an Englishman with an unusual background, even by the standards of Z Special Unit. Born in London on Christmas Day 1904, Sochon had spent most of the 1930s in Sarawak as Assistant Superintendent of Police and Prisons. He fell ill with malaria in 1938 and returned to England to recuperate. When he had, Sochon became Governor of Rochester Prison, and in 1940 he was appointed Deputy Governor of Wormwood Scrubs in London. He joined the Kent Home Guard in 1940 and no doubt envisaged that would

★ The Victoria Hotel on Northumberland Avenue, where Bobby Ross was interviewed by Major Grey Egerton Mott of SOE in March 1944.

be the extent of his military service. But in 1943 SOE contacted Sochon, having realized that here was a man who, like Tom Harrisson, could help them fill in the 'blanks' in the Borneo map. He was sent on the same 'subversive' instruction course as Harrisson – the one instigated by Bill Stirling and Bryan Mayfield in 1940 – and he impressed his instructors. He may have been in his fortieth year with a lived-in face and a middle-aged moustache, but he had shown up some recruits 15 years his junior. In his youth he had been a keen sportsman – rugby, rowing and boxing – and age had not diminished his enjoyment of confrontation. 'A useful man to have around in a scrap,' was the assessment of Sochon's instructor. 'He showed some great interest in his work and produced very good results.'[128]

Then came the parachuting, which was more of a challenge to Sochon. He had subdued plenty of unruly inmates in his time, but jumping out of an aircraft was a more frightening proposition. '[Sochon] is a little too heavy for parachuting, and some nervousness was noted in him,' said the assessor. 'He was obviously very happy when the course had finished although he had done reasonably well in view of his age and weight.'

Sochon was commissioned a second lieutenant on 1 July 1944 and the following month, now promoted to captain, he flew from England to Melbourne. 'He is a good solid type and fairly tough,' remarked SOE.

For an anthropologist such as Harrisson, his arrival at Fraser Island was like a dog being thrown a bone. Here he was confronted with Z Special Unit, a disparate band of men of different ages, nationalities, classes and motivations. Observing them was a thrill for the eccentric Englishman. There were the officers, 'complete extroverts . . . the casual man without a visible concern on earth,' such as his compatriot John Martin, who had come to Z Special via service with SOE in Palestine and Greece. He and Harrisson had great fun 'chasing hospital nurses' at Maryborough, just up the Mary River from Fraser Island.[129]

There were also 'some advanced introvert Aussies', such as Sergeant Fred Sanderson of Charlestown, New South Wales. Born in 1910 in Thailand, one of 15 children, Sanderson spent ten years as a boarder at St Andrew's School in Singapore before heading to Sydney to attend an agricultural college. He was a man who spoke only when he had something of note to say.

Harrisson appreciated this type, even before they parachuted into Borneo. They were quiet, self-sufficient and dependable, solitary by nature but with the self-discipline to work as part of a small team as and when required. 'On the whole, there was a marked – and vitalising – difference between these chaps, the large part of whom did it for "fun", and the British,' said Harrisson, 'usually in

The commando school on Fraser Island (seen here in the 1980s), off the coast of Queensland, was opened in October 1943 under the command of Major Jock Campbell. (NAA 11930449)

charge because of previous knowledge, who had much less simple reasons, were often older, wiser and far more nervous.'[130]

Once the men had undergone the basic survival, close combat, folboat and demolitions training at Fraser Island, they were taken north to Cairns, to what John Martin remembered as 'the fringe of the real jungle of North Australia.' Their instructor introduced them to the witchety grub, plucking them from dead trees and making them eat them raw. 'They taste like bully beef,' he assured his ashen-faced students.[131]

He showed them what flora to eat and what to avoid. The giant taro was particularly nutritious in the jungle, its leaves and stems providing an abundance of vitamins and its peeled and boiled stems a rich source of carbohydrate. The roots reminded Martin of a huge parsnip, but the instructor warned them they were filled with acid and only prolonged boiling would make them safe to eat.

One day the instructor, a bushman before the war, led his pupils on a snake hunt. They soon got lucky. 'This huge snake, must have been seven or eight feet, went through the bush and he was at it like a shot,' recalled Martin. The instructor trapped the snake behind its head with his v-shaped prong fashioned from a broken branch. 'He released his prong and held it behind the head and then got hold of the snake's tail and lifted it up, and it twisted itself over his arms and he had complete control . . . all of a sudden he let go of the head and like a bull whip he went like that and broke the snake's head.' Back at camp the instructor threw the snake to Martin and told him to skin it. 'I said "How do I do that?" and he said "Have you ever taken off a lady's stocking?"' Martin nodded. '"It's just like that. Get your fingers behind the head, get hold of the skin and then pull it back. There will be a bit of resistance at first, but keep pulling and the whole thing comes off, just like a lady's stocking."' Skinned and chopped, the snake was thrown in a pot and boiled with some leaves to make what Martin remembered as a 'good stew'.★

The training at Fraser Island was arduous and instructive, but it was limited in scope, according to one officer, Captain Dave Kearney. 'The school was aimed solely at producing guerrillas,' he reflected. 'There was no mention made, as far as I can recall, of obtaining intelligence in any disciplined way. There was no training in Jap army organisation, weapons or methods.'[132]

★ In early June 1945 Martin led one of four small parties to Borneo on a mission codenamed *Platypus,* the object of which was to support the main invasion of North Borneo by gathering intelligence on the Japanese line of withdrawal and organizing local resistance.

CHAPTER 13

ALLIES AND HEADHUNTERS

Operation *Semut* was scheduled to launch in October or November 1944 with its operational area in the central Kalabit Plateau and the headwaters of the rivers Limbang and Trusan that flowed north into Brunei Bay. Its instructions were to gather intelligence ahead of the main Australian coastal landing. A preliminary plan of *Semut* was submitted to GHQ, AIF, in May 1944 and an outline plan followed in September; approval was not forthcoming because the operation was low on GHQ's list of priorities. When they did get round to authorizing *Semut* it was too late 'for a submarine insertion to be effected before the break of the North-East monsoon.'

Semut was revised. The operation, which would be under the overall command of Toby Carter, would deploy by parachute and concentrate its resources on the hinterland of Brunei Bay. So the Christmas period was spent parachute training at the Richmond Royal Australian Air Force Base.

It was March 1945 when the first of four *Semut* parties (*Semut I, II, III* and *IV*) were ordered into Borneo. By then Harrisson had not endeared himself to his Australian soldiers. Fred 'Sandy' Sanderson considered him a 'bastard' and he and Keith Barrie did not '"hit it off" from the beginning'. There were too many airs and graces to the Englishman.

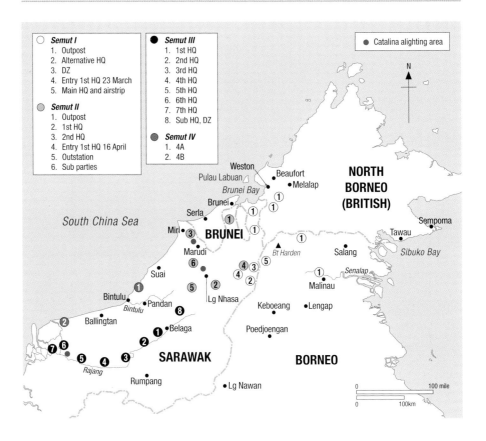

He made the mistake of believing his presence wasn't required for the 0600 PT session on Fraser Island, until Warrant Officer Peter Hill volubly disabused him of that idea. By the time the men were practising unarmed combat, Barrie had become 'disenchanted' with Harrisson's attitude. 'I remember with some satisfaction that during one of the sessions he and I became embroiled in combat in the sandpit and we both drew blood,' said Barrie.[133] The Australian didn't know it – in fact none of them did – but beneath Harrisson's obnoxious exterior lay a very perceptive man who had nothing but respect and admiration for their qualities. He called Barrie a 'short, chunkily-built piece of liquid dynamite'.

The men selected for the advance party were Harrisson, Captain Eric Edmeades, Warrant Officer Rod Cusack, and Sergeants Fred Sanderson, Douglas Bower, Keith Barrie, Kel Hallam and Jack Tredrea, remembered by Harrisson as 'a medical orderly and superb soldier'. Major Carter was not an enthusiast of parachuting, but recognized that it was the most effective means of inserting the party into its operational area. The drop zone was an upland valley about 90 miles south-east of Brunei, a location suggested by Dr Werner Schneeberger, a geologist for the Shell Company.

This photo of a longhouse, taken in Sarawak in 2001, depicts a building that has changed little from the one spotted by Fred Sanderson as he parachuted into Borneo over half a century earlier. (Getty Education Images/Contributor)

Twice the party attempted to insert but were thwarted by bad weather. It was third time lucky when they took off in two Liberators from San Jose Air Base on Mindoro Island in the Philippines on 25 March 1945. Harrisson was in the first Liberator with Cusack, Barrie and Hallam, a radio operator. 'We could see glimpses of the plain below through the cloud,' said Harrisson.★ Harrisson positioned himself on the slide, and behind him was Fred Sanderson. 'Are you all right, Sandy?' shouted Harrisson. 'Yes Tom,' replied the sergeant. The red light came on. Harrisson's eyes fixed on the colour. Green. He released his grip on the rails and shot out of the Liberator.

As Sanderson descended he took his bearings on a longhouse he could see to the west in a valley.

Harrisson had also seen the longhouse through the wisps of cloud. He spotted two red deer. The ground came up and he braced for the impact. 'Squelch! The plain proved to be a parachutist's dream, a nice wet, soft bog,' he said.

Sanderson dropped close to Harrisson and as soon as he was out of his harness he set off west to make contact with the people in the longhouse. They were Kelabits of the Dayak people,† one of the smaller ethnic groups in Borneo. The Christian missionary called Edwin H. Gomes had lived among them half a century earlier and wrote: 'They are cheerful, merry, and pleasure-loving. Fine

---

★ The Liberator that dropped Harrisson's party, flown by the renowned Squadron Leader Graham Pockley, never returned to its base and no trace of it was found.

† 'Dayak' is derived from the Malay for 'upland', and sometimes is spelt 'Dyak'. In Borneo the Dayaks encompassed the Lun Dayeh, Kelabits, Murat, Kayan, Penan and others. For the sake of clarity I refer throughout to 'Dayak'.

dress is a passion, and the love, in both men and women, for bright colours is very marked . . . they are truthful and honest, and are faithful to those who have been kind to them.'[134]

The Dayaks liked to sing and feast and play games, and hunt for heads, a tradition that the current White Rajah of Sarawak, Sir Charles Brooke, had endeavoured to extirpate. Gomes, like Harrisson, was sympathetic to the custom of headhunting. 'The Dayaks are faithful, hospitable, just, and honest to their friends,' he wrote. 'Being so, it naturally follows that they avenge any act of injustice or cruelty to them, and they are consequently bloodthirsty and revengeful against their enemies, and willing to undergo fatigue, hunger, want of sleep, and other privations when on the war-path.'[135]

Like Sioux warriors collecting scalps from their victims, young Dayaks took heads to prove their courage and, more often than not, to demonstrate to their sweethearts that they were worthy of their love. The head didn't have to belong to a warrior; it could be a woman's or a child's, just as long it came from the shoulders of an enemy tribe. To kill their prey, human or animal, the Dayaks used an 8-foot wooden blowpipe. To Westerners the craftsmanship of the blowpipe was remarkable. The 1-inch-wide bore was flawlessly smooth and straight, the hole drilled with a chisel-pointed iron rod through a hard wood log. The Dayak then pared the wood, which was different to the wood used for the darts. They were constructed from the slim splinters of the nibong palm and the poison on the tips was harvested from the epoh tree. 'Incisions are made in the tree, and the gutta which exudes is collected and cooked over a slow fire on a leaf until it assumes the consistency of soft wax,' recorded Gomes. 'It is a potent and deadly poison. Some Dayaks say that the most deadly poison is made of a mixture of the gum from the epoh tree and that from some creeper.'[136]

In the hands of a Dayak warrior, the blowpipe was accurate up to 25 yards, although it could still be effective (if inconsistent) for a further 25 yards. The tiniest nick of a dart was enough to kill a man. Harrisson estimated that overall *Semut* killed no more than 80 Japanese soldiers with the blowpipe but the demoralization it caused was disproportionate to the paltry casualty figures. 'The Japs could never cope with blow-pipes,' he remarked. 'The mere suspicion that there were blow-pipers around did more to them than a dozen machine guns. I don't know if we were breaking any of the rules of war. Frankly, we didn't care.' Harrisson had first seen the deadly and debilitating effect of the blowpipe during his 1932 expedition. It was an experience not to be forgotten. A pigeon struck by a dart dropped dead; a monkey took about 30 seconds to die; an enemy soldier fought the poison for around 20 minutes. Always in vain.

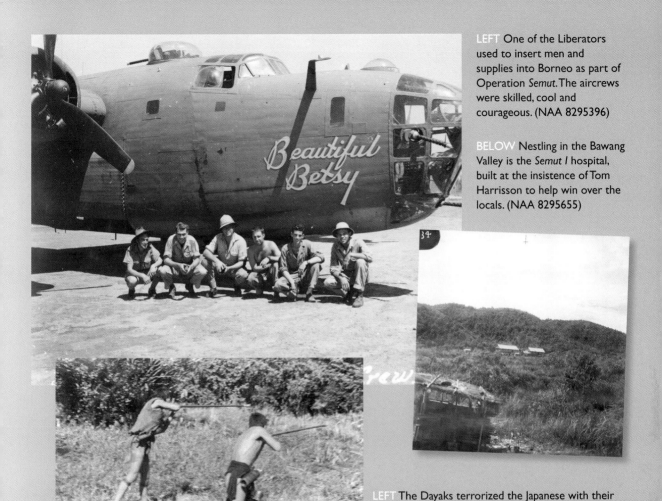

LEFT One of the Liberators used to insert men and supplies into Borneo as part of Operation *Semut*. The aircrews were skilled, cool and courageous. (NAA 8295396)

BELOW Nestling in the Bawang Valley is the *Semut I* hospital, built at the insistence of Tom Harrisson to help win over the locals. (NAA 8295655)

LEFT The Dayaks terrorized the Japanese with their eight-foot wooden blowpipe with darts constructed from splinters of the nibong palm, while the poison on the tips came from the Ipoh tree. (NAA 8295679)

LEFT Kenyah guerrillas engaged in weapons training under the watchful eye of members of *Semut II*. (NAA 8295694)

An Iban warrior armed with a rifle and his parang, a razor-sharp machete with which they hunted the heads of their enemies. (NAA 8295696)

There was, said Harrisson, a 'creeping combination of intoxication and paralysis, terrible to watch'.

Once the head had been hacked from the corpse with a parang, it was brought back to the village and smoked and preserved. The hair was used to decorate shields and the heads were displayed on a circular rack hung on the verandah. 'It's slightly depressing to gaze into the hollow eyes of an empty skull, dangling at face height as you come up the step ladder and bend to pass through the low door,' commented Harrisson.

Sanderson set off to the longhouse alone, unsure of what reception he would receive. No doubt Harrisson had told him what he had told the Royal Geographical Society in London 11 years earlier, during a lecture about his 1932 expedition to Sarawak with the Oxford University Exploration Club. 'The white man,' Harrisson explained to his audience, 'is expected to join in every sort of native activity; to drink with them; to join in all ceremonies and so on. The more native bangles and tattoo marks he has the better. If he can teach them to Charleston or do conjuring tricks he is bound to be a success.'[137]

The Dayak village to which Sanderson was headed was Bareo, and the chief, Lawai Bisarai, was already aware of the soldiers' arrival. He was partial to the British, a result of an incident in his youth, when he had a killed a rival. His punishment – handed down to avoid a tribal headhunting war – was a form of community service, a stint gardening for the British District Officer. Lawai Bisarai regarded the British as bizarre but benign, unlike the Japanese 37th Army which garrisoned Borneo. Its men had raped or killed most of the Christian missionaries they found on the island, and on their rare forays into Borneo's daunting interior they bullied and beat the villagers, slapping them in the face or striking them with their rattan sticks for no reason.

On reaching Bareo, Sanderson was introduced to Lawai Bisarai and in Malay he explained the background to his arrival. Lawai then relayed their conversation to the village elders and they discussed their next step. If they wanted a quiet life they could kill the soldiers, or alternatively they could befriend them and assist in any way they could in the fight against the hated Japanese. They chose the latter course, and Bisarai despatched three men to fetch Harrisson and the rest of his party, advising them to take a white cloth on the end of a bamboo stick as this was the white man's symbol of peace.

Harrisson had just rounded up the rest of his party when 'there appeared three tall dark figures, wearing loincloths and with leopard teeth in their ears, wading through the swamp and waving (of all things) a white flag. They were friendly. We judged this by interminable handshakes and caresses.'

The three Dayaks guided the seven soldiers out of the swamp and across an open grassland plain to the village of Bareo, where they were reunited with Sanderson. 'Bareo, like any Kelabit village, is simply one longhouse, built 15 feet off the ground on poles, with palm-leaf roof and beautiful hand-made plank walls and floors,' wrote Harrisson. 'It is divided lengthways down the middle. One half is the verandah. Bachelors and visitors sleep here. In the other half, each family lives around its own fireplace. There are no partitions between the families. Everything in Kelabit life is carried on in public.'[138]

That included going to the loo, which entailed both sexes parking their bottoms over the edge of the verandah and emptying their bowels into the pig pen below.

It was eye-opening for the Australians, but Harrisson had urged his men to respect the customs and not reject any hospitality. So they accepted the potent rice wine called borak and they ate the pork, even if, as Sanderson noted, it 'smelled like human excreta'. There were naturally some misunderstandings as the two cultures met for the first time. Unable to finish his bowl of borak, Sanderson offered it to the young woman sitting

ABOVE The *Semut* party constructed a bamboo air strip at Belawit with the help of native labour and the 'H' in this photo is the drop zone for their resupply by parachute. (Author's Collection)

ABOVE LEFT Rifles packed and ready for insertion into Borneo inside a Storepedo. The Dayaks were enthusiastic marksmen and a valuable addition to *Semut*'s guerrilla campaign. (NAA 8295312)

Beneath the parachute silk is an aid station where Semut medics are treating the natives' various ailments, an effective way of winning their 'hearts and minds.' (NAA 8295691)

next to him at the feast. She gave a girlish simper while the men roared with laughter: it was explained to Sanderson that if a Dayak man offers his borak to a woman it is an invitation to retire to the bedroom together.

As the borak flowed so the singing began. The villagers first and then, as was the custom, they expected their visitors to respond in kind. Harrisson and the Australians didn't have a great repertoire, but they eventually settled on one, which they boomed out with gusto: 'Fuck 'em all, fuck 'em all, the long and the short and the tall'. 'All the pre-embarkation briefing about security went out the window,' reflected Barrie, who was as drunk as his mates and his hosts. 'The sounds of ribald celebration [were] reverberating down the valley.'[139]

Lawai Bisarai had sent runners to all the surrounding villagers summoning the people to Bareo to meet the white men who were the first of many who would drive out the Japanese. 'Village headmen came all the way to pledge their loyalty and give us personal support in the event of our attacking the Japanese,' said Sanderson.[140]

Also brought to the village were *Semut I*'s supplies, which had been dropped by parachute in cylindrical containers called 'storepedos'. These were an invention credited to G. W. Griffiths of the Ordnance Production Directorate, who solved the problem of supplies being smashed on impact by stashing them in absorbent heavy-gauge wire netting containers.

Among *Semut*'s supplies were Jack Tredrea's medical kit. On 26 March he opened his surgery in Bareo. '[I] let it be known that I would treat anyone who needed medical attention,' he said. His first patient was an old man suffering from a large boil in his groin. Tredrea had no idea what it was. But he lanced it anyway, and out oozed a gallon of pus. He cleansed the wound with sulpha powder and hoped for the best. The old man's relief was immediate and word spread of Tredrea's healing properties. His surgery was soon packed, a waiting room of men and women, young and old, suffering from malaria, dysentery, diarrhoea and other unfortunate afflictions.

The Dayaks' loyalty was now unbreakable. These eight white men who came from the sky were good men; it was the duty of the Dayaks to help them kill the bad men who didn't heal but hurt them.

Harrisson saw how Tredrea's medical bag could win the hearts and minds of the whole region, so he instructed him to take it on tour, his kerosene tins of supplies, carried by eager Dayaks. At the same time, he was to gather intelligence on Japanese movements.

A Storepedo is carried towards the *Semut II* HQ at Long Akah. These cylindrical containers, fitted with absorbent heavy-gauge wire netting, solved the problem of supplies smashing on impact. (NAA 8295692)

Captain Eric Edmeades, a New Zealander whose parents were missionaries, and Keith Barrie departed from Bareo two days after their arrival, heading west up the Tamu Abu mountain range. His instructions were to recruit villagers to a guerrilla army ready to rise up when the Australian 9th Division invaded Brunei, and also collect intelligence about the enemy. Furthermore, they were to establish an HQ for the arrival of the *Semut II* party, led by Major Toby Carter, scheduled to arrive in the middle of April.

Sergeants Bower and Hallam set up a radio station with their radio transmitter/receiver and established regular night and day schedules with Darwin. Ron Cusack distributed stores and oversaw administration.

All members of *Semut*, 'Ants' as Harrisson called them, were encouraged – or ordered – to 'go native' as far as possible, including learning the basics of the language, and walking barefoot near or in villages so as not to leave tell-tale bootprints. He was reluctant to distribute rations, believing this made the men lazy; they should eat what the Dayaks did. They should look and learn. This caused considerable resentment, as did Harrisson's overbearing manner in general. What the young Australians didn't understand was that beneath his brusque arrogance was an insecure man, starved of affection during his youth, who was desperate to prove himself tougher than any Australian. But he was also challenging the Australians to push themselves physically, mentally and intellectually beyond the limits set by western civilization. He had hand-picked the advance party and he believed in the strength of the men he had with him; he wanted them to believe it, too.

There were tasks undertaken by *Semut I* other than intelligence gathering and guerrilla training. An American B-24 bomber had been shot down over Borneo four months earlier and its crew had been sheltering with the Dayaks ever since. Although brave and resourceful, the airmen were ill-equipped mentally and materially for such an experience, and were desperate to be rescued. Harrisson took them in hand and arranged for their air-evacuation in June.

Sanderson was often detailed to arrest natives who were working for, or collaborating with, the Japanese. It was not a task he relished. Nor did he see the sense in it, particularly when his instructions were to shoot the suspect. Sanderson refused, telling Harrisson it wasn't 'wise to start killing locals at this stage as the people might start to fear us and then turn on us and we wouldn't stand a chance'. Harrisson harrumphed, his way of acknowledging that Sanderson had a point.

Among the hundreds of Dayaks who flocked to Bareo the ones considered by Harrisson the most reliable were recruited to an espionage network, whose

reach was far and wide. The Dayaks moved swiftly and easily through jungle and over mountain ranges, gathering intelligence about the Japanese and relaying it to Harrisson through a system of runners. Nevertheless, it still took about five or six days from the east and west coasts to reach Bareo.

The Dayaks not working for Harrisson's intelligence agency were eager to attack the Japanese, but *Semut*'s instructions from Colonel Roger 'Jumbo' Courtney, Commander of Group A at Moratai, in effect the middleman between *Semut* and the 9th Australian Division, were not to commence open fighting until the invasion was underway.

By the start of April Sanderson had been sent north-west by Harrisson to the upper reaches of the Limbang, which was within reach by river of Brunei Town. It was a sign of how far word had spread of their arrival that the chief of this region, Penghulu Badak, wanted to join the great uprising against the Japanese. Sanderson undertook a circuitous route to the Limbang, first heading east through the Bawang, where he made contact with their chief, Lasong Piri, another new ally. In all, Harrisson estimated that 'something like 100,000 people had voluntarily become involved in following, to some extent, *Semut*'.[141]

The Z Special Unit men on *Semut* used the rivers of Borneo – like the Baram, seen here – to transport supplies and also to ambush the Japanese. (Author's Collection)

155

CHAPTER 14
GUERRILLA ARMY

On 16 April the next *Semut* mission unfurled over Borneo with the arrival of Major Dan Carter and *Semut II* and a quantity of storepedos, in all eight men and 24 containers. Also floating to earth was the unmistakeable figure of Major Bill Sochon. 'As he descended upon the plain, the panels of his 'chute began to peel off one by one,' recalled Harrisson, who marvelled at Sochon's extensive vocabulary as the earth rushed up. 'If he had not landed in the swamps not far from the bogs we had earlier plumped, he must have been crushed into Pentonville pulp!'

Sochon and all the men had 50-pound packs on their backs, and were wearing boiler suits with the legs and sleeves cut off. They looked an odd sight, but Harrisson was pleased to see them. Sochon didn't stay long. On 17 April he, Warrant Officer Don Horsnell and Sergeant Abu bin Kassim set off on a weary hike to Long Lelang to rendezvous with Keith Barrie. Toby Carter and his small team followed a day later, and by 24 April they were reunited. Carter and his *Semut II* party remained at Long Akah by the Baram River, approximately 100 miles due south of Bandar Seri Begawan, the capital of Brunei. Sochon, Barrie and bin Kassim established themselves farther south on the Rajang River. Carter and his men had spent months learning the art of stealth at Fraser Island, but they came to naught on their journey from the drop zone to Long

Akah. 'News of the white man's return spread like wildfire of course and our journey down the Akah was like a triumphal procession,' he said. 'The women at the villages [were] weeping for joy and the men roaring their stirring boat songs as we shot through the beautiful and sometimes dangerous rapids.' The men travelled in praus, native canoes hollowed from tree trunks.

On arriving at each village there was the customary feast. Pigs were killed and their livers scrutinized to check the omens were favourable. Then the borak appeared. Carter was shocked by the appearance of the natives. 'Most were wearing bark for clothing, malaria was rife and skin disease was bad,' he recalled. The medical orderly did what he could for the worst afflicted and Carter ordered their parachute silks to be cut up and distributed for clothing. Carter had known the regional chief before the war during his days as a Shell corporation surveyor; the reunion was heartfelt.

What the men of *Semut* were putting into practice was the culmination of the Special Training School at Lochailort five years earlier. The seeds of that school had been watered ever since by the likes of Freddie Spencer Chapman, Mike Calvert, Bill Stirling and Jim Gavin, and they had then cultivated the fruit according to the climate in which they found themselves. Mike Calvert had with Orde Wingate raised the Chindits, and their training had been as much psychological as practical. 'Most Europeans do not know what their bodies can stand, and it is the mind and willpower which so often gives way first,' said Calvert. 'One advantage of exceptionally hard training is that it proves to a man what he

The members of *Semut* relied on the skill of the locals to navigate them down rivers that were unpredictable and home to crocodiles. (NAA 8295663)

can do and suffer.'[142] Calvert's friend, Spencer Chapman, believed that the key to jungle warfare was that 'you must always hold the initiative and keep fear at bay . . . a man masters himself by mastering hazards from which there is no escape.'[143]

Tom Harrisson, Toby Carter and Bill Sochon had 'acclimatized' psychologically to Borneo in the 1930s; Keith Barrie was experiencing the jungle for the first time and it was an environment in which he felt comfortable. 'In a curious sort of way I loved the isolation of the jungle – the great dark forests interspersed with occasional shafts of sunlight fracturing the gloom, a tangle of undergrowth away from the beaten tracks,' he reflected. 'I was very much at home . . . unlike so many other less fortunate city oriented people who found the whole atmosphere intimidating.'[144]

By the time Sochon and *Semut III* were established at Belaga it was mid-May. They were approximately 300 miles south-west of Tom Harrisson and *Semut I*'s operational zone.

There were problems with resupplies and communications, forcing Sochon to move even further downstream (south). That meant encroaching on Iban territory. The Ibans had the most fearsome reputation of all Dayaks; they were Sea Dayaks as opposed to the Land Dayaks with whom Harrisson was lodging. They hated the Japanese more than their brethren in the interior because, as they lived near the coast, they had experienced their brutality more frequently; but they were initially sceptical that so few white men could bring anything other than trouble. Sochon had what Barrie described as a 'pow-wow' with the Iban and convinced them that soon many white men would land by boat and drive the Japanese out. There would be the chance to harvest many heads.

On 10 June the Australian 9th Division assault on North Borneo began with an amphibious landing at Brunei Bay and Labuan Island. Now the *Semut* parties and their Dayak allies could launch their guerrilla campaign. On 18 June a group of Dayaks arrived at *Semut III*'s camp, grinning from ear to ear and brandishing several Japanese heads. Barrie recoiled at the sight. The Dayaks had already hollowed out the heads as if they were pumpkins at Halloween. 'There was of course great excitement among all the Dayaks for it was many years since they had enjoyed such a windfall of heads,' said Barrie.[145] There was a feast that night to celebrate, the centrepiece of which was the ceremonial feeding the heads, in which the women chanted while feeding rice to the mouths of the victims. Barrie found it spine-chilling but fascinating. The ceremony over, they tucked into the plentiful food while the women smoked the heads over a low fire to drain off the fat.

Two officers and a sergeant arrived three weeks later in late June and six more Z Special Unit men arrived to reinforce *Semut III*, inserted by a Catalina flying boat that landed on the Rejang, the principal river in the Rejang watershed. Among their number was Corporal Ross Bradbury. He was part of a patrol under Captain Dave Kearney sent south to reconnoitre Kapit, where Sochon was considering establishing a new HQ. They travelled down the river by prau, portaging when they came to the rapids. They saw numerous crocodiles, most lying on the grassy mud banks of the Rajang.

From Kapit, Kearney and his patrol continued to Kanowit and from there to a place called Kidd's Estate. 'We captured this fellow after a fire fight in which a few Japanese were killed,' recalled Bradbury. 'We got a prau and with this Japanese officer paddled up river. But about halfway up the river he jumped overboard, committed hari kari . . . because once you're in the Rajang River it's full of crocodiles and flows around three or four knots.'[146]

Returning north, Kearney's men, which included some Ibans, mounted an ambush on a Japanese launch that patrolled the river. 'They could only travel on one side of the Rajang River because you couldn't travel up the middle of the River because of a tide,' remembered Bradbury. 'We dug a weapon pit and put a heavy machine gun, a mortar and small firearms. I'm waiting for the launch to come. We had some Ibans with us and they thought it was wonderful after being persecuted by the Japanese for four years. Soon enough we heard the launch coming. We were on the downside of Kanowit . . . [and] as the launch came abreast of us we opened fire. We sent up a flare and there was an awful lot of firing.'

In his diary Sochon noted that the result of the attack on the launch was '40 killed out of 60'. Keith Barrie and Ron Baker, with the help of some Dayaks, also ambushed a launch on its way to Kabit. 'During the firing I decided to hurl a grenade or two,' said Barrie. 'I couldn't get the pin out so I applied my teeth to it.' But Barrie had forgotten that he'd had his upper teeth removed prior to dropping into Borneo and replaced with dentures. 'Result: not the grenade pin but a tooth came out.'[147] Eventually Barrie managed to yank out the pin and throw the grenade at the launch.

By the end of July *Semut III* and their Iban allies had captured a series of small towns. Sochon recorded in his diary: 'To date approximately 20,000 square miles liberated by *Semut III*. Japs killed to date – 120. Launch[es] attacked: 32.'

To the north-east of Bill Sochon and *Semut III* was Major Toby Carter and *Semut II*. The natives who joined their guerrilla army weren't Ibans but Kenyahs

RIGHT Toby Carter, seen here with the Kelabit headman, was a greatly respected soldier and leader of *Semut II*. (NAA 8295674)

FAR RIGHT Major Carter, left, and Major Sochon welcoming prominent natives to their operational area in the final weeks of the war. (NAA 8295673)

ABOVE A group of Services Reconnaissance Department signallers pose at Labaun. Stan Eadie is fourth from left in the back row. (Author's Collection)

under the leadership of chief Tama Weng Ajang, the dominant leader in the Baram watershed. Carter was in overall command of the three *Semut* operations (a fourth small party, *IV*, was inserted into Borneo in July) but Harrisson was a recalcitrant subordinate, refusing to let Carter have the only working radio. There had been communications problems from the start; Doug Bower, the wireless operator who had dropped with Harrisson on 25 March was not skilled at his craft and none of his messages had been transmitted clearly to Toby Carter, who was waiting to parachute in with *Semut II*. Carter and his men had jumped into Borneo unsure whether they would be greeted by *Semut I* or the Japanese as they feared the wireless had fallen into the hands of the Japanese. 'In sending message you must be accurate,' recalled Bob Long, the signaller who inserted with Toby Carter. 'If you subtract by one digit it can make a big difference to the message.' On learning from Harrisson the reason for the communications problems, Carter took Long aside. 'Carter asked if I could stay behind with the advance party and see if I could sort out their radio problems, I agreed', he said.

'Two local fellows guided me up the side of a leech-infested mountain to a tiny shelter where the radio was and there was a jungle hammock to sleep in. I sent a message that night and then waited to see what happened.'[148]

The message was received and it was decided that Long should remain with Harrisson at *Semut I*, assisted by two Dayaks who wound the hand generator while the Australian keyed the traffic and received. 'We had a very friendly and wonderful interaction,' said Long of his assistants. 'We were dependent on them for food and we grew accustomed to boiled rice three times a day.'

Harrisson kept Long busy with regular messages asking for drops of arms and ammunitions with which to supply the growing native guerrilla force, as well as more medicine to treat the afflictions of the Dayaks. There was also intelligence to send back, gleaned from Harrisson's network of spies that branched out across North Borneo.

The fact that Harrisson had purloined Bob Long left Toby Carter short of a proficient signaller. His solution was to have Long send a message to Moratai requesting the presence of Lieutenant Stan Eadie. A 28-year-old Scot from Coupar Angus, Eadie's love of radio communications had started at an early age; his father worked for the post office as a telegraphist and his job was also his hobby. He was one of the first people in Britain to build a radio receiving set and his son inherited his passion. Eadie had joined the Royal Signals in January 1940, and in February 1944 he received his commission with his Officer Cadet Training Unit (OCTU) chief instructor concluding that 'this cadet is above

RIGHT The signal hut at Long Akah, HQ of *Semut II*, and where Lt. Stan Eadie was despatched to fix the communication problems. (NAA 8295685)

BELOW This photo was taken from an aircraft on 30 May 1945 and shows reinforcements parachuting into Long Akah. (Author's Collection)

average in all respects . . . he will make a keen and energetic officer'. A short while later Eadie was sent to Australia to train special operations' signallers prior to their insertion behind enemy lines.

It was all a bit of a rush for Eadie, who packed his wireless set along with a 9mm pistol, 50 rounds of ammunition and an American jungle knife. Eadie had never jumped before; he had not even undergone any basic parachute training. There were no spare jump overalls so he wore an outsized pair of Australian army shorts. Sergeant Leo Duffus offered to accompany him as a morale prop, an offer that was gratefully accepted by Eadie.

As they approached the Drop Zone at Long Akah, the despatcher aboard the Liberator signalled for Eadie to prepare to jump. 'They opened a trap door and out came a kiddies' slide,' remembered Eadie. 'You put a foot either side and when the light came on you slid out.'[149]

What no one had mentioned to Eadie was the buffet he would receive as he shot out of the slide. 'This gust at 130 miles an hour hitting you straight in the face . . . I didn't know what happened for the first few seconds,' he said. A little dazed and confused, and frightened, Eadie then felt the jolt as the parachute opened. Joy surged through his body. 'It was a wonderful drop, I couldn't imagine anything more wonderful . . . ranges of hills covered in forests, tropical forest, gorgeous, the whole view.'[150]

Eadie had no idea how to steer a parachute but somehow he managed to avoid landing in a river and instead came through trees and found himself suspended 6 feet above the ground. 'I wriggled out of my parachute harness and landed on the ground, no fuss at all,' he said. 'I suddenly heard people not far away cutting their way through the undergrowth . . . and there were four of the locals in loin cloth each with a parang, looking at me, yapping away and I had no idea what they were saying . . . two of them came forward and they each took one of my arms and gently led me away and took me to canoes, and we paddled across the river to a landing stage.'[151]

Waiting for Eadie and Duffus on the far bank was Toby Carter. Eadie set to work at once, examining the wireless in the hut that had been constructed just inside the forest, the aerial hidden among the trees. Eadie soon deduced that the radio had been incorrectly wired in Australia. Using his soldering iron that had been dropped in a storepedo as part of his tool kit Eadie soon had the radio working.

That was in effect Eadie's job done, but Carter asked him if he would like to remain with *Semut II* indefinitely. Eadie agreed. He had a lot of time for the New Zealander, whom he considered a gentleman. 'He would listen to anybody and anything that was being said.' He knew the importance of winning the natives' hearts and minds, and he made no secret of the fact that he was motivated not just by a desire to defeat the Japanese but also to ensure the foundations were laid for a strong post-war reconstruction in Borneo. Above all he was not profligate with the lives of the men under his command. 'We could see no point in going and killing half a dozen Japanese for no reason and putting your own life at risk,' reflected Eadie. 'We were there to get information about the right things, and get the local people on our side to support us.'

His opinion of Tom Harrisson was less favourable. 'We [*Semut II*] would not have anything to do with him,' said Eadie. 'Neither would Bill Sochon.' Harrisson visited both

Lieutenant Stan Eadie was a skilled wireless operator who was dropped into *Semut* to fix communication problems. (Author's Collection)

Semut II's and *Semut III*'s operational HQ with a view to joining forces in one big guerrilla campaign but, according to Eadie, both Sochon and Carter rejected the idea. 'He was a showman and that's all it was about,' said Eadie. 'As far as Tom was concerned he had to be the big man, and he kept moving people about. It was pathetic that's all that one can say about it.'[152]

Harrisson was not the only maverick officer making life difficult for Carter. At the end of June Major Robert Wilson and three sergeants arrived to reinforce *Semut II*. Wilson was 46, and had packed much excitement and achievement into those years. A veteran of the Great War, he subsequently qualified as a surgeon and achieved fame in 1934 by taking a photograph of what appeared to be a monster in Loch Ness. The picture was splashed across newspapers around the world.★

Not long after the outbreak of World War II, Wilson – who was also an expert on ballistics – joined SOE and he had been awarded the *Croix de Guerre* for his activities in occupied France in 1944. Wilson and his three sergeants arrived with a specific purpose. 'The powers-that-be had decided that the party I was with were not killing enough Japanese,' said Eadie. 'They had been sent in and they were going to be killing everybody left, right and centre as far as I could make out because Toby Carter was not going to do it ... but they started killing the wrong people so Toby Carter had to get them back, and [he] insisted on them staying with us and doing what he said.'[153]

It was an ill-judged decision by HQ to despatch Wilson's party. Jumbo Courtney from Group A had flown in once by seaplane to liaise with his officers, but a brief visit was no way to appreciate the challenges and pressures faced on the ground, or to understand the carefully cultivated relationship between *Semut* and the natives. Ultimately, Courtney's crass interference endangered Toby Carter and his men.

Wilson had stirred up the Japanese and they now wanted to flush out the guerrillas in their midst. 'We got word of them [via *Semut*'s network of informers] going to do this advance so we thought we would ambush them on the way up, but we hadn't enough people to do very much', said Eadie.

In previous patrols upriver the Japanese had travelled in one big launch flanked by two smaller ones. On this occasion the big launch – containing about 100 soldiers, in Eadie's estimation – was at the back of the convoy. *Semut II* opened up on the first two vessels, but the weight of fire from the big launch

★ It was not until 1994 that what became known as the Surgeon's photo was conclusively proved to be a fake, with the 'monster' constructed from a toy submarine with a neck and head made from plastic wood.

LOOKING FOR DZ ON MORNING OF
16 APRIL 45 UNDER BAD CONDITIONS.
INITIAL ENTRY SEMUT II

This photo was taken on the morning of 16 April 1945 as the crew of a Liberator searched for the *Semut II* DZ in order to despatch some supplies. (NAA 8295711)

persuaded Carter to pull back, leaving two of his NCOs to cover their withdrawal and join them at the canoes further upstream. Carter's men had just reached the canoes when they heard several bursts of machine-gun fire. A couple of minutes later the two soldiers sprinted into view. They had ambushed a group of Japanese who had waded ashore and were in pursuit of their ambushers. 'Just as we were going to get in there was a yell from further up,' said Eadie. A group of natives hurried towards them, carrying two emaciated figures. They were Indian Sikhs, who had escaped from Sarawak internment camp and been sheltered by villagers nearby. 'They were so weak they could not walk,' said Eadie. 'Toby Carter took one in his canoe and I took one in my canoe. They were just absolutely exhausted and we laid them down and took off and went up river.'[154]

CHAPTER 15
VICTORY IN BORNEO

Somewhere in the wilds of Borneo between the north-easterly edges of *Semut II* and the south-westerly edges of *Semut I* was Fred Sanderson. He had arrived in early June with Phil Henry, who had inserted with *Semut III*, and a consignment of weapons, including 15 American carbines, six Owen sub-machine guns, one .303 rifle, one Bren gun and two Stens, plus 1,800 rounds of ammunition.

His orders were to 'stir up the Ibans against the enemy' commencing on 5 June, five days before the Australian invasion began. Harrisson's orders were to desist from open fighting, but Sanderson was happy to undermine his officer by using his discretion.

On the evening of the 4th Sanderson reached the village of Rumah Kadu, on the Limbang River, where they were briefed by the headman, Penghulu Kadu. There were four Japanese outposts, lightly manned, none more distant than a two-hour trek. Sanderson wanted them all destroyed, but Kadu expressed his reluctance after he had seen the size of the Australian arsenal. 'Not enough arms or ammunition,' he told Sanderson. 'We will be taking a risk with the lives of our women and children, and our longhouses will be burnt down also if we are unable to defend ourselves from the angry Japanese.'[155] Sanderson promised the chief that a great many Australians would arrive in North Borneo on

10 June. The rest of the evening was spent planning the attack, and in the early hours the guerrillas moved into position.

The furthest target was at Rumah Brandah, a two-hour trek, where five Japanese soldiers were stationed. Shortly after sunrise on 5 June two Iban warriors, Laga and Insom, approached the outpost requesting some quinine to treat their malaria. Two Japanese soldiers appeared with the medicine. Neither was armed, neither expected trouble. With two swift strikes, the parangs of the Iban sliced off the Japanese heads. Their terrified comrades ran screaming into the jungle. The parang, remarked Sanderson, was as sharp as a razor, 'the blade shaped so that the extreme end of the weapon is heaviest, a devastating sword in the hands of an expert'.

Sanderson launched his attack by shooting dead a Japanese soldier, who was in charge of a labour party of over 70 Malay and Javanese coolies. 'The Ibans were now excited,' recorded Sanderson. 'All were dressed in their colourful padded war coats and head gear. One chap had an orang-utan on his head while another wore a rusty old fowl feathered pisspot.'[156]

With so few guns to distribute among the Iban, most warriors were armed with either their blowpipes or parangs, much to their disappointment. Stan Eadie had discovered that frightening as the blowpipe was to the Japanese, it was a banal weapon to the warriors. 'To the locals the blow pipe did not make a loud bang and that noise is important,' said Eadie. On one patrol conducted by *Semut II*, a native had discharged his rifle into the air when he saw the Japanese several hundred yards away. 'When asked why he had done this,' recalled Eadie, 'he said that by firing he expected the Japanese to run away and then there would be no fighting and no one would be hurt.'[157]

After Sanderson and his guerrillas had overrun the outpost, they paddled downriver to Rumah Guni, where the Iban had captured four Japanese soldiers. 'They were taken across the river and shot,' said Sanderson. 'The Ibans then took the four heads before they had stopped kicking. The blood squirted into the river and changed the colour of the water.'

The bodies were left for the animals and the heads brandished as trophies. Sanderson stayed the night at Rumah Guni and departed at dawn for Ukong police station, 24 miles from Brunei. Its floor was slippery with the blood of the three slain soldiers. Sanderson remained at Ukong for several days where there was an abundant supply of rice, salt and brown sugar. On the afternoon of 9 June a runner arrived at Ukong to warn Sanderson that 20 Japanese were approaching the neighbouring settlement. 'Give the Japanese food and plenty of borak and get them drunk,' was the message Sanderson gave to the runner. 'When they are helpless we will be there to help you tie them up.'[158]

RIGHT A Z Special Unit signalman takes down a message from the *Semut* operatives in Borneo at the Leanyer station using a Marconi CR100 receiver. (Author's Collection)

D.Z.

SEMUT II FIRST HQ. LONG AKAH

BARAM RIVER

AKAH RIVER

7 JUNE 1205. 8" 1000' W .200 FT 1-2

ABOVE This aerial photograph pinpoints the location of Toby Carter's *Semut II* HQ, and also illustrates how vital control of the rivers was in Borneo. (NAA 8295713)

LEFT The Leanyer receiving station was situated 'in scrub country' 12 miles from Darwin in northern Australia. The transmitter station was also in Darwin, at Cemetery Plains, 11 miles from the receiving station. (Author's Collection)

The Iban were generous in their hospitality to the 20 enemy soldiers and after a gutful of borak they began boasting that 'one Japanese soldier is equal to two American'. When Sanderson arrived, however, he was greeted with carnage: 20 headless Japanese. He was unnerved and upset, and demanded to know why they hadn't been held captive. The Iban replied that the borak had gone to their enemy's heads, and they had started to grope and molest the women and girls. They got what they deserved, they told Sanderson.

The next day the Australian invasion force landed at Brunei, and eight days later an AIF barge arrived at Ukong carrying an infantry platoon. It was the start of a tense relationship between Z Special Unit and the Australian 9th Infantry Division. On 20 June Sanderson attended a conference in Brunei and was informed that their 'information was unreliable'. Tom Harrisson, who had a high regard for Sanderson, even if he concealed it well, was not impressed. 'Sanderson's information has always been reliable but is obviously not appreciated by 9th Division,' he commented.[159]

Semut II also experienced the disdain of the 9th Division. 'We offered to supply the army with scouts for any of their movements but they declined, possibly not trusting us enough,' said Stan Eadie. 'As a result they suffered casualties in ambushes.'[160]

The 9th Division's cold attitude to Z Special Unit was misguided, particularly as their orders from the Australian government were to occupy the major towns and the coastal areas with oilfields. It was feared that incursions into Borneo's interior would result in heavy casualties; as it was, this area was increasingly controlled by *Semut*'s ever-expanding guerrilla army, who, with the assistance of the RAAF, were harassing the Japanese as they withdrew from the coast. 'Group A treated Harrisson as an uncontrollable force to be supported through thick and thin as far as relations with 9th Division were concerned,' remarked Jumbo Courtney. 'Relations between Group A and 9th Division were distant until physical contact started between SRD operatives [Z Special Unit] on the ground and forward parties of 9th Division. Thereafter there was friction owing to differences between guerrilla and regular behaviour, and the basic type of tactical intelligence provided by the former.'[161]

There may also have been a touch of Anglophilia on the part of Headquarters 9th Division. Major Jumbo Courtney was British as were Harrisson and Sochon. 'To me what was important was not the nationality but the quality of the man for leadership roles,' remarked Lieutenant-Colonel John Holland, an Australian, and a senior officer at SRD in Melbourne. 'Some Australians adopted the childish attitude of "anything the Brits can do, we can do better."' Nonetheless,

OPPOSITE Members of
Semut I participating in a
march-past in Borneo to
mark the end of the war.
(NAA 8295659)

Holland believed that it was a mistake not to appoint an Australian to Courtney's role, simply because it would have eliminated the possibility of any Anglo-Australian antagonism in their dealings with the 9th Division: 'I consider that for political reasons, better all-round relationships, and hence performance in the field for all of SRD operations, would have been achieved if from the very early days the commander had been a senior Australian officer with a reputation for leadership.'[162]

Matters came to a head on 22 June when the 9th Division asked Sanderson to be transferred from his operational area because of his 'unreliable' information. On 2 July he was asked to return because the 9th Division was desperate for intelligence about a force of 450 Japanese reportedly moving in the direction of the Lambang River. 'Orders from Harrisson were to kill as many as possible using any method,' said Sanderson. 'There was much rivalry between *Semut I* and *Semut II*; this was the reason Harrisson wanted the Japs herded into his area.' *Semut II* on the other hand urged Sanderson and his native guerrilla force to hit them in their rear, so they would 'recoil like a snake and return westward' into their territory.[163] The 9th Division's instructions were for Sanderson to drive them towards the coast so they would surrender.

When Sanderson arrived back at Ukong he was told by the Ibans that Phil Henry had been arrested by the 9th Division. His first offence was a failure to show an infantry officer sufficient respect when he led his platoon into Ukong. The Ibans, for their part, bristled at the disrespect shown to the man they called 'Tuan Phil'. They took out their anger on a native collaborator captured that morning, hacking off his head and leaving the corpse by the platoon truck. The officer 'nearly fainted' on returning to the truck and, outraged, he had Henry placed under close arrest.

For the rest of July Sanderson and his Iban army hunted the 450 Japanese. On 26 July he recorded that 'Japanese stragglers were appearing in twos and threes but no sign of the main party'. Two days later a scout arrived and told Sanderson a large force of the enemy was moving down the stream Sungei Madalam; three of his Ibans volunteered to approach the Japanese and call on them to surrender. Only one returned. The next day Sanderson and 120 Ibans paddled upriver in search of their prey. Early the next morning, 30 July, they were moving slowly along the river in their praus when one of the Iban scouts spotted a Japanese sentry. The man fired and Sanderson and his Ibans paddled to the left bank, scrambling out of the canoes and seeking cover among some thick timber. 'The river was about one hundred yards wide at this point and the ground was heavily timbered,' remembered Sanderson. 'We took up positions

and the gun duel was on.'[164] Paroo, the Iban manning the Bren, raked the bank opposite from the hole into which he had jumped. Neither side had many marksmen, and it was the trees rather than the men who took the brunt of the shooting. One Japanese officer felt confident enough to emerge from the trees on the other side of the bank and challenge his enemy to a fight. Aware that they had only a limited supply of ammunition, Sanderson effected a staged withdrawal and the Ibans suffered only one casualty. Back at his HQ, Sanderson radioed the 9th Division with the news he had discovered the 450 Japanese. 'We are under a qualified ceasefire and therefore cannot assist you,' was the reply. 'However, in the meantime continue shadowing them and keep us informed of their movements. Only fire on them in self defence.'

As August arrived Sanderson obeyed instructions, stalking the Japanese by day and tormenting them at night. The usual tactic was for an Iban to drift past every couple of hours on the fast-flowing river in a prau, firing a long burst from the Bren into where they were camped on the bank. 'It must have been a terrible experience for them,' reflected Sanderson, 'lost, starving and continually harassed.'[165]

Sanderson was ordered to leave his operational area a few days later. He reported to Harrisson at Labaun. He was worn-out, remarked his officer, and a hospital bed beckoned. But he had done well. Sanderson was honoured with a Distinguished Conduct Medal, but when he requested to submit the names of several of his Ibans for recommendations for medals he was told he was allowed just one nomination. 'The Ibans are a likeable, sober people, clean of habit and moral,' he reflected. 'Do not think too harshly of the Ibans ... these people were only defending what was theirs with the weapon they knew best – the parang.'[166]

Emperor Hirohito's Japan surrendered on 15 August. For several days prior, Bill Sochon had been endeavouring to persuade the Japanese garrison in Sibu to throw in the towel. Situated 360 miles south of Bandar Seri Begawan, Sibu was the largest port in the Rejang Basin and the destination for Japanese soldiers retreating south from Brunei. It was a city that Sochon knew well from his pre-war days in Sarawak.

He sent a series of messages to the Japanese HQ in Sibu urging the hundreds of troops to surrender. There were conflicting reports as to the intentions of the enemy. Sochon was admonished by his superiors for his attempts to broker a Japanese surrender. 'Evidently using initiative is wrong,' he wrote in his diary.

Then on 11 September he received a message from the Japanese commander in Sibu, which read: 'Quite willing to co-operate.'[167]

Sochon decided to take matters into his own hands. On 15 September Sochon despatched a messenger into Sibu to inform the Japanese commander that he and four of his officers would enter the city at 1000 hours the following morning. This was agreed and they met at a table at a road junction on the outskirts of the city, Sochon carrying a Sarawak flag in lieu of a Union Flag that he did not possess. It was, as Sochon acknowledged, all a bluff on his part. His *Semut II* party was vastly inferior in number and firepower to the Japanese garrison. 'On approaching the Japanese party they sprang smartly to attention and saluted,' wrote Sochon. The salute was returned and Sochon shook hands with his opposite number. They sat down and Sochon was asked what he sought from their meeting. 'I informed the Japanese commander that it was useless to carry on fighting, that the surrender had taken place, and if he persisted in

A Catalina on the Baram River below Long Lama. These flying boats were used to bring in reinforcements and evacuate the sick and wounded of *Semut*. (NAA 8295698)

carrying on, I had no other option than to take the law into my own hands and see that the garrison surrenders, either by passive means or otherwise.'[168]

The Japanese commander explained that he had not yet been in charge a fortnight. Then he suggested they discuss a possible surrender at his HQ in the city centre. Was it a trap? Sochon knew any hesitation would appear as a weakness: 'I made an instant decision, realising that it was still a game of bluff, and that seeing that we had started so well it would be a pity not to see the thing through.'

Sochon and his officers were driven in two cars to the Japanese HQ, through a scene of desolation with hardly a local to be seen. Sochon struggled to recognize the city he had known so well before war laid it to waste.

Once in the HQ, Sochon laid out his terms to the Japanese commander, stating 'that by 4p.m. he was to have all his troops off the mainland and contained on Sibu Island'. Sochon would have his men guard the bridges and causeway, and the Japanese commander, called Noda, would be responsible for disarming his men on the island. Then, continued Sochon, they would meet at 0900 hours the next day and sign the terms of surrender, and Noda would submit a full list of all the arms on Sibu Island. Once that was done, he and his men could depart on their vessels to the garrison at Kuching, a couple of hundred miles further south. 'All this he agreed to do,' noted Sochon with great satisfaction.

At 1600 hours Sochon arrived at the Mission Bridge to watch the last of the Japanese leave the mainland for Sibu Island. At the far end of the bridge Commander Noda took the salute of every soldier that passed. Then he stared as Sochon's guerrillas took up position on the bridge. 'I have never known anyone to be in such a rage as what Noda was when he saw our troops,' recorded Sochon. 'They were indeed a ragtag and bobtail outfit, all carried rifles, but as to uniforms some wore shirts and chawats [sandals], others just shorts and others chawats only, still they were good fighters and definitely not a case of clothes maketh the man.'★[169]

★ In total, the 82 officers and men of Operation *Semut*, along with their 2,000 native guerrillas, killed approximately 1,500 enemy troops and took 240 prisoner. Thirty natives were killed but *Semut* suffered no fatalities.

THIS TABLET IS TO COMMEMORATE
THE RE-OCCUPATION OF FORT LONG AKAH
AND THE RE-ESTABLISHMENT OF THE
SARAWAK GOVERNMENT BY THE FOLLOWING
PARATROOP PERSONNEL OF
HIS MAJESTY'S FORCES

MAJOR G.S. CARTER British Army
CAPTAIN W.L.P. SOCHON British Army
W.O.II. D.L. HORSNELL A.I.F.
SGT. C.W. PARE A.I.F.
SGT. K.W. HALLAM A.I.F.
SGT. J.K. BARRIE A.I.F.
SGT. TEH SOEN HIN A.I.F.
SGT. ABU KASSIM A.I.F.

This plaque was erected to mark the reoccupation of Long Akah at the instigation of Majors Toby Carter and Bill Sochon (here incorrectly listed as a captain). (NAA 8295690)

CHAPTER 16

SAVAGE REVENGE

On 3 July, six weeks before the Japanese surrender, ten men were taken from their cells in Outram Road gaol at the foot of Pearl's Hill in Singapore. For more than four months they had been held captive in cramped and insanitary conditions, regularly beaten during interrogation by guards who enjoyed their job. They had been detained two to a cell, all of which were cold, damp, crawling with insects and rats, and measured 5 feet by 8 feet.

Their destination could not have been more different. Raffles College was an elegant colonial building, designed by two British architects in the 1920s and named after Stamford Raffles, the 19th-century statesman who founded modern Singapore. Since 1942 it had served as the HQ of the island's Japanese garrison. It was from here, in October 1943, that orders had been issued to find and punish those responsible for the damage caused to several Japanese ships at anchorage in Singapore. Hundreds of Europeans, Chinese and Malays had been interrogated and dozens killed for their suspected role in the attack. All of them had been innocent. The Japanese now knew that the perpetrators were British and Australian soldiers, comrades of the ten men who had been brought to court to face trial for a second attempted raid on Singapore.

The president of the court was Colonel Masayoshi Towatari of Garrison HQ, known to his subordinates as a 'swaggerer and a general nuisance'. His assistants were Major Mitsuo Jifuku, who had been preparing the case for the prosecution for weeks, and Major Miyoshi Hisada.

The prosecutor was Major Haruo Kamiya, a lawyer by training, who had first become aware of the charges against the defendants in February, shortly after they were brought to Outram Road Gaol from detention in Tanjung Pagar, the HQ of the Kempeitai Water Police in Singapore. Looking down from the packed gallery in the court that had once been a professor's residence was Major-General Misao Otsuka, the Head of the Judicial Department of the 7th Area Army, the man who had ordered Kamiya to prosecute the ten soldiers in the dock.

The accused were wearing the clothes of the Japanese military and for the first time in many months they were not barefoot but wearing ill-fitting Japanese boots. They had been led into the court in order of seniority, and they now listened as their case was summarized and translated by an interpreter, Hiroyuki Furuta:[170]

> . . . all the accused persons who were selected as members of the party headed by Lt-Col Lyon, British Army, left Fremantle on September 11 on board a British submarine Porpoise and arrived at an island called Merapas where they established their base, unloaded necessary rations, signal equipment, etc, left Capt. Carey in charge of those stores and the rest of the party left the island by the same submarine.
>
> On the sea near Pontiak, Borneo, the party captured a native junk of about 100 tons, towed the same to Pedjantan Island and transferred from the submarine to the junk 15 special submergible boats, special magnetic charges called Limpets, arms, munitions, rations, etc, and [when] these preparations were completed the party sent the nine Malayan crew of the junk to Australia by the submarine, and started on this junk for Singapore port on about September 25 for attack. On passing off Merapas Island the party landed Warren and two more members to join Captain Carey and the rest continued their navigation towards Singapore sea area for the mission.

Colonel Masayoshi Towatari then asked the defendants to state their name, rank, age, birthplace and military unit, starting with the the most senior. A big man, twice the size of many of the Japanese present, spoke first:

> Reginald Middleton Ingleton, Major, Royal Marines, 26 years of age, born at No. 3 Richmond Road, Wanstead, London.

Robert Charles Page, Captain, Australian Imperial Forces, 24 years of age, born in Sydney, New South Wales, Australia.

Walter George Carey, Captain, Australian Imperial Forces, 31 years of age, born at Canberra City, New South Wales, Australia.

Albert Leslie Sargent, Lieutenant, Australian Imperial Forces, 25 years of age, born at No. 85 Templeton Street, Wangaratta, Victoria, Australia.

Alfred Warren, Warrant Officer, Australian Imperial Forces, 32 years of age, born at Port Billy, South Australia.

Clair Mack Stewart, Sergeant, Australian Imperial Forces, 35 years of age, born at Southern Cross Town, West Australia.

Roland Bernard Fletcher, Sergeant,★ Australian Imperial Forces, 29 years of age, born at Dublin, Ireland.

David Peter Gooley, Sergeant, Australian Imperial Forces, 27 years of age, born at Carran Town, Victoria, Australia.

John Thomas Hardy, Corporal, Australian Imperial Forces, 23 years of age, born at Naraburi Town, New South Wales.

Walter Gordon Falls, Able Seaman, Australian Navy, 25 years of age, born at Aberdeen, Scotland.

Major Haruo Kamiya for the prosecution then read the two charges. The first dealt initially with their clothing, and the fact that during their mission they chose to dress in a manner that made it 'difficult to recognise them as regular fighting members of either British or Australian forces'. Furthermore, the junk on which they were travelling bore a Japanese national flag, and they had with them another Japanese flag. 'With these deceptive activities they succeeded in passing the guarded area and infiltrated into the outlying area of the port of Singapore'.

Following the attack on the police launch at Kasu on 20 October, they 'exploded the junk and made individual flights towards Merapas Base with a view to catch at the base the submarine which had been scheduled to come to the base at the beginning of November.'

The charge listed the fighting that had occurred on the islands of Soreh, Tapai and Merapas, the deaths of Japanese soldiers, and the detail that the accused were engaged in hostile activity 'without wearing uniforms to qualify them for fighting'.

★ The trial records stated that Fletcher gave his rank as sergeant yet official Australian records have his rank as corporal.

Major Kamiya then read the second charge, which accused the men of gathering intelligence; specifically Major Ingleton of sketching, Captain Page of taking photographs and Lieutenant-Commander Davidson of recording detailed notes. Among the intelligence gathered were details of the strength of the Japanese Navy in the Riau Straits and the location of bauxite mines on the southern coast of Bintan Island. In addition Captain Walter Carey had, during his lengthy stay on Merapas, accumulated much information on the movement of Japanese naval ships and aircraft.

Among the evidence presented to the court was one Japanese national flag, one sketchbook, one notebook, one camera and 17 negatives. Kamiya also had witness statements from local administrators and the transcripts of the prisoner interrogations, which he read to the court.

Major Mitsuo Jifuku addressed Major Ingleton through the interpreter and asked if there was anything in the charges to which he objected.

'No,' replied Ingleton. 'I have no objection. They were quite true.'

Jifuku then talked the Royal Marine through Operation *Rimau*, information that had been tortured out of the prisoners over several months. Ingleton and his comrades were worn out. They were probably resigned to their fate. Prisoners of war who had been so brutalized would not be allowed to live to bear witness. This was nothing but a show trial.

Asked about the confrontation with the police launch at Kasu on the afternoon of 10 October, Ingleton said: 'Coming nearer, we found it a navy patroller and I thought, "Everything is over". Other people seemed to have also been surprised and there were shouting at various places in the junk . . . then I heard someone shooting and so I took up my automatic rifle and shot the patroller . . . I did not know where Lt-Col Lyon was at that time. I merely shot because I heard others shoot, and not by order of him.'

Jifuku turned to Captain Bob Page. He also raised no objection to the charges. Nor did Carey or Sargent or any of the accused. The ten men were asked if they disagreed with anything that their co-accused had said. None did.

Major Kamiya then made the case for the prosecution, manipulating the facts to suit his purpose. How much of what he said was translated – and how accurately – was not recorded. The ten accused stood silently and watched as the professional lawyer addressed the three judges. Kamiya said that the guilt of the defendants had

Wally Falls, the Aberdonian, was captured on 15 December 1944 on the island of Selajar, and beheaded seven months later in Singapore. (AWM 045408)

been 'completely proved' by their 'unrestricted and free statements'. He pointed out that sailing in a vessel with an enemy flag – the court claimed that the junk *Mustika* had a Japanese flag painted on its stern, the only prosecution assertion that Ingleton challenged – was a breach of the 1907 Hague Convention. A good defence lawyer would have countered that this is not strictly true; that Article 23 of the Convention proscribes only the 'improper use of a flag of truce, of the national flag or of the military insignia and uniform of the enemy'. Did the flying of the Japanese flag constitute 'improper use'? Japanese maritime laws in the region in 1944 stipulated all vessels must fly their flags.

Kamiya told the court that the accused had been engaged in espionage, and again he referred to the Hague Convention to consolidate his claim. It was an erroneous reference. The men may have removed their badges of rank, but nonetheless they were in Australian uniform while gathering intelligence. A diligent defence lawyer would have challenged Kamiya, pointing out that Article 29 of the Hague Convention states: 'A person can only be considered a spy when, acting clandestinely or on false pretences, he obtains or endeavours to obtain information in the zone of operations of a belligerent, with the intention of communicating it to the hostile party. Thus, soldiers not wearing a disguise who have penetrated into the zone of operations of the hostile army, for the purpose of obtaining information, are not considered spies. Similarly, the following are not considered spies: Soldiers and civilians, carrying out their mission openly.'

On the other hand, Page and Carey of the ten had admitted wearing a sarong in enemy territory and were therefore more open to the charge of espionage. But it was only for some of the time, and a defence lawyer would have argued their case. But the defendants had no legal representation. They weren't even permitted by Japanese law to cross-examine the witnesses. They probably had little or no idea of what was being said. The interpreter was a weak and devious man, whose English was not capable of keeping up with proceedings.

Kamiya, according to the court record, was unstinting in his admiration of the men's courage and daring. He even described them as 'heroes', likening them to Colonel Yokogawa Shozo and Captain Oki Teisuke, executed for sabotage by the Russians during their war with Japan in 1904. The pair were caught disguised as Mongolian lamas and subsequently shot. In recognition of their gallant deaths, the Russians disposed of their bodies in accordance with Japanese tradition, cremating the bodies and preserving their ashes.

Kamiya closed the prosecution's case with a demand that the defendants he called 'heroes' be found guilty and executed. 'When the guilt is so clear,' he said, 'it would be disgracing the fine spirit of those heroes, if we tried or thought of saving their lives . . . I am sure they would rather die than save their lives at the mercy of the captor, because dying gloriously is the way to immortalize their names on the history.'

The panel of three judges retired to consider their verdict. They returned after half an hour. In the early evening of 3 July the ten defendants learned they had been found guilty and their punishment was death.

They were escorted back to Outram Road gaol to spend their last days on earth in small, filthy, wretched cells. The sentence was confirmed on 6 July by General Seishirō Itagaki, Commander-in-Chief of the 7th Area Army, and scheduled for the following day. The five men selected for the execution under the command of Major Miyoshi Hisada, one of the three judges at the trial, were not chosen for their swordsmanship. They were guards from the jail, five thugs among many.

On the morning of Saturday 7 July the Japanese ordered the ten men from their cells. They were wearing jungle green shirts and trousers or shorts. None wore boots. They were manacled one by one to a central chain and marched outside in single file. Outside the jail were two trucks. The men were unmanacled and ordered to climb on board. It was about 5 miles to the execution ground.

The men knew they were on their way to die, but they might not have known by what method.

There was a quite crowd at the execution ground, a barren patch of land near the Reformatory School in the Juroung district of Singapore. Three pits, freshly dug, were visible to the ten men as they were hauled down from the trucks. They were blindfolded and led across the wasteland to the edge of the three pits. They were forced to their knees. Their five executioners stepped forward. They had assigned themselves two prisoners each.

It took nearly half an hour to perform the execution. One prisoner's head proved impossible to sever, despite the repeated attempts of Sergeant Nibara. But he was tossed in the pit with his comrades to die from shock and loss of blood. The graves were filled in and the Japanese left. There was no cross or any form of marker.

When the five guards returned to the jail they were in boisterous mood. Two Korean prisoners overheard them reliving the execution, laughing at the length of time it had taken. Who could have imagined it would be so hard to cut off a man's head?

For the Japanese the execution of the ten men concluded Operation *Rimau*. Lieutenant-Colonel Ivan Lyon and Lieutenant Bobby Ross had been killed in action on Soreh, Lieutenant-Commander Donald Davidson and Corporal Pat Campbell had taken their own lives on Tapei. Corporal Clair Stewart had surrendered on Soreh in October, putting his life in the hands of the Japanese rather than snuffing it out with a cyanide pill.

It had then taken the Japanese nearly three weeks to hunt down the others. Able Seaman Andrew 'Happy' Huston and Private Doug Warne had paddled away from Tapei only a few hours before Davidson and Campbell arrived. They would have heard the sound of battle on Soreh and imagined that there was no escape for their comrades. Provisioning the canoe with as many rations as they could, the pair left the remainder and the rubber raft on Tapei. It was a wise decision. Their destination was Merapas, approximately 15 miles east, where there were ample supplies. But between them and their objective were possibly many Japanese search parties. They would have to paddle hard and fast to avoid detection.

Few if any of the *Rimau* party were as accomplished canoeists as Huston and Warne. Huston was a veteran of *Jaywick*, and with the hardy Warne they reached Merapas without incident. But what did they expect to find? The last they had seen of most of their comrades was a week earlier when they encountered the patrol launch at Kasu.

On reaching Merapas, Huston and Warne were delighted to be reunited with 16 of their party: the 12 who had fled the sinking junk at Kasu, and Walter Carey and his three companions – Hugo Pace, Alf Warren and Colin Cameron – who had remained on the island throughout.

Major Reggie Ingleton was the senior officer, but he passed command to Captain Robert Page, acknowledging the Australian's greater experience and knowledge of the region.

There would have been no reason to panic unduly, although there must have been concern at the thought that Lyon, Davidson and the others might at that very moment be undergoing a ghastly interrogation. Corporal Stewart probably was. But the Australian evidently revealed nothing. October came and went, and the 18 men on Merapas had seen no sign of the Japanese. Only another week until the submarine arrived. Could their luck hold?

There was at least one powerful transmitter/receiver radio on Merapas, and although one of the signallers, Stewart, had been captured, the other, Colin Craft, was on the island. But no messages were transmitted to Australia. Lyon had arranged his one-off code with Mary Ellis based on two copies of the same book; he had left the book in Melbourne, but surely he had noted the relevant code system and disclosed it in some shape or form to Craft and Stewart.

The men also had some walkie-talkies, as did Walter Chapman, who would be on the submarine that was scheduled in a few days.

For Major Hajime Fujita, the officer in charge of hunting down the enemy, the trail had gone cold. Four of the guerrillas were dead and one was in custody, but the two survivors from the police launch that had encountered the commandos off Kasu said there had been 'about twenty people' on the junk that attacked them.

For a fortnight Fujita and his men had scoured the myriad islands around Pangkil and Tapai, but their hunt had turned up nothing. Hitherto he had concentrated his search on the area west and south of his HQ on Bintan Island, but at the start of November he extended the zone to the islands east of Bintan. The first port of call was the large island of Mapur, 8 miles east of Bintan. On the morning of 4 November a detachment of 50 Japanese landed in two barges and questioned the locals. They had nothing of note to report.

The Japanese re-embarked and set off for the next island, 5 miles south-east, which was Merapas. The barges landed on the western beach, which Lyon had called 'Kolek Bay' in a nod to the Malay vessels that he saw when the Porpoise had first arrived. The captain in charge, Sungarno left half his force on the beach with Lieutenant Orzawa and the rest followed him as he led them towards the coconut plantation. It wasn't a big island, 1 mile in length and half a mile across. The reconnaissance wouldn't take long.

Bob Page and his men had been about to sit down to lunch on Wild Cat Hill, the high ground on the north of Merapas, when their lookout reported the approach of two vessels from the north-west. They immediately went into their well-rehearsed defensive drill, fanning out into the jungle as the enemy came ashore.

Captain Sungarno was at the head of his men when the first bullets were fired. They came from a silent Sten and the captain and the soldier behind him fell dead. Further down the trail the Japanese saw their officer drop and heard the 'thwack' of bullets cutting through foliage. Soon the Japanese from the second barge joined the fight, hosing the wild sago and thick palms on Wild Cat Hill with machine-gun fire.

The enemy responded from their hidden vantage points, well concealed and well protected, chosen with care by Walter Carey and his companions during their long stay.

For the rest of the afternoon desultory gunfire was exchanged. The Japanese slaked their thirst from coconuts while Bob Page and his men sniped at any soldier stupid enough to expose himself. It was a stalemate. But one side had the resources to break it. As dusk fell, Lieutenant Orzawa despatched one of the barges to Bintan to bring reinforcements. The other he ordered to sail around Merapas continuously to prevent any escape. He and the rest of his men remained in position.

In fact by the time one barge was sent west to fetch help, several of the *Rimau* party had already slipped away on the orders of Bob Page, paddling north from the eastern beach to Mapur.

Having disabled the radio, Page and a few others escaped at nightfall, pushing off from the east coast having worked out the length of time it took the barge to circumnavigate the island. That left eight men defending Merapas: Lieutenants Albert Sargent and Bruno Reymond, Doug Warne, Colin Craft, Jeffrey Willersdorf, Grigor Riggs, Hugo Pace and Colin Cameron.

The eight were all strong canoeists; Reymond, the son of a Swiss father and a mother from the island of Makin, was the operation's navigator and an experienced mariner; Pace had been on the island for weeks and knew every nook and cranny.

They may have volunteered to cover the two previous parties to flee or perhaps they drew lots, but however they were allotted their role, the eight were in a grave predicament. The reinforcements would arrive on the morning of 5 November, in effect trapping them on a small island against scores of well-armed Japanese

They could surrender, and take their chance. Or they could fight to the last, a final stand on Wild Cat Hill. There was a third option, fantastic as it seemed when Grigor Riggs and Colin Cameron proposed it. That was to create a diversion, draw the Japanese away from the landing beach on the west coast, allowing time for their six comrades to emerge from hiding, and rush down to the beach where the Malay koleks lay on the sand. Reymond was a skilled sailor who had charts and a sextant; all they needed were a precious few minutes' headstart and the Japanese would not be able to catch them.

It was decided. Riggs and Cameron promised they would follow in the one remaining folboat. When the reinforcement hove into view they were headed for the northern shore. It was obvious what the Japanese strategy was: to storm Wild Cat Hill simultaneously from the north and the west.

Riggs and Cameron took up position either side of the trail that led from the northern shore to the supply dump to the west of Wild Cat Hill. During the night they had constructed two small gun pits from rocks collected from the shore. Their comrades were hidden, probably in the swamp in which the dump was concealed. The first Japanese to land on the northern shore had to clamber over the rocks before they picked up the trail ascending towards the high ground. Riggs and Cameron rose from their pits and opened fire. Once again there were the shrieks of men, made all the more unnerving by the fact there was no accompanying gunfire.

But this time the Japanese had come expecting a fight. They responded swiftly and vigorously. Cameron had ducked down behind his stone wall to change magazines. He bobbed up, and was shot dead. Riggs continued firing. When he had run out of ammunition for his Sten gun, Riggs pulled out his .38 Smith & Wesson Special and fired at the advancing enemy until it clicked dry. He hurled the gun down the hill and then began running.

It was a sharp ascent to the top of Wild Cat Hill, but for a fit strong man like Riggs, powered by adrenaline, it was an easy summit. Once on top he was clearly visible to the Japanese advancing from the western beach. A young local, Abdul Rachman Achap, press-ganged into joining the Japanese as an island guide, watched as Riggs sprinted down the southern slope of the high ground across terrain providing little cover. The Japanese appeared on the hill, shouting and hollering, firing at the fleeing figure, who had now disappeared into some tall timber. The Japanese who were advancing from the west joined the chase.

Riggs emerged from the tall timber, tore through a banana plantation and pulled up. He had run out of island. Beneath were rocks and surf. The young Scot turned. All he could see were Japanese. There was no thought of surrender. With a Highland roar, he charged towards his enemy and was shot three times in the chest.

The Japanese stood over the body of the handsome young man. He had died with honour and the officer in charge ordered Achap to bury the body. It was later that day, after Riggs had been put in the soil and the rest of the island had been searched – turning up no more enemy but a sketchbook, camera and a flag – that the Japanese returned to the western shore. The two koleks were missing, and the sand was scarred with numerous bootprints that weren't theirs.

Bob Page and the other nine men who had paddled from Merapas to Mapur on the night of 4/5 November had done so unseen. But what was their next move? They must have anticipated the arrival of the Japanese. Perhaps they had captured the rest of the party, and extracted details of the contingency plan from them, or failing that, they would simply head to the nearest island in pursuit of their quarry. East and south of Merapas was endless ocean; Mapur therefore was the obvious choice for men in flimsy canoes.

But inexplicably, the Japanese failed to pick up the scent. On the afternoon of 5 November they transported their dead and wounded on to the barges and returned to base, leaving behind a detachment of soldiers on Merapas in case the enemy should return to retrieve their supplies.

Once it became apparent in the next day or two that the Japanese weren't coming, Bob Page had to make a decision: continue to lie up on Mapur for a couple more weeks or attempt to make the rendezvous with the submarine at Merapas. It was due any night from 8 November, but Page must have suspected that the enemy had left a force of some size on the island. Again, Page had to consider that the rendezvous was compromised, its details revealed under interrogation by one of the eight men left behind.

There were always the walkie-talkies that could be used from Mapur to contact the submarine and divert it to their new location. But did he have one? Or had they been forgotten when they fled Merapas or perhaps damaged on the frantic paddle across the sea to their present location?

The rendezvous window closed on 7 December. Now Page and his men had to make their own way home to Australia, approximately 1,800 miles south, and in monsoon season. Page drew on his past experience, and led his men 60 miles south-west by folboat to the island of Pompong, where in September 1943 the *Krait* had dropped anchor prior to the *Jaywick* raid.

At Pompong, Page divided the party: he, Wally Falls, David Gooley and Ron Fletcher in one section, and Reggie Ingleton leading a second group comprising Walter Carey, Alf Warren, Andrew Huston, Fred Marsh and John Hardy.

The plan was to hijack a junk and sail it home, with or without the crew's acquiescence. It had been relatively straightforward to seize the *Mustika* two months earlier, but now everyone was on the lookout for the white men. The Japanese had visited the islands and vowed retribution on any villager who didn't report immediately a sighting of the wanted men.

Page, Falls, Gooley and Fletcher paddled 40 miles south to the island of Selajar, arriving on the night of 14/15 December. They were exhausted and ravenous after covering more than 100 miles in a few days. Someone saw them land, and a little before midday on 15 December, as the quartet cooked a late breakfast they were ambushed by the Japanese. Wally Falls, the Aberdonian, was shot in the hip and taken prisoner, and his comrades were all captured after an extensive manhunt.

Reggie Ingleton's party, lacking the canoeing prowess of Page's, hadn't made such swift progress after leaving Pompong. On 18 December they were about 15 miles south of Pompong, close to the Japanese seaplane base at Tjempa Island. The Japanese were alerted to their whereabouts and the canoeists were fired upon. Bullets tore through the folboat containing Fred Marsh and Andrew Huston, two veterans of *Jaywick*. Huston may have been wounded when he and his mate took to the water. Marsh managed to evade capture and, with the assistance of Carey and Warren, he reached Tjempa. Huston's body was washed up the following day on the southern shore of Buaja Island.

The canoe paddled by Ingleton and Hardy also came under fire. Hardy was hit in the shoulder. The barrel-chested Ingleton powered them to the nearest shore, the tiny droplet of land west of Tjempa called Gentung. But on 18 December a Japanese patrol arrived and captured the pair.

For nine days Marsh, Warren and Carey remained at liberty on Tjempa. Marsh's ebullient character must have been a boon to his comrades and Carey, who had lived among the natives in the New Guinea jungle for several years, would not have been cowed by their circumstance. But on 27 December the trio were run to ground. Marsh, 'Boof' to his mates, the 'larrikin' with a love of practical jokes, did not come quietly. He was bayoneted in the chest. The Japanese let the wound fester as they transported the captured men to Tanjung Pagar in Singapore. Marsh was a sick man when the new year dawned. He grew progressively weaker as the infection spread. The Japanese did nothing, other than watch him die.

Albert Sargent, Bruno Reymond, Doug Warne, Colin Craft, Jeffrey Willersdorf and Hugo Pace had emerged from hiding as the Japanese chased Grigor Riggs to the southern tip of Merapas. Hardly daring to believe their plan would succeed, they had scrambled down to the western beach and pushed the two koleks into the sea, Sargent, Craft and Reymond in one and Warne, Willersdorf and Pace in the other. At any moment they must have expected to hear the sound of shouts and gunfire as the Japanese realized the ruse; they heard nothing except the faraway burst that brought Riggs's brave life to an end. For the next month they navigated their way south, through the freckles of land that make up the Lingga Archipelago. On 1 December the two koleks put in on the southern snout of Lingga and enlisted the help of a local to carry out running repairs on their vessels. Then they were off again.

About a week before Christmas the kolek containing Sargent, Reymond and Craft seized a junk off the central west coast of Borneo. Its crew were Chinese and Malay. The Australians indicated their intention; the crew agreed. But that night they fought back. Reymond and Craft were beaten and thrown overboard. Sargent jumped into the sea to escape his assailants. The bodies of Craft and Reymond were washed ashore a while later. Sargent was rescued hours later by fishermen, who turned him over to the Japanese.

Warne, Pace and Willersdorf meanwhile were still sailing south in their kolek round the south-western corner of Borneo and then east, hugging the southern coastline. But now the indomitable Doug Warne was sick, ravaged by malaria. He was becoming a brake to the progress of his mates. He insisted they leave him, saying he was too ill to go on. Pace and Willersdorf put in at Kedapongan, a heavily jungled pimple in the Java Sea, 50 miles south of Borneo, and entrusted Warne into the care of the locals. The pair set sail once more, island-hopping east: Doang Doangan to Dewakang to Kajuadi to Romang on 17 January, an island 875 miles from where they had left Warne at Kedapongan. Pace and Willersdorf were in the home straight: Darwin was just over 400 miles south across the Timor Sea, the end of what would rank as one of the most extraordinary feats of seamanship.

They decided to rest and recuperate for a couple of days on Romang before embarking on the final leg of their voyage. Thus far they had met on the islands only the best that human nature had to offer; but on Romang, Pace and Willersdorf encountered the worst. The village where they sought sustenance was run by a man in the pay of the Japanese. He welcomed the two Australians, and then sent word to the Japanese. On 19 January Pace and Willersdorf became prisoners in Dili, Timor.

It took the Japanese a few days to torture the identities out of the Australians. When they realized they had two more of the Singapore raiders in custody, they went berserk. How had they come this far? How had they evaded their clutches? The humiliation unleashed a diabolical fury from the Japanese. Pace and Willersdorf were beaten, bayoneted and broken. Willersdorf had the life tortured out of him in early February; Pace, the athlete and Casanova, was left to rot in a dingy cell, unfed and untended. He died in June 1945.

One snippet of information extracted from Pace and Willersdorf was that they had left a sick comrade at Kedapongan. But by the time Japanese arrived there was no sign of Doug Warne, either dead or alive.

Warne was no sailor, but he was a remarkable man of iron character. Once recovered from his debilitating bout of malaria, Warne obtained a kolek from the kind locals who had tended him and took to the sea. He had no charts or sextant with him. He would have to rely on initiative and instinct. He did, for several weeks, evading the Japanese patrols who were searching for what they didn't know was the last survivor of Operation *Rimau*. Eventually, in March, he was caught and transported to a naval base in Surabaya in East Java. Warne would die but the Japanese Navy had a job for him first; along with several other prisoners, Warne was used as a medical guinea pig by a naval doctor, Dr Nakamura, as he strove to produce an anti-tetanus serum.

Warne received two shots of tetanus bacteria and over the course of several days Dr Nakamura studied with interest the effect of the bacteria on his patient – the fever, the spasms and the lockjaw. He noted everything, including the fact that it took Warne two weeks to die. His emaciated remains were buried in a cemetery with nothing to mark the final resting place of a gallant young man.

CHAPTER 17

THE ELUSIVE TRUTH

On 7 May 1945 Lieutenant-Commander P. E. Scrivener, senior naval officer at the SRD, wrote a letter that was sent to the next of kin of the 23 men who had left Australia eight months earlier on Operation *Rimau*. It ran:

> My purpose in writing this letter is to express regret that I have no more information to give you concerning your son, except that he was posted missing when, with others, he failed to return from an operation against the enemy.
>
> 2. I am indeed sorry that I cannot say more than that there is no occasion to assume that he has not been taken prisoner by the enemy.
>
> 3. Please accept my sincere sympathy in this anxious time and be assured that any information I may be able to afford in the future will be passed onto you at once.[171]

The next day, 8 May, VE Day in Europe, SRD in Melbourne began taking steps for the 'disposal of the personnel effects, cash, etc' of Ivan Lyon, Bobby Ross, Reggie Ingleton, Grigor Riggs and Donald Davidson. SRD sent a memo to SOE HQ in London advising them it would require time to assemble the personal effects of the British officers as they were scattered from western to

A radio set similar to the one taken on Operation *Rimau*. The left tin contains a spare parts box and a receiver. The right tin contains a transmitter and a vibrator power pack. (NAA 31633851)

eastern Australia. 'Please note,' said the memo, 'that owing to the correct "missing" labels being out of stock, all the packages referred to above have had the "Deceased" [label]. The word "deceased" should be blacked out before forwarding the packages to the next-of-kin.'

Among the personnel effects was Ingleton's silver cigarette case, Lyon's driving licence and a lucky charm belonging to Riggs.

★   ★   ★   ★   ★   ★   ★

Mrs Nancy Davidson received the letter from Lieutenant-Commander Scrivener at the home she shared with her husband, Donald, at 109 Domain Road, South Yarra. A similar letter was delivered to Roma Page at the same address. Robert Page's wife had been sick with worry ever since the party failed to return by 6 December, the date her husband had promised he'd be back.

Some of the *Jaywick* men in November 1943, including Ted Carse (sitting), Bob Page (right, front row), Arthur Jones (above Page) and Ivan Lyon (above Jones). (AWM 045420)

Nancy Davidson was a woman of some standing in Melbourne, not someone accustomed to being brushed off. Acting as the unofficial spokeswoman for the families of the *Rimau* men, Mrs Davidson began using her connections to make plain her feeling that they weren't being told the full story.

On 22 May an internal memo was sent within SRD HQ in Melbourne. 'I have had a complaint from Admiral Royle,★ based I should think on unfounded statements by Mrs. Davidson, that we are not being sympathetic to these people, or giving them the assistance to which they are entitled . . . I think I have satisfied Admiral Royle that we cannot give them any more, and in fact we do not ourselves know enough to say more than that Davidson and Page are missing. I think we have only one name definitely killed, and that from a source which we cannot disclose.'

The source was 'Ultra', the Allied intelligence project based at Bletchley Park in Bedfordshire, which for years had intercepted and decrypted communications of the German, Italian and Japanese military.

The first such message pertaining to *Rimau* intercepted by Ultra was in October 1944, and described an incident in the 'northern part of the Riau Archipelago' involving about 20 people, including Caucasians, who were now the subject of an extensive search.

Three months later, on 29 January 1945, SRD in Melbourne sent a top secret cable to London based on another decrypted Japanese communiqué. It ran:

> 1. Conclusive evidence received whole RIMAU party caught Oct 10th [sic] Rhio Archipelago six killed including LYON eleven captured six missing.
>
> 2. Regret under present rules we cannot communicate through our channels information from most secret sources but presume this information must be available in London from corresponding source.

How the Japanese were able to put only Lyon's name to the dead isn't known but it might have been his tiger tattoo, a distinguishing feature that the Japanese probably described to the captured *Rimau* party.

Eventually, Nancy Davidson was told some of what SRD knew, with strict orders to keep the information to herself. One of the disclosures concerned her

★ Guy Royle, a British officer and in 1945 the First Naval Member of the Australian Commonwealth Naval Board.

husband: he was a prisoner. Therefore in the middle of June, she decided to return to England with her three-year-old daughter. A Major Oughton in SRD HQ telegrammed SOE in London on 14 June to warn them they could expect a visit from Mrs Davidson in the coming weeks. It then briefed SOE on the situation as it stood, explaining that since their disappearance all 'information gained about the fate of the party was from "Ultra" sources and indicated that they had been captured by the Japanese'. The memo continued:

> Mrs. Davidson, who has many friends in high Naval circles in Australia, has been given a certain amount of this information by a very senior Naval Officer . . . she is a shrewd and intelligent woman . . . she has also been told not to contact relatives of others missing on this operation, notably General Lyon, father of Lt-Col Ivan Lyon, who will not (we hope) have received similar information from high circles.

The naval source who had disclosed classified information to Mrs Davidson was Admiral Guy Royle, a fact that left Colonel James Champion, commanding officer of SRD, 'very peeved'. He had admitted as much to Mrs Davidson on learning she knew some of the men were dead, others missing and the rest in captivity. Presumably, Royle told her that Lyon was among the dead.

SOE had received a visit from Brigadier-General Francis Lyon on 20 March 1945. He and Colonel James Champion had discussed the situation in Room 238 of the Hotel Victoria on the Embankment. The elderly general had recently received a communiqué stating that his son was 'missing'. What, he wanted to know, were the reasons for issuing such information. Champion withheld the fact that according to their intelligence his son was dead. Rather, he informed Lyon that as the *Rimau* men were long overdue it was necessary to list them all as missing. However, buck up, said Champion, for his son was 'a man of infinite resource' and that 'if it were at all possible for him to get back he would undoubtedly do so, so that one must not give up hope'.[172]

Francis Lyon found it hard to be so optimistic. The last time he had seen his son, nearly a year earlier at his Surrey home, he had told him that he would sooner die than allow himself be taken prisoner by the Japanese.

As Mrs Davidson sailed for England in the middle of June 1945, Mrs Josephine Brown of Edgware, London, wrote to the Admiralty. She appreciated 'that it is probably quite out of order to write such a letter' but it was on behalf of her daughter, Didi, who was engaged to be married to Grigor Riggs, RNVR. Since she learned her fiancé was missing she had been gripped by 'anguish and anxiety', and Mrs Brown was desperate for any information she could pass to her daughter as to whether Riggs 'is alive and possibly a prisoner'.

The letter eventually landed on the desk of Lieutenant-Commander Scrivener, who replied to Mrs Brown on 3 August. 'I fully understand your daughter's anxiety and your desire to help her,' he began. 'I regret that I have no information to give you concerning S/Lt Riggs, except that he was posted missing . . . I am indeed sorry that I cannot say more than that [but] that there is no occasion to assume that he has not been taken prisoner by the enemy. Please express to your daughter my very sincere sympathy in this anxious time.'[173]

Lieutenant-Commander Scrivener was being economical with the truth, but he hadn't lied. All that he and SRD knew was that Ivan Lyon was dead along with five of his men, 11 were prisoners and six missing. Might Grigor Riggs be a prisoner? Or might he be one of the six missing, sheltering on one of the islands in the Riau Archipelago, waiting for the war to end?

On 2 October Nancy Davidson wrote again to SOE, addressing her letter to Squadron Leader H. E. Park. 'Surely now that most of the occupied territories have been liberated, and most of the prisoners of the war released, some news should have been forthcoming,' she stated. 'I was told before I left Melbourne that my husband was taken prisoner. Do you know if there are many people still left unaccounted for? It's seven weeks since the war with Japan ended.'

She asked for the address of General Lyon and also suggested to Park that perhaps Colonel Freddie Spencer Chapman might be able to help in the hunt for her husband. He was a friend of the Davidsons from pre-war Singapore, and Nancy had read recently in the paper of Spencer Chapman's extraordinary guerrilla exploits behind Japanese lines in Malaya. 'I shall be very grateful for any news you can give me,' she concluded. 'This waiting is very trying.'[174]

On the same day that Davidson wrote to SOE, Major Cyril Wild – a former Japanese POW – and a detachment of soldiers belonging to E Group South landed on Singkep Island, about 120 miles due south of Singapore. Wild's task was a mammoth one, to trace the scores of missing Allied pilots in the region, but he was in Singkep to oversee the surrender of a small number of Japanese still holding out, and to restore the island to its ruler, Amir Silalahi, whose authority stretched to over 100 islands in the archipelago. The Amir had stolen a boat and sailed to Singapore, where he alerted the British to the presence of the Japanese on his land.

Once the Japanese were in captivity, people in Singkep began to talk, including the chief of police under the Japanese, Said Abdullah. He told Wild that in December 1944 five white men had been held at Singkep police station, including one who was wounded in the shoulder. A Malay policeman gave Wild a piece of paper on which were the names of three men who were held in one cell. The names had been written by one of the men: Captain Carey, Warrant Officer Warren and Able Seaman Marsh. Wild asked to see the Singkep Police Station Admission Book and among the names was that of R. M Ingleton, Major, Royal Marines, admitted 19 December, and several unidentified 'white men' around the same time.

Major Wild's wasn't the only team pursuing missing Allied personnel, but on learning of what had happened at Singkep, SOA asked all investigative units to keep an ear to the ground about the missing *Rimau* men. The breakthrough came when several Royal Naval launches arrived at Kidjang on Bintan Island on 8 October with Captain John Ellis of SOA among their number. He was soon questioning the garrison commander, Major Hajime Fujita. He told Ellis a great deal, from the confrontation between the junk and the patrol boat at Kasu on 10 October to the storming of Merapas nearly a month later in which one Australian had been killed and a number of items recovered including a walkie-talkie and a silent Sten. A detachment of soldiers had been left on Merapas but no further Australians were killed or captured.

Also interrogated were Abdul Wahad, the head man of Mapur Island and Raja Mun, the informer, who had reported the presence of Lyon and his men on Pangkil to the Japanese, information for which he received $70. He told Ellis that two Australians had been killed on Soreh and another two on Tapai Island.

There were many other witness statements collected by Ellis in the following days, some contradictory and others vague, but in his report of 13 October, he stated that it was his opinion that 'there are still members of this party roaming around the islands in this area, not aware of the Jap capitulation'.

Wild and Ellis were making headway in discovering the fate of the *Rimau* party, although the bones of Lyon and Ross still lay under the trees of Soreh and the skeletons of Davidson and Campbell were propped up against the large rock on Tapai. Attention now switched to reports emerging in Singapore that ten white men had been executed on some wasteland in early July. Furthermore, most of the Japanese officers implicated in the deaths were in custody, including the prosecutor, Major Haruo Kamiya, and his superior, General Misao Otsuka, the Head of the Judicial Department of the 7th Area Army. They had nothing to hide, they told Wild. The men had been given a fair trial but the evidence of their espionage was

TELEPHONES

SERVICES RECONNAISSANCE DEPARTMENT

39 Ackant Street

South Yarra

No. GDA/549.

Box 2141 T.,
G.P.O.,
Melbourne.

17th December 1945

Mrs. T.S. Ross,
"Brackens",
Dormans Park,
EAST GRINSTEAD,
Sussex.

Dear Mrs. Ross,

As I have been handling all incoming reports on your son's party, Lt.Col. Rigg has passed your letter of the 21st November on to me. I had already written to Col. Ross on the 30th November, as I felt you would like to have all possible details.

I can now let you have further information resulting from Japanese interrogations. The Japanese state that Lieut. Ross and Lt.Col. Lyon, the party leader, were killed fighting a Japanese patrol on a small island called ASORE Island, just north of PANGKIL Island in the RIOUW Straits, on or about the 10th October 1944 and that they made fine graves for them. This will of course be investigated by the War Graves Unit and you will be informed of the results.

I feel I must be frank with you and say that in my opinion the details we have received are correct and that there is no chance that Lieut. Ross may have escaped on to the mainland of Malaya or that he is being held in the Dutch Islands.

As regards your request to be put in touch with the parents of another missing member of the party, I think the best address for me to give you is that of Col. Lyon's parents. His wife, Mrs. Ivan Lyon, who is out here at the moment, will be coming home with me in January. The address is -

 Brig/Gen. F. Lyon, C.B., C.M.G., C.V.O., D.S.O.,
   "Gorsehanger",
    FARNHAM,
    Surrey.

Please accept from myself and the members of this Unit our deepest sympathy in your great loss.

     Yours sincerely,

     George Dilley

     Major.

overwhelming. As proof of what they were saying, the pair told Wild to read the court proceedings. He did, and unfortunately he believed what he read, that the ten men had been treated with honour, equity, dignity and even admiration by their Japanese accusers. In a subsequent article for *Blackwoods* magazine, Wild recounted the mawkish closing statement of the prosecutor, Major Kamiya:

> With such fine determination they infiltrated into the Japanese area. We do not hesitate to call them the real heroes of a forlorn hope. It has been fortunate for us that their intention was frustrated half-way, but when we fathom their intention and share their feelings we cannot but spare a tear for them . . . when the deed is so heroic, its sublime spirit must be respected, and its success or failure becomes a secondary matter. These heroes must have left Australia with sublime patriotism flaming in their breasts . . . the names of these heroes will remain in the heart of the British and Australian people for evermore.[175]

Wild may have been gullible or by publishing verbatim the fictious statement of Kamiya he may have been trying to ease some of the pain felt by the dead men's families.

According to Kamiya, Major Ingleton 'thanked the court for referring to them as patriotic heroes' and he and his co-defendants admitted their guilt and 'shall humbly accept any punishment that is due'.

The Japanese documents then stated that between the verdict and their execution, the ten men were given increased rations and treated in a manner befitting 'patriotic heroes'. 'Every other possible means for warm treatment was given and all through these days the attitude of them was really admirable. They were always clear and bright and not a single shadow of dismal or melancholic mood did they show.'[176]

The Japanese account of the execution differed from that of the Koreans in Outram Road gaol who saw the ten men dragged from their cells and then manacled to one another. According to the Japanese version handed to Wild: 'All of them were given cigarettes and rested. Then, in accordance with their request, they were allowed to shake hands with each other. They all stood up, shook hands merrily and even laughingly in very harmonious air, and bid farewell [to] each other.'

The interpreter, Hiroyuki Furuta, shed many crocodile tears for the ten men whom he had grown to so admire and respect. Indeed, he told Wild during his interrogation, he had 'dreamt of trying to help them get away'. So overcome with emotion was Furuta that on the day of the execution he declined the invitation to attend among the official party. But he changed his mind at the last minute and made his way to the execution ground, where he watched their gallant deaths from behind a bush. He had to stifle a cry when Major Ingleton, having stopped laughing with his mates, addressed his executioners and declared: 'We have one regret. This is that we cannot see at this place Mr Furuta who has been so kind to us. We wanted to thank him once more but I suppose he has his duty. Please tell him we thanked him before we died.'★ [177]

Nowhere in any of the trial documents did it mention that it took half an hour to sever the men's heads from their bodies.

But there was an upside to the weak and devious character of Hiroyuki Furuta. Desperate to distance himself from any involvement in the execution, other than acting as their tender-hearted interpreter, he told his interrogators everything he knew about the fate of Operation *Rimau*. And he had been briefed about it. He knew, for instance, that after leaving Walter Carey on Merapas, Lieutenant-Colonel Lyon had returned to the island to deposit three more men, one of whom was Warrant Officer Warren. He knew also that after the police launch had been attacked, Lyon 'decided that as they had been discovered the operation must be cancelled owing to the necessity of ensuring the secrecy of the SB equipment'. Furuta told his interrogators: 'The party split into four groups under command of Lt-Colonel Lyon, Lt-Commander Davidson, Captain Page and Lt Ross. Each group had rubber boats and were ordered to make their own way back to Merapas.'

What Furuta didn't know, because none of the prisoners had revealed the fact, was that Bobby Ross and Andrew Huston had been on Subar when the police launch intercepted *Mustika*. Had they not been on the island, then almost certainly they would all have struck out for Merapas. But Lyon couldn't abandon two of his men, so, taking Davidson, Campbell, Warne and Stewart, the strongest canoeists, he headed to Subar.

When Furuta was unsure of the timeline he invented it, claiming that the raiders had been run to ground by the Japanese on an island. There was a fight and Lyon and Ross were killed, 'and the Japanese made very fine graves for them'. They hadn't, of course, but Furuta may not have known the truth, otherwise why blurt out a lie that would be easy to expose?

★ In *Kill the Tiger* the authors say that post-war a clergyman in Tokyo, acting on behalf of the Page family, attempted on several occasions to meet with Furuta, who claimed to have been particularly close to Bob Page. But Furuta 'never kept the appointments'.

Asked the name of the island, Furuta replied 'Soreh', but his accent was misinterpreted by his interrogator, an Australian by the name of Lieutenant-Colonel Pritchard, who wrote down 'Sole'. This was a puzzle as no such island could be found. Eventually it was suggested that Furuta had meant 'Pulau Asore', another name by which Soreh was known.

After the death of Lyon and Ross, claimed Furuta, the rest of the men headed towards Merapas but Davidson 'was killed en route'. The rest reached Merapas but were discovered on 4 November. 'Certain Japanese were killed in this action but the Australian party suffered no casualties,' said Furuta. 'They then split into small parties and moved south.'

Grigor Riggs and Colin Cameron were killed on Merapas, and the Scot had been buried by the Japanese on the southern tip. An Allied investigative team had discovered the unmarked grave but presumed it to be that of a Japanese soldier.

Asked if he had any further information, Furuta replied that Lieutenant Sargent and two other men whose names he did not know (Reymond and Craft) had reached an island east of Timor. Here Sargent was taken prisoner, and he had heard it said that one of his accomplices was killed by a Chinese and the other eaten by a shark. In total, continued Furuta, 11 of the party were caught and brought to Singapore but one, Able Seaman Marsh, died of illness.

Major Wild had by now identified the waste ground where the ten men had been executed as well as their graves. There were ten crosses on the graves, which, explained a Korean, had been hurriedly planted by the Japanese just a few days before their surrender.

Wild and his investigative team collated all the information about the fate of the *Rimau* party and published it in a memo:

Executed after court-martial Singapore	10
Died of illness in Singapore (Marsh)	1
Killed in action on Asore Island (Lyon, Ross)	2
Killed in action on Regah Island (Davidson & 3 unidentified)	4
Died in Romalg Island [sic, it was Romang], unidentified (1 killed by shark, 1 by Chinese)	2
Died at sea off Temiang, unidentified	1
Killed in Merapas, unidentified	1
Shot and buried at Selear (Temiang) [sic, it was Selajar] unidentified	1
Died escaping at sea off Boeia unidentified	1

The bodies of the ten beheaded men were exhumed by a Japanese labour team in November 1945. Inexplicably, it wasn't until February 1946 that the bones of Lyon, Davidson, Ross and Campbell were retrieved (by the Dutch). They were all laid to rest in Kranji War Cemetery in Singapore. But for the relatives of Grigor Riggs, Colin Campbell, Colin Craft, Hugo Pace, Doug Warne, Andrew Huston, Fred Marsh, Bruno Reymond and Jeffrey Willersdorf there was not even the consolation of having a body to mourn.

'Eight men sailed to sink fleet' was the headline of the article that appeared in the *Daily Mail* on 6 November 1945, a story similar to the one that was run by several other newspapers that week, including the *Daily Telegraph*. The *Mail*'s 'special correspondent' in Singapore described how Lt-Colonel Ivor Lyon and a major of the Royal Marines 'made a daring attempt last year to blow up the Japanese Fleet in Singapore Harbour. They were captured in a junk ten miles from Singapore, court-martialled and executed by the sword, according to documents found in Singapore'.

The report was read by Gabrielle Lyon who, with her four-year old son, Clive, had recently returned to Australia after more than three years in a Japanese internment camp. Among her frequent visitors were Lieutenant-Colonel Jack Finlay of SOE and Major Francis Chester, both friends of Ivan Lyon, who played games with Clive as they told his mother what they knew about her husband's last operation. 'She is quite lovely and most sensible,' said Finlay in a letter to London in which he stressed the need to ensure she and her boy were looked after by SOE. 'She feels that she doesn't want to go back to England until she feels sure that the Lyon family want her,' said Finlay.[178]

Gabrielle Lyon had discovered on returning to Australia that her parents had not survived their internment in a Saigon internment camp. That news, together with the newspaper speculation about her husband, left her deeply distressed. But in early December she received word from England that her parents-in-law wanted nothing more than to welcome her and their grandson into their home. SOE arranged for Mrs Lyon and her son to fly home because Gabrielle felt 'she could not stand the strain of sympathetic strangers on a sea trip'.

Nancy Davidson experienced first anguish and then apoplexy when she read newspaper reports describing how the *Rimau* men had been beheaded. A friend had sent her the clipping from the *Daily Mail* and Davidson enclosed it in a letter she wrote to Squadron Leader Park, in which she said she considered it 'disgraceful that such appalling news should drift through to me via a letter from a friend.'[179]

In fact the press coverage of Operation *Rimau* had already forced the hand of the War Office, which had been erring on the side of caution, despite the fact the evidence pointed to the deaths of all involved. There had been a glimmer of hope that one or two might have been hiding out on remote islands, but after the investigations of Cyril Wild and John Ellis that now seemed highly unlikely.

On 7 November SOE sent an internal memo advising that the status of the 23 men should be changed from 'missing' to 'missing, believed killed'. By the end of the month letters were sent to the men's next of kin, written by Colonel James Champion. The one received by Mr and Mrs Ross at their Sussex home ran:

> I feel, after reading through all available reports on searches carried out that the position is serious and I must be frank with you and say that the chances of your son's recovery are very slight.
> I would therefore like to let you have all possible details on his activities. Lieut. Ross was a member of a specially selected and highly trained party of English and Australians who left Australia in September 1944 on an operation with the object of sinking enemy shipping in Singapore Harbour.
>
> The party was unlucky enough to be surprised by a Water Police Patrol when nearing Singapore and were forced to make a rapid withdrawal, splitting up into small groups. These groups received instructions to make their way back to an island base some 70 miles from Singapore.
>
> Whilst carrying out this fighting withdrawal, several skirmishes occurred with the enemy, in which some of our personnel were killed. The party succeeded in inflicting many casualties on the Japanese but the latter, under interrogation, were unable to produce any identification. We cannot therefore establish which group your son was with.
>
> Some of the party were picked up and taken back to Singapore but he was definitely not amongst these. We are continuing with our efforts and should any definite information come to hand you will be informed immediately.

This operation was one of the most gallant and courageous feats ever attempted in the Pacific and we, as a Unit, are proud to have been associated with your son and the other members of his group.

There was of course a reason why Champion had stressed to Mr and Mrs Ross that their son was not among those captured and taken to Singapore. If there was any consolation for his grieving parents it was that he wasn't among those beheaded a month before the end of the war. But when Colonel Champion wrote to the parents and wife of Major Reggie Ingleton he had to expect that they had read the newspaper reports. So he chose his words carefully, doing everything to minimize their pain. Having been captured, he explained, Major Ingleton and the others were taken to Singapore, 'where, from all reports, they were well treated'. Champion quoted some of the remarks of Hiroyuki Furuta, the interpreter, who with the rest of the court, had been in awe of the prisoners' courage, which was an example even to the 'great Nipponese army'.

Champion made no reference to the manner of Ingleton's death, other than to say: 'We have been informed that the burial took place just outside Singapore. The army authorities will advise you full details of the location of the grave.'[180]

As devastating as the news was to the families of the 23 men, at least the agony of waiting was over. Their sons and husbands and brothers and fiancés weren't coming home. Notices began appearing in the 'Roll of Honour' column in newspapers, such as the one in the *Sydney Morning Herald* on 20 February 1946:

LYON.—Lieut.-Colonel Ivan Lyon, M.B.E., the Gordon Highlanders, husband of Gabrielle and elder surviving son of Brigadier-General and Mrs. Francis Lyon, Gorshanger, Farnham, previously reported missing, is now reported presumably killed in action, whilst in command of a raid against shipping in Singapore Harbour in October, 1944, aged 29.

Fred Marsh, the Able Seaman and practical joker, left behind many grieving relatives and friends in Brisbane. Everyone had liked him and admired him. Indomitable to the end.

'In memory of Fred,' ran the notice placed in a local paper by his Auntie Ivy and Uncle Len. 'Loved in life, let us not forget him in death.'[181]

EPILOGUE

'WAR'S PRETTY GRIM'

OPPOSITE The
Krait arrives in
Sydney in 1964
with (left to
right) Harold
Nobbs (Royal
Volunteer
Coastal Patrol)
and four
veterans of
Jaywick: Moss
Berryman,
Horace Young,
Arthur Jones
and Ted Carse.
(NAA 1649073)

On 23 November 1948 Gabrielle Lyon wrote to John Chapman-Walker. Since her arrival in England three years earlier she and her son, Clive, had been living with Ivan's parents in Surrey. The reason for her writing to her husband's former boss in the Services Reconnaissance Department was a memorial for which funds were being collected. The memorial was to be erected on Garden Island in Western Australia, and Gabrielle enclosed a guinea from herself and 'a contribution from my small son Clive to the memory of his father and all fallen members of S.R.D.'

Jack Finlay had earlier shown Mrs Lyon the design of the memorial and as she told Chapman-Walker it met with her approval. It was of two face stones, each stone 7 feet tall by 3 feet 10 inches wide.

'I thought it excellent,' she wrote, 'as the very strength & solidity of the memorial materialises the undaunted spirit and sublime bravery of every member of SRD; & stone upon stone symbolise the gallant achievements that one after the others led to victory.'

She did have one quibble, however, and that was the wording on the memorial. In her opinion, it should be 'shorter and simpler as I know it is a jealous principle of SRD that no reward & no praise should be bargained for'.

Gabrielle Lyon ended her letter to Chapman-Walker by saying: 'I shall always feel very proud that Ivan, whom I loved, served amongst the bravest.'

The bodies of Lyon (left) and Ross (right) were reinterred at Kranji War Cemetery in Singapore in 1946. (Author's Collection - Courtesy of the Ross Family)

The memorial was unveiled on Sunday 6 November 1949 in the presence of Duncan McLarty, the Premier of Western Australia. The wording on the memorial read: 'Erected in memory of members of Services Reconnaissance Department who gave their lives for king and country in the Pacific campaign during WW2.'

Underneath was a map of the Pacific area, including Australia, and a list of the place names of the major SRD operations. On the reverse face the names of the fallen were inscribed.

John Chapman-Walker was unable to make the trip so a wreath was laid in his absence by a Colonel Spry. Gabrielle and Clive Lyon had sent a cheque for 30 shillings with an order that a wreath was laid on their behalf. It was placed at the foot of the memorial by Arthur Jones, the only member of the six *Jaywick* canoeists who had survived the war.

In 2003 Arthur Jones was interviewed as part of an Australian Government initiative called The Australians at War Film Archive. He talked at length about his early life, his enlistment in the navy and, of course, his remarkable part in Operation *Jaywick*. He also admitted that six decades after the war he still sometimes lay awake at night and thought of his mates who were lost on *Rimau*. 'It's all I ever think about of a night if I'm not sleeping,' he explained:

I used to think, 'how would I have been if I'd have gone on that raid? How I would have stood up to being possibly in prison for six months and then being let out to be executed?' I feel for those fellows because knowing them so personally, particularly Wally Falls and Bob Page, they were both executed, and I really feel for them and their parents, and Bob Page had married just before he went away . . . so this is why I still often lay awake. Perhaps I might wake up during the night and I just think about it, you know, but it doesn't worry me very much now old age has taken over.[182]

For 30 years after the end of the war the documentation regarding Z Special Unit and its operations was classified information. There had been a few articles published in the press in the summer of 1946, with grudging authorization from the War Office. An SOE memo on 6 August that year stated: 'As you know our reluctance in the past to release any information on the *Rimau* Operation arose out of the fact that this operation was built up around a large quantity of most secret equipment'. This was the submersible metal canoe, the Sleeping Beauty, which Britain believed was a weapon far ahead of its time, details of which should be kept secret from any potential future enemy.

The story was released to the press but no details were given about the 'secret equipment'. A typical piece was published by a local paper in England, in the *Coventry Evening Telegraph*, on 22 August 1946, which said:

> The party captured a junk off Borneo on September 28 and continued their journey in it. After meeting a police boat from Singapore on October 6, Colonel Lyon decided to cancel the operation in order to protect their secret equipment. They destroyed the junk and split into four groups. By using rubber boats they reached an island where they clashed with the Japanese. Colonel Lyon and Lieut. H.R. Ross, of the British Army, were killed. Most of the others died, or were made prisoner.

When the files were declassified in the 1970s it enabled historians and relatives to learn a great deal more about the fate of *Rimau*. But it was too late for the parents of the dead men. Fortunately, there were still siblings and widows and children, who finally got to hear the truth; if not all of it, at least more than they had hitherto heard.

The widow of Bob Page, Roma, honoured her husband with this cushion at St George's Church in Singapore. (Author's Collection - Courtesy of Jerome Lin)

The Australian Commando Association was at the forefront of establishing how *Rimau* had unravelled; they also struck 23 medals for presentation to relatives of the dead men. The driving force behind this initiative was Alan Davidson, brother of Donald, who travelled from his home in Australia to present the medal to Mrs Mary Rose David of Sussex, the sister of Bobby Ross. 'Rosebud', as her brother had called her, had been devastated by his death and still cherished his letters and telegrams. The memories stirred by the visit of Alan Davidson were bittersweet; old wounds were reopened, but there was a quiet pride in learning of the manner of his death. He had wanted to be tested, and he had, and her Bobby had not been found wanting.

In April 1986 Rosebud travelled to Singapore to lay a wreath on the gravestone of her brother, buried in Kranji War Cemetery alongside Ivan Lyon.

When Ross's sister visited Kranji two of the gravestones in the cemetery close to where her brother and Lyon lay were nameless. It was another four years before they were identified by the Commonwealth War Graves Commission as those of Donald Davidson and Pat Campbell. That was made possible by the determination and dedication of one man, a former Australian soldier called Tom Hall. As a 24-year-old officer in 1958 he heard a story from the Australian novelist and World War II veteran Ronald McKie which, while a distortion of the facts, piqued his curiosity, perhaps because it seemed so fantastic. McKie was researching a book about Ivan Lyon and his men, published in 1960 as *The Heroes*, and he told Hall about three soldiers in 1944 who canoed more than 2,000 miles during a commando raid.

EXECUTION OF CAPTURED RIMAU COMMANDOS

Three of the Rimau Commandos, 1943. Captain Charles Page (left) was among the 10 who were executed. Lieutenant-Colonel Ivan Lyon (centre) and Lieutenant-Commander Donald Davidson (right) were both killed in action. Courtesy of Australian War Memorial.

Operation Rimau ("tiger" in Malay) was the second Allied commando attack that targeted Japanese ships in Keppel Harbour. It took place from late September to early October 1944 during the Second World War. Unlike the first attack (Operation Jaywick, 26-27 September 1943), Operation Rimau failed as the commandos were spotted by the Japanese. Thirteen of them were killed in action and 10 others were captured, tried without defence and beheaded near Dover and Clementi Roads.

The commandos travelled in a Malay junk during Operation Rimau to hide their presence from the Japanese. Courtesy of National Archives of Australia.

For more information, visit www.nhb.gov.sg

National Heritage Board

A marker in Singapore near the spot where Robert Page (pictured left in the photograph at the top of the marker, next to Lyon and Davidson) and his nine comrades were beheaded in 1945. (Author's Collection - Courtesy of Jerome Lin)

He was referring to Hugo Pace, Jeffrey Willersdorf and Doug Warne. It was one of many inaccuracies in McKie's book, which he wrote based on the scant information he had available about Operation *Rimau*. Nonetheless, it set Hall on a path of discovery that spanned 30 years and culminated in the publication in 1990 of *The Heroes of Rimau*, written in collaboration with the Australian author Lynette Silver.

Since the files relating to *Rimau* (and other operations) had been declassified, Hall had sifted through them and, among his discoveries, was the gruesome fate of Douglas Warne. He also cleared up the confusion about the location of the island where Lyon and Ross met their death after tracking down the interpreter Hiroyuki Furuta. It was Soreh, he confirmed, and not Sole, which is how the Allies had lazily transcribed it from his interrogation – despite the fact there was no island on the map called Sole. It was indicative of the sloppy investigation into Operation *Rimau* in 1945 and 1946.

In 1981 Hall went island-hopping in the Riau Archipelago, much as Ivan Lyon had done in the late 1930s. In Hall's case, however, he was after eyewitnesses. He found them, all able to provide undimmed memories of what they had seen in late 1944. When Hall complimented one man on his powers of recall, the Indonesian replied: 'It was important to remember. One day we knew that someone would come back to ask about the white men.'[183]

Among the items that Hall found on this trip was a human skull on Merapas Island. He smuggled it back to Australia where a forensic analysis identified it as belonging to either Grigor Riggs or Colin Campbell. In a time before DNA testing, the scientists studied photographs of the pair but 'were unwilling to make a positive identification.' Hall returned to the islands in May 1989 accompanied by Lynette Silver. They were joined on Merapas by Abdul Rachman Achap, who as a young man in November 1944, had been forced by the Japanese to act as their guide. Achap had helped Hall find the skull eight years earlier, but what he hadn't said at the time was that there was another body at the southern tip of the island. This was because Hall's cover story was that he was looking for the remains of his uncle and having found the skull, Achap assumed his amateur excavation was complete.

Achap led the two Australians to the spot where he had buried Grigor Riggs 45 years earlier and explained that the manner of the man's death had left such an impression on him he had never forgotten him. Furthermore, he revealed that the dead man had worn a silver wrist bracelet, which, before it was snatched by the Japanese, Achap had examined. He wrote for Hall and Silver the two letters he remembered: it had begun with a 'G' and ended with an 'S'. He also drew a symbol that he remembered had been engraved on the bracelet, which corresponded to that of the Royal Naval Volunteer Reserve.

Once Achap had buried Grigor Riggs, the Japanese who were left to garrison Merapas constructed a marker for his grave that included some writing in Japanese. That was why Captain John Ellis during his examination of Merapas in October 1944 had believed the man who lay beneath the marker was an enemy soldier and not one of the *Rimau* party.

On 26 August 1994 the remains of Grigor Riggs and Colin Campbell were buried with full military honours in Kranji War Cemetery close to the other men of Operation *Rimau*. Among those present were Abdul Rachman Achap, and Mrs Muriel Buie and Miss Barbara Riggs, Grigor's two sisters. 'It has been a traumatic experience, having heard nothing for more than 40 years,' said Miss Riggs.[184]

While Tom Hall had been scouring for the missing pieces of *Rimau* he had also been searching for a scapegoat, and he found two in Hugh 'Rufus' Mackenzie and Walter Chapman. Hall had interviewed Mackenzie, a retired rear admiral, in the early 1980s and the latter was not left with a 'very good impression'. It may have been the insinuation of some of Hall's questions.[185]

When Lynette Silver and Hall published their book in 1990 neither Mackenzie nor Chapman was portrayed in a good light. The assertion was that if Mackenzie had arrived off Merapas on the night of 8 November 1944 – the first night of the one-month rendezvous window – he would have rescued the *Rimau* party. But no, this gung-ho commander was off chasing targets.

These claims resurfaced in the British press in the summer of 1994 prior to the burial of Riggs and Campbell in Kranji War Cemetery, including a report in *The Times* on 4 June. Mackenzie felt compelled to refute the accusations on behalf of himself and Walter Chapman, who had been dead for 30 years. He wrote:

> I deny strongly that I either 'failed to obey' or 'ignored' my orders in regard to Tantalus's [sic] part in the operation. On the contrary, these were very much in the forefront of my mind throughout that patrol . . . further, your account of Major Chapman's conduct at Merapas Island, forty miles off Singapore [sic], is a complete distortion of fact . . . Chapman was a very brave man who carried out with his companion, Corporal Croton of the Australian forces, a most detailed search of the island: the reason he found no survivors was, as I learned later, that the Japanese had already intervened and ensured there were none, well before the earliest date given for possible pick-up by Tantalus.
> He remained my friend until his tragic death in 1964 and I have no reason to believe that *Rimau* lay behind that.

The letter was read by Jeremy Chapman, one of Walter's two sons, who had followed his father into the army. He contacted Mackenzie and received a lengthy reply. 'I am so glad to be in contact with you . . . for ever since first meeting him I have always admired and had great respect for your father,' wrote Mackenzie.[186]

He then discussed the Tantalus patrol of October and November 1944 and admitted that he 'felt concern and anxiety' over the delay in the submarine reaching Merapas. However, as it had subsequently been proved that the Japanese had already assaulted the island, such worry had been 'removed'.

Mackenzie had nothing for which to reproach himself. The operational order he received from Captain Shadwell on the eve of his departure from Fremantle stated:

> **The commanding officer HMS Tantalus is responsible for the safety of the submarine which is to be his first consideration and [he] has discretion to cancel or postpone the operation at any time . . .**
> **a) Subject to patrol requirements HMS Tantalus will leave her patrol at dark on 7th November and proceed to the vicinity of Merapas Island.**

In a Progress Report on Operation *Rimau*, dated 21 October 1944, it was recorded that Tantalus had sailed from Fremantle in place of Porpoise and 'will effect withdrawal of RIMAU party on *completion* [author's italics] of her operational patrol'.

On 3 November Mackenzie had received a signal from Fremantle ordering the Tantalus 'to proceed to the entrance of the Singapore Strait to do air sea rescue duties on the surface for the proposed raid on Singapore by B.29s on 5th November.'

Mackenzie lurked in the Strait until the early afternoon of 7 November when he resumed his aggressive patrolling, heading north up the east coast of Malaya, in the hope of firing some of his 15 torpedoes that remained. His was an important contribution to the war; like the sinking of the ships on Operation *Jaywick*, it wasn't so much the tonnage sunk that counted, rather than the psychological damage on an enemy that knew the enemy was at its door.

At no point at this time was he instructed to rendezvous at Merapas: his order stated that he had a month to make the pick-up, from 8 November to 7 December. There had been no radio signal from *Rimau* to indicate that they were in trouble so Mackenzie correctly prioritized the sinking of enemy shipping before the collection of a small party of commandos.

Indeed if the Tantalus had rendezvoused at Merapas on the night of 8 November, and if Walter Campbell and Ron Croton had paddled ashore, they would have almost certainly been caught by the Japanese. They had stormed the island on 4 and 5 November, and a detachment of soldiers had subsequently been left behind to garrison Merapas.

For how long they were posted on the island isn't known; during his interrogation by Captain John Ellis of SOA in October 1945 Major Hajime Fujita claimed that Merapas had been garrisoned for four months. But it is inconceivable that Chapman and Croton traversed the island on 22 November 1944 without encountering any of this garrison. In all likelihood the men were withdrawn after a couple of weeks when they decided the raiders had fled the region.

During the 24 hours that the Tantalus loitered off Merapas, there was considerable enemy air and sea activity in the area, which was not surprising as the Japanese were still hunting the men who had evaded capture nearly three weeks earlier; it was not a healthy spot for a submarine to remain. Mackenzie was right to put to sea on learning of Chapman's and Proton's fruitless search for the Rimau party. He had a crew of 61 in his submarine; they were more important than trying to locate a few commandos who may or may not have been in the vicinity.

Mackenzie was also criticized for approaching the island from the north-west in contravention of Donald Davidson's instructions to surface on the eastern shore. This would have allowed Chapman and Croton to paddle ashore on a sandy beach and then undertake a relatively easy trek to the rendezvous at Hammock Tree on the north coast. But Davidson had visited Merapas for only a few hours and was ignorant of the sea conditions. As Mackenzie explained, it was impossible for a canoe to approach from the north-east or east 'because the NE monsoon was blowing and a swell was running on that side of the island . . . it [the canoe] would have been broken up by the water'.[187] That was why Chapman and Croton landed at Punai Point on the north-west tip of Merapas, even though it meant an exhausting scramble over slippery rocks to reach Hammock Tree just after first light.

Finally, there is the question of communications. Lyon took four transmitter/receivers with him, but at no point did he send a message to Australia. Why he didn't do so after the confrontation off Kasu is a mystery. Had Lyon mislaid the code or had he left it, along with the radios, on Merapas? Why didn't Bob Page radio a message requesting an immediate pick-up after he and the others had returned to Merapas? Were the radios faulty, like the one taken into Borneo by the Semut II party? Those had been incorrectly wired in Australia and it was

TOP A memorial stone commemorating the site of the Guerrilla Warfare School at Wilsons Promontory, south of Melbourne, where the Special Training School was established in 1941. (Author's Collection - Courtesy of Jerome Lin)

ABOVE The headstones in Kranji Cemetery of the ten *Rimau* men executed in 1945, including Alf Warren, far right and alongside Clair Stewart. (Author's Collection - Courtesy of Jerome Lin)

ABOVE Fate was cruel to Francis Chester, who died of fever in 1946 after outstanding war service and was laid to rest in the Anglican Cemetery at Sabah in Malaysia, formerly British North Borneo. (Author's Collection - Courtesy of Jerome Lin) only the arrival by parachute of Lieutenant Stan Eadie, complete with his tool kit and soldering iron, that enabled messages to be sent.

In 1945 Staff Sergeant Mary Ellis discovered that Lyon had left behind in Australia the book that they had used to devise their code; that led to speculation in some quarters that it was always his intention to be incommunicado in order to prevent the higher-ups aborting the operation. That seems highly unlikely. Davidson would surely have run through the communication procedure with Lyon and the signallers at some point, and he would not have allowed Lyon to act so recklessly. Not that Lyon would. He would not have jeopardized the lives of his men in such a foolhardy manner.

But it wasn't the radios that were to blame for the failure of *Rimau*; the reason the operation was doomed from the start was because of Lyon's determination to use the Sleeping Beauties. No doubt he was encouraged by the Royal Navy in England, who were keen to introduce them into service and saw *Rimau* as an ideal testing ground. One might even say the men on the *Rimau* operation were guinea pigs. Yet the men had only a few weeks to train on this very experimental weapon. As Donald Davidson noted in his journal throughout July and August, the SBs proved unreliable and the men themselves struggled to master the innovation. 'They were very temperamental things apparently,' reflected Arthur Jones. 'Their range was very small, their batteries wouldn't last too long and their speed wasn't too good, either. I believe from fellows that I know that trained in them, they were very, what shall I say, uncontrollable at times. You only had to shift your weight a little bit and they'd go over to one side.'[188]

There must have been a nagging doubt in the minds of the pilots selected to navigate the SBs as to their efficacy. For men already under great strain it was an anxiety that they could well have done without.

Furthermore, the SBs were in size and weight the antithesis of the folboat; they were impractical, forcing the men to hijack a junk and then spend more than a day unloading them from a submarine while deep inside enemy territory. *Jaywick* was a brilliantly simple and effective operation, relying on the initiative and endurance of the men involved, with a 'return' that far exceeded its investment. *Rimau* was anything but simple, and as a result it was vulnerable to misfortune.

In an interview in 2003 Lieutenant-Colonel John Holland, a senior officer at SRD in Melbourne in 1944, stated that in hindsight Operation *Rimau* should not have been authorized. 'He [Lyon] was very persuasive and he desperately wanted to carry out another operation in the same place with more modern equipment, and he had the more modern equipment,' he said. What Lyon didn't have, however, in Holland's opinion, was a strong commander able to resist his persuasive power. 'It should have been knocked on the head early in the piece . . . [by] a very strong commander, who will say, "My boy, this will not go ahead"'.[189]

That is not in any way to apportion blame to Ivan Lyon, one of Britain's most daring, imaginative and accomplished guerrilla fighters of the war. That he failed was no one's fault, certainly not Mackenzie's or Chapman's, and the traducing of their characters in recent decades is unconscionable. The charges of cowardice and dereliction of duty are unjust and unwarranted and in making them the perpetrators reveal an all-too-common fault in modern society: that of judging the past through the prism of the soft and safety-obsessed 21st century.

Mackenzie was fighting a war. As a submarine commander deep inside enemy territory he was under extraordinary pressure, far beyond the comprehension of any of his modern critics. His priority was his submarine, his crew and his duty as a submariner. The fate of a handful of brave and intrepid commandos was of secondary importance. He expressed regret at their deaths: in an interview with the Imperial War Museum in 1990 he described *Rimau* as 'one of the bravest operations I'd heard of during the whole of the war and it's a tragedy that none survived to tell the tale'. But he didn't feel responsible or bear any guilt about its tragic conclusion, and nor should he. It wasn't his fault.

Like Mackenzie, Ivan Lyon pursued his enemy with single-minded ruthlessness. The pair were realists, not idealists, but neither was reckless. On the contrary they planned their patrols and operations assiduously, eliminating as much risk as they could. But war – and here again is a concept difficult to grasp for many in the risk-averse 21st century – is fraught with risk no matter how well one plans. The odds had always been stacked against Lyon, but on *Jaywick* the cards fell his way. On *Rimau* they didn't. '*C'est la vie*', as Gabrielle Lyon might have said, or as Lyon did say in 1942: 'War's pretty grim.'[190]

POST-WAR LIFE

In 1948 Lieutenant-Colonel John Chapman-Walker corresponded with the parents of Ivan Lyon about the imminent unveiling of the memorial to Z Special Unit in Western Australia. In one letter, Chapman-Walker wrote: 'You may possibly not know that after consultation with General [Thomas] Blamey, and with his fullest approval, I recommended Ivan for the VC. General Blamey had himself discussed the matter with the authorities in London, and it was a very great disappointment to him, and I need hardly say to me also, that he did not get it for a more or less technical reason. Awards of the VC are regulated rather differently from other awards as the regulations are proscribed by a special status.'

Ivan Lyon was without doubt one of the most remarkable characters of World War II. A soldier by profession, but a sailor by instinct, his versatile and innovative mind made him one of the great guerrilla fighters of the conflict, the equal of Paddy Mayne of the SAS or Anders Lassen of the SBS. Yet Lyon is largely unknown in his native land. The same applies for Donald Davidson, who was just as bold, adaptable and enterprising. To a large extent this is because Z Special Unit was a very small outfit, and a short-lived one, and post-war its legacy was understandably absorbed into the Australian military.

Z Special Unit received a flurry of attention in 2012 when the Duke and Duchess of Cambridge asked to see the graves of the *Rimau* men during a visit to Kranji War Cemetery, and in 2020 several British newspapers carried the obituary of Moss Berryman, the last member of *Jaywick*, who died aged 96. The purpose of this book is to shine a light on the bravery of a small band of men who fought a brutal enemy and a hostile environment and set a standard of excellence that has provided inspiration for generations of subsequent special forces soldiers.

The Services Reconnaissance Department unveiled a memorial to its members at Garden Island, Western Australia, in 1949. (Author's Collection)

Keith Barrie: Spent many years working as a surveyor in Malaya and Singapore, returning to Australia in 1959 where he established Australian Aerial Mapping, which had a hand in many of the country's largest civil engineering projects in the 1960s and 1970s. He died in 2005 aged 91.

Moss Berryman: After *Jaywick*, for which he was mentioned in despatches, Berryman left Z Special Unit and served out the war in the destroyer HMAS *Vendetta*. Upon demob, he married his childhood sweetheart and joined a firm of stockbrokers where he remained for 46 years. In 1993 he attended a ceremony at Kranji War Cemetery in Singapore to commemorate the 50th anniversary, and was introduced to Clive Lyon, whom he described as 'the spitting image of his father'. He died aged 96 in 2020, the last member of Operation *Jaywick*.

Ted Carse: Returned to HMAS *Magnetic*, the land base at Townsville, Queensland, after *Jaywick*, and left the navy in 1946. Along with Jones, Horrie Young and Moss Berryman, Carse was a guest of honour when the *Krait* entered Sydney Harbour to start her new life as a museum ship. He died in 1970.

After the war the *Krait*, seen here in Sydney Harbour in 1976, worked for a spell in the Borneo timber trade before being bought by Australia in 1964. It is now on display at Sydney's National Maritime Museum. (Getty Fairfax Media Archives/ Contributor)

Toby Carter: Returned to Borneo after the war where he worked in the oil industry and was instrumental in the raising of memorials to the Allied POWs who died in the island's Japanese POW camps and the native population. Upon his death in 1988 aged 77, Jumbo Courtney, his Z Special Unit CO, said: 'It is still my belief that we would have been in very big trouble had Toby Carter not been our leader in *Semut II*.'

Walter Chapman: After the war, Chapman resumed his career as an architect, while remaining an active member of the Territorial Army. He accepted an invitation from the officers of the Tantalus and Porpoise to attend an annual Submarine Officers reunion in the 1950s, where he showed the film he had taken on the Tantalus during their patrol. In 1963 he was hired by Mackenzie to make some alterations to his house in Surrey. The following year he committed suicide by taking the suicide pill he had kept from Operation *Rimau*. A local newspaper that reported his death wrote that he 'killed himself in his car outside Amersham General Hospital last week with hydrocyanic acid which he had kept from his war-time days. Throughout the whole inquest, held in Amersham Hospital on Friday, there was no indication given of any mental stress, but among Mr. Walter William Chapman's documents in his car were found a few unpaid bills.'

In recent years it has been claimed by several Australian writers that Chapman took his own life after discovering that most of the *Rimau* party had still been alive when he and Croton made their sweep of Merapas on 21/22 November. Neither Mackenzie nor Tibbs believed this, pointing to marital problems as the cause of his death. Chapman was aware of the fate of the *Rimau* party shortly after the war and, while deeply saddened, he did not hold himself responsible. He is remembered with great love by his two sons.

John Chapman-Walker: Returned to his pre-war profession as a solicitor and entered local politics in the 1950s as a councillor representing the cities of London and Westminster. He died in 1958 aged 50.

Francis Chester: Like Carter and Sochon, Chester returned to Borneo after the war, but in August 1946 he died of blackwater fever (a complication of malaria) aged 47. He was buried in Kota Kinabalu Anglican Cemetery and the inscription on his grave states: 'A Pioneer of Victory in Borneo and a Lovely Man.'

Major Hajime Fujita: Spent two years after the war as a POW in Singapore repairing war damage, and he also oversaw the erection of four large tombstones of red granite to the Japanese war dead 'away from the eyes of the British'. One of the tombstones was to those Japanese executed for war crimes, people Fujita preferred to describe as 'martyred patriots'. He remained unrepentant about Japan's role in the war and in an article in 1978 he boasted that 'he had never been defeated in battle', and had helped capture Ivan Lyon and his men.

James Gavin: Enjoyed a distinguished post-war career in the military, including spells as Commandant of the Intelligence Centre and Assistant Chief of Staff, Intelligence. On leaving the army he was for many years Technical Director of the British Standards Institution. He died in 2000 aged 89, the last surviving member of the 1936 Everest expedition.

Tom Harrisson: For nearly 20 years after the war, Harrisson was the Curator of the Sarawak Museum, an appointment not without controversy as he was accused of stealing museum collections, although he was exonerated. He also undertook during this period some important excavations in the Niah Caves in northern Sarawak and authored several books, including his war memoir, *World Within, A Borneo Story*.

In December 1962 Borneo experienced a brief insurgency in the oil-rich British protectorate of Brunei. Harrisson, then curator of the Sarawak Museum, recruited an irregular force from the local population to counter the insurgency, serving alongside the British Army.

Harrisson continued to divide opinion among the men who served under him. 'He was an egotistical man, but a thinking man,' said Bob Long, his radio operator. 'He was pretty brilliant in his way but not very popular.' In his memoirs, Keith Barrie reflected that the Englishman was tenacious and methodical in planning their insertion into Borneo, and his advice and insistence on 'going native' was invaluable in helping the men adapt to their unforgiving environment. 'Having said that,' continued Barrie, 'it does not make me like him any more as he remained an arrogant, abrasive and in some ways a shifty character.'[191]

In a letter to Jack Finlay in May 1966 Harrisson made some interesting observations on the characteristics of the men who served in Z Special Unit. Harrisson and his third wife were killed in a car crash in Thailand in 1976.

Arthur Jones: Awarded a DSM for his part in *Jaywick*, Jones left the navy in 1946 and married the following year. He spent his life in the printing trade and died in 2013 aged 91. Asked in a 2003 interview if he'd had a 'philosophy' of life as a result of his war experience, he said: 'No, I don't think so . . . I don't have any real philosophies; I've just gone along with life and been happy with my life.'[192]

Gabrielle Lyon: Lived with her in-laws in Surrey with her son Clive, who followed his father to Harrow School. After the death of Ivan Lyon's parents (his father died in 1953 and his mother in 1961), Gabrielle remained in Surrey and never remarried. In the late 1960s Tom Harrisson and Jack Finlay corresponded about the idea of writing a book about Ivan Lyon and his operations. Harrisson wrote: 'It would be possible perhaps, to pursue my own line on Lyon, and extend it to: why did these fellows do what they did? Coupled, of course, with the question: and was it worth doing, anyway? I mean, worth doing except as bravery, as individualism, as indeed a sort of protest at mass war inside war itself.' The book never materialized, however, for reasons unstated, although Gabrielle Lyon might have intervened. In a letter dated 5 September 1968, Harrisson discussed returning some material about Ivan Lyon to the Frenchwoman, describing her as 'half way round the bend and behaving in a very nasty way for no reason anyone knows of. Certainly I am not to blame - for once'. She died in 1978.

Rufus Mackenzie: Upon his death in 1996 aged 83, Sir Hugh Mackenzie was described by one Scottish newspaper as 'one of the most distinguished submarine captains of the Second World War'. Awarded a DSC and DSO he was promoted Rear Admiral in 1961 and became Flag Officer Submarines. His final appointment was Chief Polaris Executive, introducing to the Royal Navy the British Naval Ballistic Missile System.

Roma Page: Married a former member of Z Special Unit in 1950, but never forgot her first love and gave several interviews to historians and journalists. Upon the death of her second husband, Roma changed her name back to Page. She died in 2016.

Fred Sanderson: Awarded the DCM for his exploits in Borneo, he and his family bought a dairy farm in NSW, which he named 'Bario Hills' because the land reminded him of Bario in Borneo. Despite his criticisms of Tom Harrisson, he teamed up with him again in the 1960s when they carried out British intelligence work during the communist insurgency in Sarawak. He died in 1997 aged 87.

Bill Sochon: Remained in Borneo after the war working for the Civil Administration and in 1953 he was appointed Commissioner of Prisons in Singapore. In the 1960s he and his family settled in Australia and became Deputy Controller of Prisons for Queensland, where his emphasis was on rehabilitation. Sochon died in 1989 and the eulogy at his funeral was read by his former Z Special Unit comrade Keith Barrie, who called Sochon 'an engaging, friendly unpretentious Englishman who made Australia home and in doing so endeared himself to many people.'

Michael Tibbs: On leaving the navy Tibbs went to Oxford University and then joined the Sudan Political Service. He later served the Royal College of Physicians as their secretary for 18 years, for which he was awarded an OBE. At the time of writing in April 2021, Michael Tibbs, 99, is the only living person to have been involved with Operation *Rimau*. He remains fully supportive of all the decisions made by Hugh 'Rufus' Mackenzie during the Tantalus patrol, writing in his autobiography in 2013: 'All of us, particularly Rufus, were worried our delay in the pick-up date might have contributed to the disaster. However, it is fairly clear that if we had tried to pick the party up on 8th November, the Japs would have been waiting and we should have been clobbered.' Tibbs also shares Mackenzie's view that Walter Chapman's reputation has been unfairly traduced by historians being wise with hindsight.

Horace Young: Left Z Special Unit after *Jaywick* for the navy and was demobbed in 1946. He became the district radio inspector for Papua New Guinea in the 1950s and finished his career as the deputy assistant director general in Australia's radio regulatory section. He died in 2011 aged 90.

GLOSSARY

AIB	Allied Intelligence Bureau, formed in 1943 by the Americans to unite all irregular units in the Far East.
AIF	Australian Imperial Force, formed in September 1939 from volunteer personnel.
Borak	Home-brewed rice wine popular in north-central Borneo.
Dayak	Also spelt Dayk; the Dayak people encompass a number of tribes in Borneo, among whom are the coastal Ibans, or the Sea Dayaks, as opposed to the Land Dayaks of the interior.
DCM	Distinguished Conduct Medal, the equivalent of the DSO – second only to the VC – and awarded to NCOs and other ranks.
DNI	Director of Naval Intelligence.
DSO	Distinguished Service Order, awarded for meritorious or distinguished service by wartime officers.
Folboat	Collapsible canoes made of canvas on a wooden frame.
ISD	Inter-Allied Services Department, a cover name for SOA
Junk	Traditional Chinese sailing vessel, also found in Indonesian and Indian waters. Constructed with a high stern and projecting bow, junks have five masts on which are set square sails of linen panels or matting flattened by strips of bamboo.
Kempeitai	The Japanese military police which, in the occupied territories, was responsible for suppressing anti-Japanese activity.
Kolek	The traditional boat, constructed from wood, used by fishermen in parts of Indonesia.
Longhouse	The traditional home – constructed of wood and raised on stilts – of the Dayak in Borneo, housing the whole village, with families living in separate rooms.
MI (R)	Military Intelligence (Research), the forerunner to SOE (which was formed in 1940), was Britain's Military Intelligence section, itself derived from GS (R) (General Support (Research)).

GLOSSARY

OP	Observation Post
Orient Mission	The SOE codename for their activities in the Far East.
Parang	A machete used in Borneo for a variety of functions.
Prahu	The traditional sailing boats of Indonesia, which vary in size but typically have a built-up hull rigged with tripod masts.
Prau	Similar to a canoe, made from a tree trunk, and used to negotiate Borneo's rivers.
POW	Prisoner of War.
RAAF	Royal Australian Air Force.
RAN	Royal Australian Navy.
RTU'd	Returned to Unit, the term for special forces recruits who failed selection.
Sarawak	Comprising the north-western part of the island of Borneo, Sarawak was recognized as a separate state by Great Britain in 1864, and in 1963 became part of Malaysia.
SB	Sleeping Beauty, SOE's one-man submersible canoe that was 12ft 8in in length and carried a 425-pound warhead.
SEAC	South East Asia Command.
SOA	Special Operations Australia, established in April 1942 by British officers Majors Edgerton Mott and Ambrose Trappes-Lomax of SOE Far East.
SOE	Special Operations Executive, formed in 1940 to conduct espionage and sabotage in occupied territory.
SRD	Services Reconnaissance Department, formed in March 1943 and recruited from the ranks of SOA, and available for operations within the South East Asia Command.
Storepedo	Cylindrical containers containing shock-absorbent heavy-gauge wire netting that were dropped by parachute to resupply special forces.
STS	Special Training School, formed in Lochailort, Scotland, in June 1940 to instruct recruits in irregular warfare. Branches were later opened in Singapore and Australia.
Ultra	The Allied signals intelligence based at Bletchley Park in Bedfordshire, which for years had intercepted and decrypted communications of the German, Italian and Japanese military.

NOTES

Introduction

1   'Hutchinson, Christopher (Oral History)', (C. Wood, Interviewer), Imperial War Museum, DOI: 9137 (1985)

2   Kemp, Peter, *No Colours or Crest: The Secret Struggle for Europe* (London: Cassell, 1958), p.16

3   Ibid.

4   Calvert, Michael, Unpublished manuscript (Imperial War Museum,1975)

5   Chapman, Freddie Spencer, *The Jungle is Neutral* (United Kingdom: Chatto and Windus, 1952), p.5

6   'Jellicoe, George (Oral History)', (C. Wood, Interviewer), Imperial War Museum, DOI: 13039 (1993)

7   Moynahan, Brian, Jungle Soldier (Quercus, 2009), p.93

8   Scapula Mission, National Archives WO 193/603 and 193/604

Chapter 1

9   Bell, Mary Haley, *What Shall We Do Tomorrow?* (Philadelphia and New York: J. B. Lippincott Company, 1969), p.16

10   Scapula Mission, National Archives WO 193/603 and 193/604

11   Ibid.

12   Jenkins, Roy, *Churchill* (London: Macmillan, 2001), p.681

13   *Daily Mail*, 26 October 1945

14   'Broome, Richard (Oral History)', (C. Wood, Interviewer), Imperial War Museum, DOI: 8255 (1984)

15   Ibid.

16   Skidmore, Ian, *Escape from the Rising Sun* (Leo Cooper, 1973), p.97

17   'Broome, Richard (Oral History)'

18   Ibid.

19   Wynyard, Noel, *Winning Hazard* (Sampson Low & Marston & Co.,

1944), p.14

20   Skidmore, Ian, *Escape from the Rising Sun*, p.102

21   'Broome, Richard (Oral History)'

Chapter 2

22   Fergusson, Bernard, *Beyond the Chindwin* (Fontana Books, 1955), p.19

23   Calvert, Mike, *Fighting Mad: One Man's Guerrilla War* (Jarrolds, 1964), p.54

24   *The Cairns Post*, 6 July 1943

25   Saunders, Cecil, available at https://www.far-eastern-heroes.org.uk/Experiences_of_Cecil_Saunders/html/japanese_pow.htm

26   Wynyard, Noel, *Winning Hazard* (Sampson Low & Marston & Co., 1944), p.11

27   Jones, Arthur, Australians at War Film Archive, DOI: 1010, available at http://australiansatwarfilmarchive.unsw.edu.au/archive/1010-arthur-jones

28   Ibid.

29   Operation Jaywick, National Archives WO 208/1538

30   Jones, Arthur, Australians at War Film Archive

31   Operation Jaywick, National Archives

32   Jones, Arthur, Australians at War Film Archive

33   Operation Jaywick, National Archives

34   Mackay, Jack, Australians at War Film Archive, DOI: 784, available at http://australiansatwarfilmarchive.unsw.edu.au/archive/784-jack-mackay

35   Jones, Arthur, Australians at War Film Archive

36   Wynyard, Noel, *Winning Hazard* (Sampson Low & Marston & Co., 1944), p.17

Chapter 3

37   Hunter, Claire, 'They told us it would be exciting' (27 September 2018) Australian War Memorial website, available at https://www.awm.gov.au/articles/blog/moss-berryman-and-operation-jaywick

38   Jones, Arthur, Australians at War Film Archive, DOI: 1010, available at http://australiansatwarfilmarchive.unsw.edu.au/archive/1010-arthur-jones

39   Ibid.

40   *The Queensland Times*, 13 August 1946

41   Wynyard, Noel, *Winning Hazard* (Sampson Low & Marston & Co., 1944), p.18

42   Young, Horace, Australians at War Film Archive, DOI: 1815, available at http://australiansatwarfilmarchive.unsw.edu.au/archive/1815-horace-young

43   Ibid.

44   Ibid.

45   Ibid.

Chapter 4

46   Jones, Arthur, Australians at War Film Archive, DOI: 1010, available at http://australiansatwarfilmarchive.unsw.edu.au/archive/1010-arthur-jones

47   Wynyard, Noel, *Winning Hazard* (Sampson Low & Marston & Co., 1944), p.39

48   Young, Horace, Australians at War Film Archive, DOI: 1815, available at http://australiansatwarfilmarchive.unsw.edu.au/archive/1815-horace-young

49   Jones, Arthur, Australians at War Film Archive

50   Operation Jaywick, National Archives WO 208/1538

51   Jones, Arthur, Australians at War Film Archive

52   Hunter, Claire, 'They told us it would be exciting' (27 September 2018) Australian War Memorial website, available at https://www.awm.gov.au/articles/blog/moss-berryman-and-operation-jaywick

53   Young, Horace, Australians at War Film Archive

54   Ibid.

55   Jones, Arthur, Australians at War Film Archive

56   Jones, Arthur, Australians at War Film Archive

57   Hunter, Claire, 'They told us it would be exciting'

58   Wynyard, Noel, *Winning Hazard* (Sampson Low & Marston & Co., 1944), p.87

Chapter 5

59   Jones, Arthur, Australians at War Film Archive, DOI: 1010, available at http://australiansatwarfilmarchive.unsw.edu.au/archive/1010-arthur-jones

60   Operation Jaywick, National Archives WO 208/1538

61   Jones, Arthur, Australians at War Film Archive

62	Operation Jaywick, National Archives
63	Jones, Arthur, Australians at War Film Archive
64	Operation Jaywick, National Archives
65	Jones, Arthur, Australians at War Film Archive
66	Wynyard, Noel, *Winning Hazard* (Sampson Low & Marston & Co., 1944), p.108
67	Ibid.
68	Ibid.
69	Jones, Arthur, Australians at War Film Archive
70	Ibid.
71	Ibid.
72	Ibid.
73	Operation Jaywick, National Archives
74	Wynyard, Noel, Winning Hazard, p.116

Chapter 6

75	Young, Horace, Australians at War Film Archive, DOI: 1815, available at http://australiansatwarfilmarchive.unsw.edu.au/archive/1815-horace-young
76	Ibid.
77	Ibid.
78	Ibid.
79	Hunter, Claire, 'They told us it would be exciting' (27 September 2018) Australian War Memorial website, available at https://www.awm.gov.au/articles/blog/moss-berryman-and-operation-jaywick
80	Jones, Arthur, Australians at War Film Archive, DOI: 1010, available at http://australiansatwarfilmarchive.unsw.edu.au/archive/1010-arthur-jones
81	Ibid.
82	Ibid.
83	Ibid.
84	Ibid.
85	Hunter, Claire, 'They told us it would be exciting'
86	Jones, Arthur, Australians at War Film Archive
87	Operation Jaywick, National Archives WO 208/1538

Chapter 7

88	'Private Papers of Lieutenant H.R. Ross', Imperial War Museum,

DOI: Documents 653

89   Operation Rimau/Hornbill, National Archives HS 1/254

90   Walter William Chapman, National Archives HS 9/297/3

91   Connell, Brian, *Return of the Tiger* (Pan, 1960) p.125

92   Ibid.

93   Ibid.

94   Ivan Lyon, National Archives HS 9/953/2

Chapter 8

95   Jones, Arthur, Australians at War Film Archive, DOI: 1010, available at http://australiansatwarfilmarchive.unsw.edu.au/archive/1010–arthur-jones

96   *The Canberra Times*, 26 November 1983

97   'Bradbury, Ross William (Oral History)', (J. Bannister, Interviewer), Imperial War Museum, DOI: 30279 (2007)

98   Silver, Lynette, *Deadly Secrets: The Singapore Raids 1942–45* (Sally Milner Publishing, 2010), p.211

99   Oakley, Derek, *Behind Japanese Lines* (The Royal Marines Historical Society, 1996) p.110

100   'Bradbury, Ross William (Oral History)', (J. Bannister, Interviewer), Imperial War Museum

101   Diary of Lt-Cdr Donald Davidson, National Archives, Kew. All future diary references are from the same source.

102   Ibid.

103   Ibid.

104   Operation Rimau/Hornbill, National Archives HS 1/254

105   Davidson

106   Ibid.

Chapter 9

107   HMS Porpoise: 16 January 1945, National Archives ADM 358/4421

108   Diary of Lt-Cdr Donald Davidson, National Archives, Kew

109   Ibid.

110   Ibid.

111   Ibid.

112   Ibid.

113   Ibid.

NOTES

Chapter 10

114   Connell, Brian, *Return of the Tiger*, (Pan, 1960), p.160

115   Thompson, Peter and Macklin, Robert, *Kill The Tiger*, (Hodder Australia, 2002), p.170

Chapter 11

116   Tibbs, Michael, *Hello Lad, Come to Join the Navy?* (The Memoir Club, 2013), p.160. The author also corresponded with Tibbs on several occasions via email in the spring of 2021.

117   Pick-up of Rimau party by HMS Tantalus, National Archives

118   National Archives

119   Appendix 1 to report of Sixth War Patrol of HMS Tantalus by Lt-Cdr Hugh Mackenzie, National Archives

120   Report on Attempted Pickup of 'Rimau' Party by HMS Tantalus by Major W.W Chapman, National Archives

121   National Archives, Kew

Chapter 12

122   Gomes, Edwin H., *Seventeen Years among the Sea Dayaks of Borneo* (Seeley, 1911), p.122

123   Francis George Leach Chester, National Archives HS 9/305/8

124   Howarth, Patrick, *The Men and Women of the S.O.E.* (Routledge & Kegan Paul, 1980), p.174

125   Cottee, Leonard Lindsay, Australians at War Film Archive, DOI: 1477, available at http://australiansatwarfilmarchive.unsw.edu.au/archive/1477-leonard-cottee

126   Tom Harrisson's adventures in Borneo with Z Special Unit were recounted in a series of four articles for the *Brisbane Telegraph* in March 1947

127   'Private Papers of Lieutenant Colonel J.E.B. Finlay', Imperial War Museum, DOI: Documents.16406

128   William Lomas Philipe Sochon, National Archives HS 9/1387/7

129   'Private Papers of Lieutenant Colonel J.E.B. Finlay', Imperial War Museum

130   Ibid.

131   Audio interview with John Martin, Imperial War Museum

132   'Collection of accounts about Operation SEMUT in Borneo 1945 compiled by Major J. Truscott', Imperial War Museum, DOI:

Documents.16755

Chapter 13

133   Barrie, Keith, 'Borneo Story', Australian War Memorial website: DOI: AWM2017.7.126, available at https://www.awm.gov.au/collection/C2582923

134   Gomes, Edwin H., *Seventeen Years among the Sea Dayaks of Borneo* (Seeley, 1911), p.62

135   Ibid.

136   Ibid.

137   *Belfast Telegraph*, 13 June 1933

138   *Brisbane Telegraph*, 8 March 1947

139   Barrie, Keith, 'Borneo Story', Australian War Memorial website

140   Long, Bob, *Z Special Unit's Secret War: Operation Semut 1* (Australian Print Group, 1989), p.49

141   Harrisson, Tom, World Within – A Borneo Story (Opus Publications 1959), p.220

Chapter 14

142   Michael Calvert papers, IWM

143   Moynahan, Brian, *Jungle Soldier* (Quercus, 2009), p.292

144   Barrie, Keith. Borneo Story, Australian War Memorial website: DOI: AWM2017.7.126, available at https://www.awm.gov.au/collection/C2582923

145   Ibid.

146   'Bradbury, Ross William (Oral History)', (J. Bannister, Interviewer). Imperial War Museum. (2007)

147   Barrie, Keith. 'Borneo Story', Australian War Memorial website

148   'Long, Bertram Charles "Bob" (Oral History)', (J. Bannister, Interviewer), Imperial War Museum, DOI: 30277, (2007)

149   'Eadie, William Stanley (Oral History)', (R. Bailey, Interviewer), Imperial War Museum, DOI: 29953

150   Ibid.

151   Ibid.

152   Ibid.

153   Ibid.

154   Ibid.

NOTES

Chapter 15

155   Long, Bob, *Z Special Unit's Secret War: Operation Semut 1* (Australian Print Group, 1989), p.62

156   Ibid.

157   'Private Papers of Lieutenant W S Eadie', Imperial War Museum, DOI: Documents.16752

158   Long, Bob, *Z Special Unit's Secret War: Operation Semut 1*, p.68

159   Ibid.

160   'Private Papers of Lieutenant W.S. Eadie', Imperial War Museum

161   'Collection of accounts about Operation SEMUT in Borneo 1945 compiled by Major J. Truscott', Imperial War Museum

162   Holland, John, Australians at War Film Archive, DOI: 222, available at http://australiansatwarfilmarchive.unsw.edu.au/archive/222-john-holland

163   Long, Bob, *Z Special Unit's Secret War: Operation Semut 1*, p.70

164   Ibid.

165   Ibid.

166   Ibid.

167   'Notes and reports from Sergeant John Keith Barrie', Australian War Memorial, DOI: AWM2017.7.213

168   'Account by Maj William Sochon on operation Semut III', Australian War Memorial, DOI: AWM2017.7.192

169   Ibid.

Chapter 16

170   Comprehensive details of the trial of the ten commandos, and the post-war interrogations of those responsible for their conviction and execution are housed in the National Archives, Kew. These include: the interrogation of interpreter Hiroyuki Furuta, Major Haruo Kamiya and two Korean prisoners, and a translation of the proceedings of Military Court of 7th Area Army.

Chapter 17

171   Donald Montague Noël Davidson, National Archives HS 9/397/5. One example of the letter is contained in the SOE file of Donald Davidson, National Archives, and another in the papers of H. R. Ross, IWM. All further correspondence between Nancy Davidson and the authorities come from the same source, as does that of the Ross family.

172   Ivan Lyon, National Archives HS 9/953/2

173   James Grigor Mackintosh Riggs, National Archives HS 9/1260/1

174   Donald Montague Noël Davidson, National Archives HS 9/397/5

175   Wild, Cyril, 'Expedition to Singkep', *Blackwoods's Magazine*, Vol. 260 (October 1946)

176   A translation of the proceedings of Military Court of 7th Area Army, National Archives

177   Interrogation of Hiroyuki Furuta, National Archives

178   'Private Papers of Lieutenant Colonel J E B Finlay', Imperial War Museum

179   Donald Montague Noël Davidson, National Archives HS 9/397/5

180   Reginald Middleton Ingleton, National Archives HS 9/776/4

181   Simpson, Robert, 'Able Seaman Frederick Walter Lota Marsh MiD', ANZAC Biographies, available at https://www.anzac-biographies.com/2017/06/01/marsh-able-seaman-frederick-walter-lota-mid/

Epilogue

182   Jones, Arthur, Australians at War Film Archive, DOI: 1010, available at http://australiansatwarfilmarchive.unsw.edu.au/archive/1010-arthur-jones

183   Silver, Lynette, 'Unravelling the Mystery of Rimau', *The Listening Post* (Autumn 1993)

184   *The Herald of Glasgow*, 8 August 1994

185   Mackenzie was 'profoundly unhappy' when he read 'The Heroes Of Rimau: Unravelling The Mystery Of One Of World War II's Most Daring Raids' by Lynette Silver and Major Tom Hall. His displeasure was aired to a documentary maker called Jane Flowers, who typed up the notes of Mackenzie's version of events. Mackenzie sent a copy of this document to Jeremy Chapman, the son of Walter Chapman, who passed it to the author of this book.

186   This exchange of correspondence was forwarded to the author by Jeremy Chapman.

187   Interview with Jane Flowers, 5 March 1996 (Hugh Mackenzie died in October 1996).

188   Jones, Arthur, Australians at War Film Archive

189   Holland, John, Australians at War Film Archive, DOI: 222, available at http://australiansatwarfilmarchive.unsw.edu.au/archive/222-john-holland

190   'Came too late, Captain misses family', *Cairns Post*, 6 July 1943

Post–war Life

191   Barrie, Keith. Borneo Story. Australian War Memorial website: DOI: AWM2017.7.126, available at https://www.awm.gov.au/collection/ C2582923

192   Jones, Arthur, Australians at War Film Archive, DOI: 1010, available at http://australiansatwarfilmarchive.unsw.edu.au/archive/1010-arthur-jones

INDEX